EFFECTIVE
WRITING

EFFECTIVE WRITING

CHOICES AND CONVENTIONS

Karen L. Greenberg

Hunter College

St. Martin's Press

Library of Congress Catalog Card Number: 87–060511
Manufactured in the United States of America
21098
fedcba

For information, write St. Martin's Press, Inc.,
175 Fifth Avenue, New York, NY 10010

cover design: Darby Downey
text design: Helen Granger

ISBN: 0–312–00289–0

ACKNOWLEDGMENTS

Chapter 1
Writing with Power: Techniques for Mastering the Writing Process by Peter Elbow (excerpt). Copyright ©
1981 by Oxford University Press, Inc. Reprinted by permission.
Writing Without Teachers by Peter Elbow (excerpt). Copyright ©1973 by Oxford University Press, Inc. Reprinted by permission.
"Interview with Maya Angelou," from *Arthur E. Thomas Interviews Leaders on Black America*, edited by
Emily Rovetch. Copyright © 1981 by Central State University. Reprinted by permission of the publisher,
E.P. Dutton, a division of New American Library.
Chapter 2
Writing with Power: Techniques for Mastering the Writing Process by Peter Elbow (excerpt). Copyright
©1981 by Oxford University Press, Inc. Reprinted by permission.
Dying to Please: Anorexia Nervosa and Its Cure (excerpt), © 1983 by Avis Rumney. Reprinted by permission
of McFarland & Co., Inc., Publishers, Jefferson, N.C.
Firefighter photograph reprinted by permission of The Image Works © by Dan Chidester.
Chapter 3
The Woman Said Yes: Encounters with Life and Death (excerpt) copyright. © 1976 by Jessamyn West. Reprinted by permission of Harcourt Brace Jovanovich, Inc.
"Evicted Family." Reprinted by permission of Photo Researchers, © by Arthur Tress.
Karen Buchanan, "Dancing Grandma" in *Student Writers at Work*, pp. 43–45. Copyright © 1984. Reprinted with permission of St. Martin's Press.
Chapter 4
"The Base Stealer." Copyright © 1948 by Robert Francis. Reprinted from *The Orb Weaver* by permission
of Wesleyan University Press.
"Survey: Work in the 1980's and 1990's," reprinted with permission from *Working Woman* magazine.
Copyright © 1983, HAL Publications.
Drawing by Donald Reilly; © 1981. The *New Yorker* Magazine, Inc.

Acknowledgments and copyrights continue at the back on page 342, which constitutes an extension of the copyright page.

PREFACE

The title of this text, *Effective Writing: Choices and Conventions*, echoes Mina Shaughnessy's belief that effective writing grows out of the choices and decisions writers make in their selection of words, sentence structures, and rhetorical strategies. In addition to making choices that are consistent with their purposes and with the expectations of their readers, writers must also edit their writing so that it conforms to the conventions of Standard Written English. This book encourages writers to try out a variety of forms and strategies, to examine the relationships between their choices and their intentions, and to cast their choices in the conventions of academic English.

Each chapter of this book presents tasks that enable students to examine their writing processes and to expand and improve those processes in specific writing contexts. Both the content and the structure of this book can help inexperienced writers appreciate the fact that effective writing is determined by the writer's purposes and strategies and by the reader's concerns and expectations. Moreover, the content of every writing assignment and exercise comes from the "real" world—from the workplace, the physical and social sciences, and the humanities. Thus, the text provides intellectual challenges while it encourages students to practice composing and revising.

The most unique feature of this text is its format: every exercise is composed of either a paragraph or an essay, allowing students to practice skills within the connected discourse of paragraphs rather than in the isolated, arhetorical sentences found in almost every other composition text. Writing teachers know how common it is for their students to complete textbook exercises correctly, only to produce paragraphs full of the very errors that they had just seemingly mastered. Part of the reason for this failure to "transfer" knowledge is that the learning context of arhetorical, disconnected sentences eliminates the relationship between content and form. In the exercises in this text, the practice of skills is merged with genuine rhetorical goals. Finally, all of the writing assignments in this book are student-centered—even the research assignments ask students to draw upon personal experiences as they plan and compose—and the many models of student writing provide realistic examples of the skills that student writers can attain.

Overview of the Text

The organization of this text reflects the findings of recent composition researchers that developing writers need to begin from the "top down" with "large" elements (paragraph-level elaboration of ideas and rhetorical objectives) and move to "smaller" elements (features of syntax, grammar, and mechanics). This progression also represents the most logical pedagogical approach. It is pointless to ask writers to begin the semester examining subjects and verbs, especially if they have not yet done any writing that requires them to use subjects and verbs. If the purpose of writing is to communicate one's ideas and feelings effectively to specific readers, then writing instruction and texts should begin by acknowledging this purpose and by presenting students with purposeful, meaningful writing activities. Working on grammar or syntax has little purpose or meaning if it is divorced from writers' efforts to make their writing more appropriate for their readers.

This text is organized into four parts: "Drafting," "Revising," "Editing," and "Applying Your Writing Skills." Each part presents writing as a recursive process of thinking, writing, rethinking, revising, editing, and rewriting. Each chapter within these parts begins with a shared writing task for groups of students to work on collaboratively (or for a whole class to try together), and each chapter includes a variety of different tasks to assign to individuals. In addition, every chapter ends with a stimulus relating to the topic of the chapter—a picture, a cartoon, a piece of writing—for students to think and write about; each also includes guidelines to help students develop and organize a response to the stimulus.

Every chapter also presents students with a revising checklist to help them examine and improve their writing, and every chapter (except the first) ends with suggested issues for students to explore in their journals. These issues come from two sources: some of them are based on ideas that have been presented in the preceding chapter, and some of them present issues that will be discussed in the chapters that follow. This variety in suggested journal topics encourages students to think and write about the material that they have recently finished reading in the text. It also enables them to record and explore their immediate responses to controversial issues that will be presented in writing tasks throughout the book.

Part One, "Drafting," helps inexperienced writers appreciate the complexity of the writing process and discourages them from doing the premature revising and editing that research indicates causes so many of the rhetorical and syntactic breakdowns in their writing. Chapter One focuses on students' perceptions of their own writing processes. Chapter Two introduces students to a variety of prewriting techniques. Chapter Three helps students think about their focus, purpose, and audience. Chapters Four and Five present strategies for developing and elaborating ideas.

Part Two, "Revising," asks students to revise and refine some of the ideas and experiences they discussed and wrote about in the first five chapters. Chapter Six focuses on revising ideas and details, Chapter Seven on revising organization and improving coherence, and Chapter Eight on revising sentence structure.

After students have done extensive writing and revising in the first eight chapters of this text, they are ready for Part Three, "Editing." Here they examine the problems that their errors may cause in readers' interpretation of their meaning. Chapter Nine focuses on editing sentence structure, Chapter Ten on editing diction, Chapter Eleven on editing grammar and usage, and Chapter Twelve on editing spelling and punctuation.

Part Four, "Applying Your Writing Skills," encourages students to apply the skills and awarenesses that they have developed to special writing assignments in and out of school settings. Some of the tasks presented here include keeping a double-entry notebook; analyzing different writing assignments; writing summaries, analyses, and evaluations; analyzing and writing essay examinations; and writing a brief research essay.

To recapitulate, every chapter in this text stresses the recursive processes involved in writing and helps students see the relationships between improvements in their processes and improvements in their products. The book ends with a series of individualized progress logs that students can use to keep track of their writing problems and progress. There are separate logs to record feedback on paragraphs and essays, spelling errors, and conference discussions.

Acknowledgments

This book would never have been written if Harvey Wiener—the master writer, gifted teacher, and loyal friend—had not spent a year nagging me to translate my classroom lessons and materials into a text that others could share. I am equally indebted to Susan Didriksen Anker for showing me that writing a textbook did not mean that I had to compromise my pedagogy or my ideals. She is everything a writer could want an editor to be: patient, caring, discerning, funny, and very smart. Michael Weber, another editor and friend at St. Martin's Press, also read each draft of my manuscript with incredible care and attention; he and project editor, Vivian McLaughlin, who worked tirelessly with me through the production stage, provided invaluable guidance. In addition, the following reviewers, whose thoughful comments provided excellent criticisms and suggestions, helped me gain new perspectives and improve each draft: Patricia Bates of Louisiana State University in Shreveport; Harry Brent of Baruch College—CUNY; Mariestelle Brown of North Iowa Area Community College; Jan Delasara of Metropolitan State College; John Ganio of SUNY Cobleskill; Alice Gillam-Scott of the University of Wisconsin–Milwaukee; George Haich of Georgia State University; Joseph LaBriola of Sinclair Community College; Patricia Mannix of the Community College of Rhode Island; Susan Meisenhelder of California State University–San Bernardino; Katherine Stone of Georgia State University; Josephine Koster Tarvers of Rutgers University; Monica Torres of New Mexico State University; Harvey Weiner of LaGuardia Community College; and Nancy Woodson of Otterbein College.

I am also indebted to the scholars whose thinking and teaching have shaped my life as a composition teacher: Peter Elbow, James Moffet, and Donald Murray. In particular, Peter's ideas about the nature and importance of prewriting have had a substantial impact on my writing process and pedagogy. And I am grateful to John Mayher, a linguist who taught a whole generation how to teach and who nurtured their scholarly writing abilities. Finally, I thank my husband Kenneth and our son Evan for their seemingly endless patience, support, and love. This book is dedicated to my students, who have always challenged and inspired me, and to the memory of my father, William Klein, who always believed in me.

K. L. G.

CONTENTS

Chapter 3 Shaping Ideas   43

PART II REVISING   121

Chapter 6 Revising Ideas and Details   123

Chapter 11   Editing Grammar and Usage   252

PART ONE

DRAFTING

CHAPTER ONE

EXPLORING YOUR THOUGHTS AND FEELINGS ABOUT WRITING

Writers kid themselves—about themselves and other people. Take the talk about writing methods. Writing is just work—there's no secret. If you dictate or use a pen or type or write with your toes—it is still just work.

SINCLAIR LEWIS

INTRODUCTION: WRITING ATTITUDES

Everyone is a "born writer." Young children love to tell stories, and young storytellers are thrilled when someone else can read their artful squiggles and understand their stories. Some of us manage to preserve this sense of the magic of the written word and, as we grow older, continue to find pleasure in expressing our experiences in writing. Others lose touch with the magic because no one delights in our stories or because the criticisms we receive start to overwhelm us. Gradually, we lose our natural spontaneity, and writing becomes more and more difficult.

How do you feel about writing? Because attitudes toward writing usually influence writing habits and processes, it is important for you to understand your beliefs and feelings about writing. For example, are you one of the many people who believe that "good" writers always enjoy writing and have the ability to create perfect prose every time they write? This is simply not true! In fact, many professional writers have problems developing and organizing their thoughts and getting them down on paper. For example, here is a discussion of this problem by a professional writer who also teaches writing:

I can't write. I'm trying to begin, I can't think of anything to say. No—there's too much to say, but first I have to find a good title, a good first word, an arresting, unforgettable first sentence. And then everything has to be beautifully organized—how? I can't do this, it's too hard, too confusing, too frightening; I put up a good front most of the time, my friends believe me, I've hoodwinked my teachers (some of them; or they were kind); but if I write badly I will, finally, be exposed; people will laugh, or they will feel sorry for me—and I will vanish.

I can't simply say what I want to say (whatever that is), I have to say it cogently, intelligently, brilliantly. I can't.

Somehow, growing up, I lost both my fluency and my spontaneity when it came to writing—it was all those red penciled comments in the margins. Eventually those can be useful, when it comes to editing; but the real problem is to get something to edit—words—on paper.

Patricia Cummings
Free Writing!

Another misunderstanding that some people have about writing is that it is a neat, orderly process. It usually isn't; in fact, writing is often a messy business. Even fluent writers who enjoy writing usually write notes all over their first drafts and draw circles and arrows connecting new ideas to old ones. Most successful writers have to write several drafts of a story, an essay, or a report. In each draft, they get closer and closer to what they want to say and how they want to say it. Also, most experienced writers show their drafts to concerned readers who help them revise, edit, and proofread their writing.

Students who have misunderstandings about the process of writing often become overwhelmed by the prospect of trying to produce a "perfect" piece of writing in one draft. They become convinced that they cannot write well and may develop negative attitudes toward writing—fear, anxiety, contempt. These negative attitudes make it even more difficult for them to produce and to shape ideas. Regardless of whether you think that you write well or poorly, you may have some attitudes about writing that are interfering with your ability to express or to revise these ideas. In order to change these attitudes, first you need to understand them. This chapter is designed to help you examine your feelings and beliefs about writing and explore your writing habits.

PAIRED WRITING TASK   INTERVIEWING YOUR PEERS

In order to discover how other people feel about writing, interview a classmate and take notes as you interview the person. Before you begin, examine the questions below and decide which ones you want to ask. If you think of any other questions about writing attitudes or habits that are not on the list, write them down in the space provided at number 12. When it is your turn to be interviewed, tell the truth. There aren't any "correct" responses to these questions. If you feel uncomfortable about answering a particular question, tell your classmate to skip that question. As you interview your classmate, write your notes about his or her responses on a separate piece of paper.

Feelings
  1. How would you describe your feelings about writing?
  2. How do you feel when you sit down to write something?
  3. How do you feel when you finish writing?

Habits
  4. How would you describe your writing habits?
  5. What kinds of writing "rituals" do you follow? For example, do you do certain things to prepare for writing? Do you need quiet or some kind of noise? Do you write in pen or pencil or do you type?
  6. What do you do when you begin writing? How do you know when you are finished writing?
  7. To whom do you show your writing? Who helps you with it?

Beliefs
8. Do you think that you write well? Why or why not?
9. Do you think that anyone can learn to write well? Why or why not?
10. Do you believe that a person has to like to write in order to write well? Why or why not?
11. Do you usually revise or edit your writing? Why or why not?
12.

When you are finished with the interview, use your notes to write a paragraph describing the person's writing attitudes and habits. The classmate you interviewed will use your paragraph to help get a better understanding of his or her writing attitudes.

A STUDENT RESPONSE

How do your feelings about writing compare with those of the students who wrote the brief uncorrected essays that follow?

I have mixed feelings about writing. Sometimes I like to write, especially when I am writing to friends and have something very important to tell them. But sometimes I hate to write and those times are usually when I am writing an essay for school or for work and I know that the person who will read my writing will judge me by it.

Even when I am writing something that I enjoy, I find it hard to write. It's so much easier to talk to people. I never seem to have any trouble thinking up ideas or organizing them when I am speaking, but I always have trouble when I am writing. I think I get so nervous about having to write that my mind clams up.

I hope that my writing courses will make it easier for me to write and will help me improve my writing. I envy writers who can sit down and pour out their ideas on paper and polish them up so that when you read them you understand exactly how the writer's mind works. I also believe that writing well is a skill that will be very valuable to me in college and my future. I am studying to be a nurse and nurses must know how to write clearly and effectively. So I am putting a lot of effort into improving my writing.

Aida Vasquez

I usually do not enjoy writing. I have great difficulty getting my thoughts together and putting them down on paper. When I know I have to write something for school, I get very nervous about it and put it off till the last possible minute. Then I sit down and write very fast and try to get all of my ideas out of my head before I lose them. If I think that the teacher is going to look at my writing, I'll go over my paper before rewriting it. After I hand it in, I try not to think about it.

My approach to writing is very different from my approach to things that I like doing. For instance, I love to run. I'm on the track team and the way I prepare for a race is almost the opposite of the way I prepare for writing a paper. I start thinking about the race and planning for it about a week in advance. I stay calm and do lots of practice runs. I give the race everything I've got and if I lose, I try to

```
figure out what went wrong and how to win the next time.

I wish I could write as good as I run.
```

Allen Parkinson

WRITING ACTIVITY EXPLORING YOUR FEELINGS ABOUT WRITING

Write a paragraph about the ways in which your feelings about writing are similar to or different from the ones expressed by Aida Vasquez or by Allen Parkinson.

PERCEPTIONS OF THE WRITING PROCESS

People's attitude toward writing are influenced by their perceptions of how writing "happens." Most students and some teachers have misconceptions about the writing process. They think that clear, correct writing flows magically from the pens of successful writers. Indeed, successful writers may foster this belief because they usually do not talk or write about the thinking, planning, and organizing that they do before they sit down to write. In fact, skilled writers may *not even be aware of* the **prewriting** that they work through—all of the thinking, deciding, focusing, organizing, and developing that they do—before they begin to write. However, prewriting activities such as thinking, planning, and focusing are absolutely necessary for the production of effective writing. These activities enable writers to come up with enough ideas and information so that when they start writing, they have the luxury of selecting and arranging only the most promising ideas. Writers who don't do any prewriting have no clear idea of what they want to say and have very little sense of why they are writing or of the audience who will read their writing.

In addition, many people also do not understand the importance of **revising.** They think that revising consists of correcting errors in spelling and grammar or "polishing" their writing. In reality, error correction is usually the *last* stage in the writing process of most skilled writers. Before they edit their errors, skilled writers usually read and revise their work over and over again. First, they reshape their ideas and organization, making sure that they have communicated their meaning. Then they may shift their attention to their sentences and words, checking for accuracy and appropriateness. Then they might cross out whole sentences or paragraphs and add new details, or they might throw out what they have written and start all over again. If a piece genuinely matters to them, skilled writers may revise it nine or ten times before they are satisfied that it has expressed their ideas and concerns. For example, here is the fourth draft of this paragraph:

```
            FOURTH DRAFT OF MY PARAGRAPH

      Also, many writers do not understand the importance of

postwriting activities.  These people think that revising

means correcting errors in spelling or grammar.  They are

wrong.  Skilled writers usually read and revise their work

over and over.  Then, they reshape their ideas and

organization.  Then, they look at sentence structure or

vocabulary.  Some throw out everything that they have written

or add new sentences or paragraphs or new details.
```

How does my fourth draft of this paragraph differ from the final version that precedes it?

Another misconception that causes problems for some writers is their perception of writing as a series of four separate stages or processes: prewriting, writing, revising, and editing. They believe that writers start with the first activity and move on to the next without any backsliding or returning to a previous activity. This description of the writing process is also inaccurate. Most experienced writers move back and forth among these activities whenever they write. In other words, they may do some planning and writing, stop, and then do some more planning. Next they may do some revising and then more planning and organizing and writing. Although this book discusses "writing" and "revising"—part one (chapters 1–6) takes up writing, and part two (chapters 6–8) covers revising—in reality, the two processes often occur simultaneously.

A PROFESSIONAL RESPONSE

Read the following essay that a well-known writing teacher wrote about his writing processes. How are his processes similar to or different from your own?

In high school I wrote relatively easily and—according to those standards—satisfactorily. In college I began to have difficulty writing. Sometimes, I wrote badly, sometimes I wrote easily and sometimes with excruciating difficulty. Starting early and planning carefully didn't seem to be the answer: sometimes it seemed to help, sometimes it seemed to make things worse.

Whether or not I succeeded in getting something written seemed related only to whether I screwed myself up into some state of frantic emotional intensity: sometimes about the subject I was writing about; occasionally about some extraneous matter in my life; usually about how overdue the paper was and how frightened I was of turning in nothing at all.

The saving factor in college was that I wasn't sure whether I cared more about skiing or about studies. But then I went to graduate school and committed myself to studies. This involved deciding to try *very hard* and plan my writing *very carefully*. Writing became more and more impossible. I finally reached the point where I could not write at all. I had to quit graduate school and go into a line of work that didn't require any writing. Teaching English in college wasn't what I had in mind, but it was the only job I could get so it had to do. . . .

My difficulties in writing, my years as an illiterate English teacher, and a recent habit of trying to keep a stream of consciousness diary whenever life in general got to be too much for me—all combined to make me notice what was happening as I tried to write. I kept a kind of almost diary. There were two main themes—what I called "stuckpoints" and "breakthroughs." Stuckpoints were when I couldn't get anything written at all no matter how hard I tried: out of pure desperation and rage I would finally stop trying to write the thing and take a fresh sheet of paper and simply try to collect evidence: babble everything I felt, when it started, and what kind of writing and mood and weather had been going on. Breakthroughs were when the log-jam broke and something good happened: I would often stop and try to say afterwards what I thought happened. . . .

Trying to begin [to write] is like being a little child who cannot write on unlined paper. I cannot write anything decent or interesting until after I have written something at least as long as the thing I want to end up with. I go back over it and cross it all out or throw it all away, but it operates as a set of lines that hold me up when I write, something to warm up the paper so my ink will "take," a security blanket. Producing writing, then, is not so much like filling a basin or a pool once, but rather getting water to keep flowing *through* till finally it runs clear.

Peter Elbow
Writing Without Teachers

WRITING ACTIVITY   DESCRIBING YOUR "WRITING HISTORY"

Write a paragraph about some of the experiences and people who have influenced your writing ability. Consider the following questions to help you get started with this paragraph:

- Who taught you how to write? How old were you?
- How did you feel about writing when you were in elementary and in secondary school?
- How often did your teachers or parents ask you to write?
- How often did you write on your own?
- How did your parents or siblings feel about writing?
- How did your friends feel about writing?
- How difficult or easy did you find writing?

Reminder: The questions above are for you to think about. Do not feel obligated to answer each or all of them.

THE PROBLEMS CAUSED BY PREMATURE EDITING

A common misconception that many inexperienced writers share is that skilled writers revise and edit while they are writing. Certainly some professional writers do stop after every paragraph, or even after every sentence, to make sure that it expresses their meaning accurately. However, most experienced writers write and revise a first draft in its entirety before they look for any errors in it. This is because they know that they are discovering their ideas *while* they are writing. Furthermore, most experienced writers develop their own methods or systems for indicating problems that they will return to in order to clarify or to correct them when they are finished writing. For example, when I am writing or revising, I use the following system. I put

- a ✓ in the margin next to any sentence that I haven't thought out clearly;

- an ✗ in the margin next to any word that sounds wrong or funny to me; and

- a ⌒ around any word that I am not sure how to spell.

- a — in place of a word when I can't think of exactly the right word to use in the sentence.

This system allows me to keep writing without stopping to edit (which would break my train of thought). Unfortunately, many inexperienced writers keep interrupting their writing in order to edit or to correct their work prematurely. Their main concern is avoiding errors that teachers often circle in red. Given some teachers' preoccupation with "rules" and with correctness, it's no wonder that many writers—professional and inexperienced—worry more about correcting errors than about communicating clearly. Some people worry so much about their errors that they find it agonizingly difficult to commit words to paper. If you are one of these people, try to relax. Allow yourself to make mistakes. In fact, assume that you *will* make mistakes and that you will learn from these mistakes. Don't let your fear of making mistakes or your concern with editing your errors cripple your writing abilities.

EXERCISE   **ANALYZING YOUR WRITING HABITS**

Below is a list of writing habits that may be interfering with your ability to get your ideas down on paper and develop these ideas clearly. In the space next to each description, write "Yes" if you have this habit or "No" if you do not.

I get nervous and worry a lot about what I am writing.

My lips keep moving but my pen or pencil doesn't.

I frequently erase and correct what I have written.

I keep wondering whether my writing is good or bad.

I pause a long time after each word or sentence.

I often cross out what I have written and start over again from the beginning with a new idea.

I often recopy what I have written and hope that I can catch all the errors.

Some of the writing habits in the list above may be causing you problems with writing. Try to concentrate *more* on figuring out your ideas and details and *less* on worrying about errors or whether your writing is good or bad. If you want to improve your writing, you have to change some of your negative attitudes and behaviors. Chapter 2 of this text will help you master some useful writing habits.

SOME DIFFERENCES BETWEEN SPEAKING AND WRITING

Another common misconception about writing is that it is merely "speaking with the pen instead of tongue." While both speaking and writing involve creative use of the language to express ideas, they are different processes. A clearer understanding of the differences between speaking and writing may help you to change some of your attitudes about writing. The major difference between the two behaviors is that speech develops naturally. All children go through the same stages in speech development. No matter what language children hear, if they are physically normal, they will begin to speak that language at about eighteen months of age, and they will have mastered its basic grammatical structure at about the age of five. In contrast, five-year-old children have very little writing ability because writing must be learned and practiced. Furthermore, regardless of one's age, writing is a skill that requires patience, training, and feedback.

Writing and speaking differ in other ways that can make the process of writing much more difficult than the process of speaking. When people speak, they see their audience and know the extent to which they share experiences, attitudes, and beliefs about the world. Writers have to consider how much their audience of readers is likely to know about a topic, or, if they know their audience, they have to figure out exactly what their readers need to know. Moreover, speakers can look at their listeners' expressions and know immediately when they are being unclear, incomplete, or confusing. Writers rarely get this immediate feedback, so they must make their ideas as clear and as explicit as possible. Also, speakers simply open their mouths and talk (unless they are making an oral presentation), whereas writers must first learn handwriting, spelling, and punctuation skills in order to communicate. Finally, spoken sentences are often less descriptive and less complex than are written sentences. Thus, writing skills are far more complicated and difficult to acquire than are speaking skills. In order to get a better understanding of some of the differences between speaking and writing, read aloud the conversation transcribed below and the course description that follows it. Stressed words have been italicized.

CONVERSATION OVERHEARD
ON THE FIRST DAY OF ENGLISH 100

"What's *this* course about? What are we gonna be . . . I mean, what will we *do* in here?"

"This is a *writing* workshop. So we'll be doing a lot of writing and . . . And a lot of revising."

"But what's the *syllabus*?" I mean, aren't you gonna hand out a *schedule* of readings and assignments?"

"No, but . . . well, the *schedule* depends on *your* interests and progress. *You'll* be responsible for *thinking up* the topics and for *writing regularly*. Let's just say that you'll be *writing* in every class session and every night."

"But what if I *can't think* of anything to *write about*? You know, if I don't have anything to *say*."

"Well, then you'll write about *that*. About *not having* anything to say. And then, you know . . . you can write about *whatever* it is that you were thinking about *before* you started writing."

"That, uh, doesn't *sound* like it's gonna help me *write* better."

"Well, it *depends* on what you mean by *better*. Doesn't it? Let me try to explain. . . . *Continuous* writing or *freewriting* might not help you *correct* your writing . . . but it will help you get in *touch* with your *ideas* and *feelings*. What I mean is that *it* will help you figure out what matters to *you*."

"Is that *important*?"

"Writing something that *matters* to *you* is *very* important. If your writing *doesn't* matter to you, why should it matter to *anyone else* who reads it?"

"Oh . . . I guess *this* course is gonna be *real* different from my *other* English courses."

HANDOUT FOR ENGLISH 100

This course is a Writing Workshop: We will be doing a great deal of writing and revising. Students will be responsible for writing every day, in class and at home, on topics of their choosing. Techniques for getting started will be taught and students will do extensive freewriting to get in touch with their ideas and feelings and to learn how to write things that matter to them.

EXERCISE   **IDENTIFYING DIFFERENCES BETWEEN SPEAKING AND WRITING**

Work on this exercise with another classmate. Reread the teacher's comments in the conversation transcribed above. Circle every word or phrase (group of words) that makes this teacher's speech sound very different from her written handout.

EXERCISE   **EXPLORING SPEAKING AND WRITING DIFFERENCES**

Ask a friend, a family member, or a classmate to let you make a tape recording while he or she is speaking. Ask the person to speak for one minute on *one* of the following topics:

- What do like best about yourself?
- What would you like to change about yourself?

- What angers you more than anything else?
- What is your favorite activity?

If you do not have a tape recorder, ask the person to speak slowly while you try to write down the words. After you have recorded the speech, ask the person to write for one minute about the same topic. When he or she is finished writing, compare the speaking with the writing. Make a list of the similarities between the two and a list of the differences.

By doing the preceding exercises, you have seen that writing is different—and usually more difficult to do—than speaking. However, one of the major advantages that writing has over speaking is that it can be shaped and reshaped over and over. Speaking is permanent: once you've said something, you can't "unsay" or change it. Writing, on the other hand, can be reshaped and revised until it expresses exactly what you want it to communicate. For this reason, writing can be a far more powerful communication tool than speaking. In addition, writing enables you to express your ideas, reflect on them, and clarify them. You can use writing to explore new concepts and news ways of thinking. Writing can also be a tool for self-discovery, enabling you to gain insights about yourself that can lead to personal growth. The ability to write well in a variety of situations provides you with the opportunity to realize your true potential.

"STANDARD WRITTEN ENGLISH" (SWE) DIALECTS

Some people feel that they don't write well because the form of English that they use is different from the kind used in books, newspapers, and magazines. In reality, however, the English language consists of many forms or *dialects*—the social, regional, and racial variations of the language. These dialects can differ in pronunciation, in vocabulary, and in grammar. Here are examples of five current American English dialects:

1. I plan to go to graduate school and my sister.
2. Usually, I be the one who leaves class first, but today I gonna stay late and talk to him.
3. I no want no favors from that professor.
4. I'm majoring in Ed. 'cause I've always wanted to be a teacher.
5. I am majoring in Education because I have always wanted to be a teacher.

Some of these examples may sound strange, but each is an example of an English dialect that is found in America today. These dialects, as well as all of the other dialects of our language, are rule-governed and are equally logical. No dialect is superior to another one, but they are not all equally appropriate for academic or business writing. The fifth example is **Standard Written English (SWE)**. This is the dialect of our language that is appropriate for professional, business, and academic writing. Nobody speaks Standard Written English. For example, no one always speaks in complete sentences or pronounces the final letter of every word. However, many people learn to "translate" their spoken dialect into SWE when they write. The following sentences show the "translations" of the four dialects into SWE.

The first is Ozark English:

1. I plan to go to graduate school and my sister does too.

The second is Black English Vernacular:

2. Usually, I'm the one who leaves class first, but today I'm going to stay late to talk to him.

The third is Chicano English:

3. I don't want any favors from the professor.

The fourth is Informal Standard English:

4. I'm majoring in Education because I've always wanted to be a teacher.

Everyone's spoken and written dialects are governed by contextual factors that include the age, sex, race, and social background of the speaker or writer and of the audience. Depending upon whom we are addressing and on what we are discussing, we can switch from the most informal slang to the most formal language. For instance, here are two examples of Standard English speech. How do you think a teacher might respond to each one?

"Hey, teach, you gotta give me a break today!"

"Professor, please excuse my negligence today."

Now examine the following examples of Standard Written English. How do they differ? Would you react differently to them? If so, how?

Please send me your answer right away.

You are requested to reply immediately.

The correct use of SWE is a survival skill necessary in most academic, professional, and business situations. Chapters 9–12 in the "Editing" section of this book will help you improve your ability to translate your spoken dialect into SWE.

WRITING ACTIVITY   TRANSLATING SPEECH INTO WRITING

Below is the opening paragraph of a novel entitled *Sitting Pretty*, by Al Young. Although this paragraph is fictional, it is characterized by many of the conversational features of genuine speech and it also includes features that identify it as a dialect that differs from Standard Written English. In the space below Young's paragraph, rewrite his paragraph in Standard Written English. You will have to make changes in spelling, punctuation, grammar, vocabulary, and sentence structure.

Maybe it was on accounta it was a full moon. I don't know. Its a whole lotta things I use to be dead certain about—like, day follow night and night follow day—things I wouldnt even bet on no more. Its been that way since me and Squirrel broke up and that's been yeahbout fifteen-some-odd years ago, *odd* years—July the Fourth.

Your SWE translation:

How does your paragraph differ from Young's?

SOME GOALS FOR YOU TO CONSIDER

For most people, the goal in taking a writing course is to improve their academic writing ability. The best way to achieve this goal is to work at mastering smaller, more manageable tasks like the ones listed here:

1. Try to care more about writing. Every time you sit down to write something, try to find something to say that matters to *you*.
2. Keep an open mind about the strategies offered by your teacher and this text, and try them out even if they seem silly or irrelevant.
3. Try to understand and to change the negative writing attitudes and behaviors that are causing you problems.
4. Take more time to think about what you want to say in your writing.
5. Focus more on getting your ideas down and less on worrying about whether your writing is good or bad.
6. Try to develop many specific details to support your ideas so that your readers will understand your generalizations.
7. Work on organizing your details in a logical order so that your reader can follow the development of the ideas.
8. Get into the habit of writing several drafts of any piece of writing that matters to you.
9. Revise a piece over and over again until it says what you want it to say in a way that is appropriate for you and your reader.
10. Edit your *final revision* for correct Standard Written English grammar, usage, spelling, and punctuation so that your readers can comprehend your ideas.

As you succeed in achieving these ten goals, you will probably feel better about writing and you will improve your writing performance in *all* of your courses and in your job.

SOMETHING TO THINK ABOUT

Here is an excerpt of an interview with the writer Maya Angelou conducted by Arthur E. Thomas. As you read it, underline the sentences with which you most agree. Circle any sentence that presents an idea that had not previously occurred to you.

Thomas: Beautiful, brilliant, fantastic black woman—why does it make you almost want to cry, and sometimes cry, when reviewers tell you that you're a natural writer?
Angelou: Well, because it costs so much to write well. It is said that easy reading is damned hard writing, and of course that's the other way around, too. Easy writing is awfully hard going to read. But to make a poem or an article, a piece of journalism, sing—so

that the reader is not even aware that he or she is reading—means that one goes to the work constantly: polishing it, cleaning it up, editing, cutting out, and then finally developing it into a piece that hopefully sings. And then one shows it to an audience and a critic says, "She's a natural writer." There's nothing natural about it. It costs a lot.

Thomas: There's a tremendous amount of work in writing.

Angelou: Hard work. It's hard work. I think everything is hard work. Everything that I've seen that one wants to excel in. I push toward excellence. Always. I think that we've become a country which accepts mediocrity, rudeness, crudeness, coarseness as the norm. We have stopped asking not only for excellence from others, we've stopped demanding excellence from ourselves individually. Too many of us, that is.

Thomas: I know you have worked all day and sometimes more than one day on just two lines.

Angelou: All day! I've worked on one poem six months. One poem. Because, first, I never wanted to write dust–catching masterpieces. And I'm happy that my work is required reading at almost every university in this country, either the autobiographies or the poetry. When I write a poem, I try to find a rhythm. First, if I wanted to write a poem about today and my experience in southern Ohio, just today, I would write everything I know about today: every picture I've seen, every person I've met, what I know about the new friends I've made, how my mother's responding to this trip, you, the car—I would write everything. That would take about fifteen pages. Now I might end up with four lines.

But then I would find rhythm. . . . *Then* I start to work on the poem, and I will *pull* it and *push* it and *kick* it and *kiss* it, *hug* it, everything. Until finally it reflects what this day has been.

It costs me. It might take me three months to write that poem. And it might end up being six lines.

WRITING ASSIGNMENT   DESCRIBING YOURSELF AS A WRITER

In this chapter, you have explored your writing attitudes and those of your classmates. You have also learned about the differences between speaking and writing and about the qualities of effective writing. You have examined your writing habits and processes, and you have read about the writing process of a well-known author. Using the information that you have read and written for this chapter, write a brief essay that describes your writing attitudes, abilities, and processes. Use the Prewriting Guidelines below to help you plan, focus, and develop your ideas for this essay.

Prewriting Guidelines

1. The audience for this essay is your instructor (and your class-mates). Think about the information you will have to provide them with so that they understand who you are and why you feel the way that you do.
2. Try writing *nonstop* for ten minutes about the topic to get your ideas flowing.
3. Reread everything that you wrote for this chapter and take notes as you are reading. Then, write a list of all the ideas that pop into your mind when you think about the assignment.
4. Keep reminding yourself of your purpose in this essay: to describe your attitudes and feelings about writing and your writing abili-ties and processes for a reader who does not know you very well.
5. Examine the paragraph written about you by the classmate who interviewed you. How accurately did your classmate describe your writing attitudes and habits? What details did he or she omit? What details would you emphasize differently?
6. When you write the first draft of your essay, make a conscious ef-fort *not* to revise or edit as you are writing. Don't worry about problems or errors. Just concentrate on getting your ideas down on the page.

When you finish the draft, reread it aloud. Then, revise it until it is as clear and as detailed as you can make it. Use the following ques-tions to help you revise or ask a classmate to use the questions to give you feedback about the strengths and the weaknesses of your draft.

Revising Questions

1. What is the main point of your essay? If the main point is not clear, why not?
2. Which specific details describe the writer's feelings and attitudes? If there are not enough specific details, what details should the au-thor add?
3. If there are any confusing details, what are they and why are they confusing?
4. What are the writer's attitudes toward writing?
5. How can you tell whether the writer is writing to herself or some-one else?
6. What words make the essay sound complete or make it sound like author simply got tired of writing and stopped?

CHAPTER TWO

GETTING STARTED

*I sometimes begin a drawing with no
preconceived problem to solve, with only the
desire to use pencil on paper and make lines,
tones, and shapes with no conscious aim; but
as my mind takes in what is so produced, a
point arrives where some idea becomes
conscious and crytallizes, and then a control
and ordering begin to take place.*

HENRY MOORE

INTRODUCTION: SOURCES OF IDEAS

The writing process begins with a need to express something to someone. Sometimes writers are asked to respond to a question or a topic that a teacher has assigned. Other times, writers' ideas may come from their diaries or journals or from something they see or hear that moves or puzzles them. And still other times, writers' ideas reflect their innermost feelings or important insights that they want to share. Many people start to write with only a vague idea of what they want to say—oftentimes they don't really know exactly what they are going to write before they get their thoughts down on paper. Also, each time a person writes something, his or her strategies for developing ideas differ because the writer is influenced by a variety of factors including the topic, purpose, intended reader, time available to write, and context (for example, in a class, on the job, graded, ungraded, and so forth). People's writing processes are also affected by their attitudes toward the topic and by their mood and energy level.

In other words, for each piece of writing you do, you may have a distinct process for developing it—for finding and organizing information, for exploring the relationships among your ideas, and for drafting and revising your writing for the specific purpose and readers. Whenever you write something, try sorting out your ideas and feelings by thinking about your answers to the following questions:

- Why are you writing? What is your point? What do you hope to accomplish by writing?
- What do you know about the topic, and how do you feel about it? What else do you need to find out about it, and how will you get this information?
- Whom are you writing to or for, and what is this audience like? If you don't know your audience, imagine the type of people who might be interested in your topic. Try to describe these people to yourself so that you can get an idea of how familiar they are with the topic. What information might they want or need to know about it?
- How much time do you have to write and revise? How many drafts do you think you will be able to write?
- To whom can you show a draft for feedback or help?

GROUP WRITING TASK PLANNING DIFFERENT TYPES OF WRITING

Form a group with two or three classmates so that you can share ideas and learn from one another. Consider how you might go about planning each of the following writing assignments and answer the questions below each. Choose one person to record the group's answers on a separate piece of paper. Don't write the assignments; just answer the questions.

1. A letter to an old friend describing a new friend
   a. What would you want your old friend to think or to feel (about your new friend or about you)?
   b. What kinds of information would you include?
2. An essay for your English teacher about your religious beliefs
   a. How comfortable do you feel writing about your religion for your teacher?
   b. What might you need to know about your teacher?
   c. What would you try to convince your teacher about you or about your religious beliefs?
3. A description of your academic accomplishments and your previous employment for a company executive who is interviewing you for a job
   a. What do you need to know about the company and the company executive?
   b. What specific details do you think the executive wants to know about you?

TECHNIQUES FOR GETTING STARTED AND FOR DEVELOPING IDEAS

Writers can get ideas from private or from public sources. The most private source is their feelings, perceptions, and insights: writers can think about these and record them in ongoing diaries or journals. The most public source is the library where writers get ideas and information by taking notes from books, magazines, newspapers, files, and other public documents. In between the journal and the library are many types of sources: people whom writers can interview and places and things that writers can observe and describe. You can get ideas for writing simply by opening your eyes and your ears to what is going on inside of you and all around you. However, if you don't keep a record of your observations, experiences, and reactions, then your best ideas may be lost to you forever. Here are some strategies for recording and developing ideas.

Journal Writing

Writing in a journal constitutes the best way of "talking to" and "listening to" yourself, of examining your ideas and emotions. A journal is simply a notebook in which writers record their observations, thoughts, and feelings. It differs from a diary in that a diary is a record of each day's events. A journal, on the other hand, is used to record particularly interesting or meaningful events or observations *and* the writer's reactions to these events. For example, here is an entry from my diary:

> 6/11/85   I finished the first section of Chap. 2. It's a tough chapter. I picked up Evan from nursery school. He had a fight with his teacher—remember to call her. Ate out at Burger King—again!

And here is an entry from my journal for the same day. How does it differ from the diary entry above?

> 6/11/85   A lovely golden day, a day for dreaming outside. But I had a rough day today—spent most of it writing (when Evan wasn't demanding attention). Chapter 2 of the new book is going very slowly. Why is it so difficult? Is this chapter touching a raw nerve—reflecting on my own anxiety about "getting started"? After fifteen years of writing professionally, I still get so nervous and cramped when I sit down to write. Can I work out some of this problem by following my own advice in this chapter?

The most important thing about journal writing is that it be done regularly, at least once or twice a day. The point of recording your thoughts and responses in a journal is to "behave" like a writer: to get into the habit of recording feelings and impressions in writing. A journal constitutes the place to let your ideas percolate, the place to write reactions to a topic, a class, a reading, or a piece of writing on which you are working. The more regularly you write in a journal, the more comfortable you will be with exploring your ideas in writing. A journal also provides a permanent record of your ideas and observations, a record that is always available to you when you need a topic or some ideas for an essay or term paper. Although a journal should never be graded or evaluated by others, some teachers do check students' journals to make sure that they are writing regularly or to learn about their concerns and reactions. If you write anything in your journal that you do not want others to read, fold over the page on which the entry is written and staple it or tape it.

A STUDENT RESPONSE

Here is an uncorrected entry from the journal of a student who wishes to remain anonymous:

2/10/84   I am still so nervous about writing in this little book. I know that its a private place and I can try out new ideas and stuff in it. But whenever I write, I always feel like someone's going to grade it or criticize me. I don't even want anyone to look at this book. I'd just die. I'd be so embarrass. I want to use this journal to figure out who I am and what I am becoming. I want to put down all the scary feelings that I have that aren't okay or ready for anyone else to read. Greenberg says that doing this will help me get over my awful fears about writing. Well, we'll see.

JOURNAL-WRITING REMINDERS

1. Write in your journal every day.
2. Always tell the truth.
3. Include details about what you see, hear, feel, taste, smell, and think.
4. Write about your reactions to your observations and your experiences.

You can also use your journal to record pieces of writing that you like: poems, quotations, paragraphs from books and magazines, road signs, and graffiti. Everything you read and record becomes material for you to sort and develop when you need ideas for essays. For example, here is an old journal entry of mine that I recently expanded into an essay on sexist language:

9/15/83   A sign I passed on the parkway today said "Slow—men working." Evan was in the back and wanted to know what the sign said, so I read it to him. As I slowed down by the construction, I saw two men and a woman in bulldozers, tearing up the shoulder of the road. My first reaction was "That sign's inaccurate—it's not true" (always the English teacher, looking for accuracy!). Then, I started to think about the effects of the sign. My young son—and all the kids who see the sign or get their parents to read it to them—are going to learn that only *men* work on roads and build and construct. Why can't the signs in our country read "People Working"?

WRITING ACTIVITY   WRITING JOURNAL ENTRIES

If you do not keep a journal, start today. Get a notebook that you will use only as a journal. Put today's date at the top of the first page, and write at least two entries for today. For your first entry, you might want to record your reaction to this writing assignment: how do you feel about keeping a journal? Why do you think you feel this way? If you are having difficulty getting started on your journal entries, think about something that really bothers you or upsets you. Explain what that thing is and why it annoys you so much. Other possible journal topics include a wonderful or a terrible experience or a person whom you like or dislike very much.

A journal is an excellent place to record images—sensory descriptions of people, things, places, and events. Images are a writer's most important tools because they enable readers to experience the writer's perceptions and feelings. Sensory details make writing interesting. How sharp are your senses? Before you can create images with words, you have to sense them fully. Here is an exercise that will help you do this.

EXERCISE **COLLECTING SENSORY OBSERVATIONS IN A JOURNAL**

Below is a picture of a firefighter. Examine it carefully. In your journal, describe this picture by making five separate lists:

1. *Sights:* Imagine that you are the firefighter. Exactly what can you see?
2. *Sounds:* As the firefighter, what do you hear? Describe these sounds in detail.
3. *Aromas:* What do you smell?
4. *Flavors:* What does the smoke taste like?
5. *Textures:* What are you holding? What does its surface feel like?

If you start a journal and then find that you are having trouble writing in it regularly, set aside a specific time each day (or every other day) to write in your journal. For example, I write in my journal for at least ten minutes at 8:30 p.m. every evening during the week. (I usually skip weekends.) Thus, keeping a journal has enabled me to create a special time and place for me to reflect on my thoughts and feelings. I review my day, consider how satisfied or dissatisfied I am with my behavior and accomplishments, and think about the next day.

Freewriting

Often, writers feel that they know what they want to say, but that they're not sure about how to express it. Freewriting can help writers with this problem. Freewriting means writing continuously about

whatever is in one's mind. Here is what the professor who created the term freewriting—Peter Elbow—has to say about it:

> Freewriting is the easiest way to get words on paper and the best all-around practice in writing that I know. To do a freewriting exercise, simply force yourself to write without stopping for ten minutes. Sometimes you will produce good writing, but that's not the goal. Sometimes you will produce garbage, but that's not the goal either. You must stay on one topic, you may flip repeatedly from one to another: it doesn't matter. Sometimes you will produce a good record of your stream of consciousness, but often you can't keep up. Speed is not the goal, though sometimes the process revs you up. If you can't think of anything to write, write about how that feels or repeat over and over "I have nothing to write" or "Nonsense" or "No." If you get stuck in the middle of a sentence or thought, just repeat the last word or phrase till something comes along. The only point is to keep writing.

Teachers may collect students' freewriting and may write comments on it or ask questions about it. However, freewriting is never graded. Here is an example of some freewriting that I did before I wrote the first draft of this section:

> Let's see me practice what I preach—or is it practice what I teach. How shall I begin this section? With a reading? an example. a student piece. myself—no I'm too boring. Uh oh, I'm running out of ideas and I just started writing. Get back to it. To what? What do I think will help my readers. I guess <u>whatever it is that helps me and other writers</u> that I know. <u>journals, charts, clusters.</u> And of

course <u>freewriting.</u> OK. so now I know my topic, but what am I going to say about it? I guess I better do some more freewriting about it. How can freewriting help me and my students? Well, it gets a person connected to her ideas and feelings and to thoughts she might not have realized were on her mind. Oh, Karen, get your act together!

Freewriting is a warm-up activity: it loosens up your hand and your mind, and it gets you into the habit of thinking on paper. In addition, it solves the two most serious writing problems: getting started and getting ideas. If you get used to freewriting regularly, you won't panic when you are faced with a writing assignment. Instead of staring anxiously at the topic, you can record your immediate responses to the topic, your questions about it, and all of the associated ideas that occur to you. Also, by freewriting, you can find your own "voice"—your own way of seeing and saying things. Just remember that the only "rule" for freewriting is to keep writing for as long as possible or for as long as your teacher specifies. If your mind goes blank, that's what you write about ("I can't think of anything to say. My mind is blank. Help. What can I write about?"). Your goal is to get all of your ideas down on paper as quickly as possible. When you are done freewriting, read over what you have written and underline any word or sentence that strikes you as particularly important or interesting. These underlined ideas can serve as starting points for further thinking and writing.

EXERCISE FREEWRITING

Take out a piece of blank paper and write continuously for five minutes. During this time, do *not* put your pen or pencil down, and do *not* go back to read over what you have written. Write about whatever occurs to you. When you are done writing, consider the number of times you started to worry about using the wrong word or making errors. Set yourself a goal of reducing this number.

FREEWRITING REMINDERS ⸻⸻⸻

1. Write *nonstop* for as long as you can.
2. Use words and phrases; don't worry about writing complete sentences.
3. Write as quickly as you can about everything that comes into your mind.
4. Don't evaluate your ideas or your writing; just write.

WRITING ACTIVITY FREEWRITING

Do five minutes of freewriting about *two* of the following topics:

1. a childhood experience that you remember clearly
2. a recent or an old dream that disturbs you
3. a favorite activity or hobby
4. a job you really liked or disliked
5. a recurring fear
6. a problem that you have overcome
7. a belief or principle that guides your life
8. a characteristic or quality that is unique to you
9. a characteristic of yours that you want to change
10. a reason why you are going to school

A STUDENT RESPONSE

Here is a student's uncorrected five-minute freewriting about her favorite place:

> Candy T. — My Favorite Place
> My real favorite place is the dance floor at the Gaslight Club — great music, terrific dance floor. I was there last night, I go three or four nights a week. I better not write that cause then Prof. Greenberg's gonna ask me when I have time to do all of my homework! Well I make time. Because I love to dance. I learn all the new dances from my friends and from watching people at the club. And then I get on the dance floor and fly. I feel the music in my heart and my head and my feet fly. I feel like a bird. Dancing is so easy for me,

it makes me feel light and free. I could dance all night every night. Maybe I should think about becoming a professional dancer. Only I don't like it when I have a clumsy partner.

Brainstorming

Brainstorming is freewriting with a focus. It works best in a group of three or four. Either you or your teacher specifies a topic, and then you call out every idea that occurs to you about the topic. Someone else's idea may stimulate you to think of a totally new idea. As you write down the group's ideas, your goal is to list as many ideas as possible, as fast as you can think them up. If you or your group get stuck, here are some suggestions:

- *Describe* the topic by answering the "familiar five." These are basic question words journalists often use to start thinking about a story: who? what? when? where? why? (and how?)
- *Associate* the topic with familiar things: How does it make you feel? Why? What does it make you think of?
- *Compare* and *contrast* the topic to other things: What is it similar to, and how is it similar? What is it different from, and how is it different?
- *Analyze* the topic: What are its parts or categories? What are its effects on you or your friends or relatives? To whom is it important? Why?
- *Debate* the topic: Why do I like it or dislike it? Why are you for or against it?

When your brainstorming time limit is up, stop listing and start examining what you have written. Circle the words or phrases that seem most important and draw lines between circles that seem related in some way. Then look at these circles and select the two or three that seem most interesting to you or that have enough material for your assignment.

EXERCISE BRAINSTORMING IN A GROUP

Get into a group of four, and take out a blank piece of paper. Brainstorm together for five minutes about the benefits of exercising. When your group is done, circle the best ideas on your list.

A STUDENT RESPONSE

Here is an example of a student's individual brainstorming list that was done in response to the assignment "Describe your favorite place." Note that after he was finished brainstorming, the writer grouped similar ideas together and gave each group a label.

```
              MY FAVORITE PLACE: MY CAR

        79 Camaro--my first car!!    My own money!

        great condition--they took good care of it

        big blue machine     new paint      sparkles

  see   V-6 fuel-injected engine that's takes off

  smell inside--clean blue leather

             my favorite smell--leather and oil

             great stereo--Akai cassette deck

               new speakers!

  what  sit in the car and blast the radio

  I do in think and dream    my OWN space

  my car or cruise the streets with Lynne

        or go places cars and buses just can't go

        or race friends at the drag strip

        always wanted to be a race-car driver
```

(continued on next page)

how I feel about it

CHALLENGE, speed, power

No one bothers me in my car   it's PRIVATE!

good place to hide, get away and think

lots of space and privacy--I love that feeling

I even like just being alone in my car and not

doing anything--just sitting in there and

thinking

My real home   MINE!

Allen Brower

Purpose

Try to make people understand how I feel about

my car and why I feel so strong.

BRAINSTORMING REMINDERS

1. Try to work in a group or in pairs.
2. Say anything that comes to mind about the topic or problem, no matter how silly or irrevelant it seems.
3. Write words and short phrases, not sentences
4. Don't judge, evaluate, or ridicule anybody's ideas (including your own).

EXERCISE BRAINSTORMING

Do five minutes of brainstorming about your favorite place and what it means to you. Here are some questions to help you get started:

- Exactly what do you see when you're in this place? What sights stand out? Describe these sights in detail (colors, shapes, sizes, textures, etc.). Why do these sights have special meaning for you?
- What sounds do you usually hear in this place? How near by or far away are these sounds? What do the sounds remind you of? How do they make you feel?
- What can you smell in this place? What does the air smell like?
- What textures can you feel? What do the surfaces and the edges of things in this place feel like?
- What does being in this place make you think of?
- What does being in this place make you feel?
- Why do you like this place so much?

When you are done, think about the main impression that you have of the place—how do you feel about it and what makes you feel that way about it? Write down this main impression, and then do five more minutes of brainstorming about it.

A PROFESSIONAL RESPONSE

Here is a description of a place written by Helen Keller, a woman who was blind and deaf almost from birth. How does this woman enable you to experience her favorite place?

I spent the autumn months with my family at our summer cottage, on a mountain about fourteen miles from Tuscumbia. It was called Fern Quarry, because near it there was a limestone quarry, long since abandoned. Three frolicsome little streams ran through it from springs in the rocks above, leaping here and tumbling there in laughing cascades wherever the rocks tried to bar their way. The opening was filled with ferns which completely covered the beds of limestone and in places hid the streams. The rest of the mountain was thickly wooded. Here were great oaks and splendid evergreens with trunks like mossy pillars, from the branches of which hung garlands of ivy and mistletoe, and persimmon trees, the odour of which pervaded every nook and corner of the wood—an illusive, fragrant something that made the heart glad. In places the wild muscadine and scuppernong vines stretched from tree to tree, making arbours which were always full of butterflies and buzzing insects. It was delightful to lose ourselves in the green hollows of that tangled wood in the late afternoon, and to smell the cool, delicious odours that came up from the earth at the close of day.

Our cottage was a sort of rough camp, beautifully situated on the top of the mountain among oaks and pines. The small rooms were arranged on each side of a long open hall. Round the house was a wide piazza, where the mountain winds blew, sweet with all wood-scents. We lived on the piazza most of the time—there we worked, ate and played. At the back door there was a great butternut tree, round which the steps had been built, and in front the trees stood so close that I could touch them and feel the wind shake their branches, or the leaves twirl downward in the autumn blast.

Underline the sensory words that Keller uses to help you experience this place.

A STUDENT RESPONSE

Here is a brainstorm that was written in response to the assignment "describe an experience that changed your life" by a college freshman named Joan Brown:

(Tommy's birth) - problems - different
Found out he's retarded

(Mongeloid) - never be normal - slow to develop
Family upset   physically &
                      mentally

Special kid - sweet, happy, good, loving

Mom and Dad had to work - I had to take care of him

(My Favorite brother) - I fed him, washed him
                        dressed him, played with him

Now - he's walking and talking
      learning (slowly)

Future - who knows his potential?
         (Doctors sure don't - they've been
          wrong about him all along)

I'll always take care of him

He made me grow up Gave me courage

                    faith

Special love.

Clustering

Clustering is a form of brainstorming that enables you to see different kinds of relationships among your ideas about a topic. You begin a cluster by writing your topic in the middle of a page and by putting a circle around the topic. Then you record all of your ideas about the topic in other circles around the topic and connect them. Each new idea may lead its own circle of clusters. For example, here is Joan Brown's cluster:

As you can see, clustering may be messy. Just make sure that you can follow the connections among your ideas.

CLUSTERING REMINDERS _____

1. Write as many words and phrases as you can think of, no matter how irrevelant they may seem at first.
2. Try to develop a cluster around each circle.
3. Keep the connecting lines in each cluster clear.

EXERCISE CLUSTERING

Choose a topic, or ask your teacher to suggest one, and make a cluster for it on a separate piece of paper. If you get stuck, ask yourself some of the questions that were discussed in the section on brainstorming. Try to continue clustering for ten minutes. Fill up the entire page with connected clusters. When you are finished, look for the group of circles that seems most interesting or that seems to connect several logically related ideas. Give that group a label, and write a sentence explaining the main point of the group.

Write a sentence or two describing the different types of essays that you could use to develop the different groups of circles in your cluster.

TECHNIQUES FOR DEVELOPING
A DISCOVERY DRAFT

A discovery draft consists of a writer's first attempt at developing an idea in paragraph or essay form. After you have explored your thoughts and feelings through freewriting, brainstorming, and clustering, you are ready to put some of your ideas together in sentences and paragraphs. However, as the name of this draft implies, you are still discovering what you want to say about a topic. In fact, as you write a draft, you should continue to ask yourself questions about the topic, questions such as the ones that follow:

- What points do I want to make about this topic?
- Who are my potential readers and what do they want or need to know?
- What do I want to make my reader think or feel or do about this topic?
- What else do I need to know about this topic in order to write intelligently about it?
- Why is this topic important?

Remember that your goal in writing a discovery draft is to write details that develop the ideas in your drafting activities. Therefore, it is extremely important that you do not edit prematurely at this stage: do *not* worry about spelling, punctuation, or grammar. Just concentrate on selecting, developing, and connecting the ideas that you wrote about in your freewriting, brainstorming, and clustering. Your discovery draft can be as messy as you like, since it will be revised several times before other people read it. However, remember to leave wide margins, on all four sides of your paper, for the comments and symbols that you will be writing on it. Also skip lines (or type with triple spaces) so that you have room for revisions.

STUDENT RESPONSES

Below is an uncorrected draft of the paragraph that Joan Brown wrote, based on her brainstorming on page 34 and on her clustering on page 35 of this chapter. Note that she did not edit any errors.

A Special Birth — Joan B.

When my little brother Tommy was born my life change. He is a Mongeloid, he's retarded ~~and different~~ and he will never be normal and he's developing very slowly — both physically and mentally. At first my family (and I) were very upset. He has so many problems that the family has to take ~~good~~ special care of him. I have helped him the most. Since my Mom and Dad have to work, I have been responsible for feeding him. washing him dressing him and playing with him. He's such a wonderful kid — he's gentle and happy and loving and I adore him. He made me grow up. Taking care of him taught me about life and made me

*strong. I love him. I'm glad
he's my brother. His life
definitely change mine for
the better!*

    Here is the uncorrected discovery draft that Allen Brower developed from the brainstorming list on page 31 of this chapter.

FIRST REVISION: MY FAVORITE PLACE

    My favorite place in the world is my car. Its the first car that I have ever owned and I really enjoy being in it. I like to sit inside and breathe the smell of the leather and oil. The car is a 1979 Camaro and its previous owner took care of it. The blue paint gleams and the chrome sparkles. Its really smooth. The blue leather is worn but clean. And the stripes on the sides of the car really look fine. Also there's an stereo radio and cassette deck with four speakers that can blast me to heaven. I feel like this car is my real home. It's private. No one bothers me when I'm driving around or even sitting in the car. I can use it to go places that buses and trains just can't go. Its a terrific place to think and dream. Also, I like to race friends in the local drag strip. Even when I'm doing this, I feel alone and I love the feeling of space and privacy. I zoom along feeling powerful and free. I also use my car simply as a place to hang out, cruising the streets with my girlfriend. And I enjoy being alone in the car. Its my own space and my own machine and I love it.

Allen Brower

Look at Brower's brainstorming list on page 31. Circle the details from this list that are incorporated in the discovery draft above.

Which details on his list did he leave out of his draft?

Why do you think he left out these details?

SOMETHING TO THINK ABOUT

Here is an excerpt from a book about anorexia nervosa, the disease which often causes young women to starve themselves. The writer is Avis Rumney, a therapist who once had the disease. In this excerpt, Rumney discusses the traumatic experience that may have triggered her first anorexic episode.

My recollection of the circumstances surrounding my grandmother's death are hazy. I do recall that it was early one morning while my father was away on a business trip and I was sleeping in my mother's bed that my grandfather called to say that his wife (my mother's mother) had just died in an operation to remove some abdominal cancer. I remember feeling scared and lost. I didn't know what to do to help my mother, who was shaking with tears, or what to do with my own feelings about my grandmother's death. My mother needed to leave early that morning to help arrange for the funeral, and my father curtailed his trip and returned early the next day. Meanwhile, friends and neighbors were very helpful. However, my mother had asked me "to help" and I interpreted that to mean she expected me to take care of the situation in any way that I could. I took charge of packing school lunches for my brothers and myself, making plans for dinner and getting laundry done. I resented my mother's leaving, both because I didn't know how to take care of my feelings about my grandmother's death and because I didn't really know what to do to make the situation better, or how to "take care of" the rest of the family. I had loved my grandmother, and had warm memories of spending Christmas holidays with her, helping her bake cakes and cookies and sitting on her lap when grandfather took us on long drives through the country. I didn't go to the funeral—it was in New Jersey, a thousand miles away from our home in Illinois. I stayed home and in about a week my mother returned. After that, I would still go for a week or two in the summer to stay with my grandfather, and cook and shop and prepare meals for him just like I remembered my grandmother doing, using all her lovely flowered china, a separate salad plate, which was square and had the same pattern, cut glass stemware or big glasses with pictures of Christmas trees on them. I was not aware of experiencing any guilt for my grandmother's death, but only of feeling an emptiness, and wishing that I could do *something* instead of feeling ineffective or incompetent because I couldn't replace my grandmother, neither for my mother nor for my grandfather. I don't remember even talking with my mother about my grandmother's death. I only recall wanting to somehow comfort her, although I didn't know how.

WRITING ASSIGNMENT **WRITING A DISCOVERY DRAFT**

The topic for this discovery draft is the same one that Joan Brown and Avis Rumney wrote about: an experience that affected your life or that taught you something important. Your purpose is to let readers see what you saw, hear what you heard, and experience what you felt. Your audience for this draft is your teacher.

Prewriting Guidelines
1. Do some freewriting on the topic. Write for fifteen minutes about everything that comes into your mind when you think about an experience that changed your life.
2. Select several ideas from your freewriting that seem to explain why this experience had such an impact on your life. Do five minutes of brainstorming or clustering about these ideas.
3. Reread your freewriting *and* your brainstorming or clustering. Select the most interesting ideas and connect them into a paragraph. Do *not* worry about spelling, punctuation, grammar, or sentence structure.
4. Get feedback on your discovery draft by following the guidelines below.

How to Get Feedback About Your Discovery Draft
Read the directions below carefully *before* you follow them.
1. Get into a group of two or three students, and take turns reading your discovery drafts aloud to one another. When it is your turn to

read, speak slowly and clearly, and don't interrupt your reading with comments about the draft. Just read it through in its entirety.

2. When it is your turn to listen to a classmate, put your draft away where you cannot see it. Try not to think about your draft; instead, concentrate on your classmate's draft. Listen closely to each classmate, and try to understand the ideas that each is trying to communicate. Do *not* write while your classmate is reading. Do not evaluate or judge their writing. Do not make any criticisms.

3. *After* each person reads his or her draft, you have three minutes to take notes on what you have heard. Write down what you think were the author's main points and important details. Write down any words or phrases that you remember clearly. Also write down any point or sentence that seemed particularly interesting or that you want to know more about.

4. After everyone in the group finishes reading and writing, take turns reading what you have written about each person's draft.

5. When it is your turn to listen to your classmates' responses, take out your draft and write notes on it. Note the ideas, sentences, or words that your classmates point out and note the places where they may have misunderstood you or where they want more information.

The goal of giving and getting this feedback is to help each other become more aware of the strengths in your writing and to make each other more aware of the impact of your writing on readers. After you go through this "group feedback" experience, you will have a clearer sense of your discovery draft as a "whole" piece of writing. Your classmates' comments should help you see where it is strong and where it is confusing or misleading. You can use your classmates' comments and the following questions to help you revise your discovery draft.

Revising Questions
(Answer these by yourself or ask a classmate to help you.)

1. What is the focus of this draft? If the focus is not clear, why not?
2. Which specific details describe the author's feelings and attitudes? If there are not enough specific details, what details should the author add?
3. If there are any confusing details, what are they and why are they confusing?
4. How do the details seem to be organized? If the logic breaks down, where does it do so and why?
5. What words make the draft sound complete or make it sound incomplete?

ISSUES FOR YOUR JOURNAL

Use your journal to record things that stimulate your thinking: ideas, observations, notes, questions, outlines, quotations, lists, signs, titles, and anything else that you might want to think or write more about at a later date. At the end of every chapter in this book, I have included several ideas for you to explore in your journal. These issues and questions are based on material discussed in the preceding chapters and on paragraph and essay topics in the chapters that follow. In other words, you can use your journal to think and write about most of the writing assignments in this book.

1. What is your impression of your writing course or of this writing textbook so far? What do you like about the course or the book? What do you dislike about either one (or about both)?
2. How did you feel about working with your classmates? How did you react to giving or getting feedback on each other's writing?
3. What interesting or strange things have been happening in your life recently? How have you reacted to these events?
4. Look at the list of topics on page 29 of this chapter. Choose one of them to write about in your journal.
5. Who is the person you care about most in your life now? In your journal, describe this person in detail. What is it about this person that makes you care so much about him or her? Why is he or she so special? What have you learned about yourself from caring for this person?

SHAPING IDEAS

How do I know what I think until I see what I say?

E.M. FORSTER

For me the initial delight is in the surprise of remembering something I didn't know I knew.

ROBERT FROST

We do not write in order to be understood, we write in order to understand.

C. DAY LEWIS

INTRODUCTION: FOCUS, PURPOSE, AUDIENCE, AND SUPPORTING DETAILS

Once you have gotten your ideas flowing in a discovery draft, you can begin to shape your material so that it has a focus and a development that a reader can follow. Your discovery draft may seem clear and logical to you, but chances are that it may not make much sense to anyone else. As you prepare your writing for readers, you have to clarify the connections between your ideas. You also need to consider your readers' concerns and attitudes and to develop examples and reasons that will convince readers of your points. Most experienced writers begin shaping a draft for readers by thinking more carefully about their focus, purpose, and audience. The **focus** is the main point that a writer wants to make about the topic. It is the aspect of the topic that the writer wants to discuss or the point that the writer wants to communicate. Some writing assignments will specify the general focus, and then the writer's job is to narrow this focus down so that it is manageable. To do this, the writer must consider how much he or she wants to—or has to—write (a paragraph, a 500 word essay, a 2,000 word essay, a long research essay) and how much information readers need.

Writers must also think about their **purpose** or reason for writing. They must ask themselves why they are writing the particular piece: To explain something? To tell a story? To describe something or someone? To analyze something? To convince someone of something? Sometimes, writers may not know their purpose until they begin writing—as they sort out their ideas and figure out what they want to say, they discover their own purpose for writing a particular piece. Whenever you write something, ask yourself how you want readers to feel or what you want them to think or do after they finish reading your writing. Even if you are writing to yourself—to explore an idea, to clarify your feelings, or to learn something—you should keep your purpose in mind.

Finally, writers must consider their **audience** (their readers). Are you writing to yourself, your family, your friends, classmates, teachers, or employers? When you write for these people, you have a sense of how familiar they are with you and with your topic. If you don't know your audience, then you have to invent one. Keeping an audience in mind while writing helps writers figure out how much information their readers already know about the topic. It also helps them analyze what their readers want to know or need to know about the topic. In addition, keeping the audience in mind enables writers to select details and words that their readers will understand and that will not offend their readers in any way. Finally, an awareness of the audience lets writers choose a tone that is appropriate for their readers. One's focus, purpose, and audience influence everything that one writes, from the first discovery draft to the final revision. The activities in this chapter will help you clarify your focus, purpose, and audience and will give you many options for developing appropriate details.

GROUP WRITING TASK   EXAMINING FOCUS, PURPOSE, AND AUDIENCE

Work on this activity with two other students. Think about the essay that you might write for each of the topics below. List all of the details that you would include in each essay.

- Topic 1: Write a description of your town or city. The purpose of this description is to share your feelings, impressions, and observations about your town. The audience consists of people your age who live in your town and whom you know.

- Topic 2: Write a description of your town or city. The purpose of this description is to inform your readers about your town and to explain why it is an appealing or an unappealing place to live. The audience consists of couples who have young children and who are considering moving to your town.

When your group is done writing the two lists, discuss the ways in which the lists differ. Consider the following questions:

- How does the information included in the lists differ?
- How does the vocabulary in the lists differ?
- How formal or informal is each list?
- Which list was easier to write? Why?
- How did the purpose determine the details in each list?
- How did the audience determine the details in each list?

TECHNIQUES FOR INVENTING AUDIENCES

If you do not know your audience (because you do not know the intended reader or because the audience has not been specified in your writing assignment), then you have to invent some readers. You will have to make up a person or a group of people who might be interested in or concerned about your focus, and you will have to consider their knowledge, attitudes, and feelings about the topic. Jot down some notes about the members of your imaginary audience:

- How old are they?
- What are their ethnic and religious backgrounds?

- How much education have they had?
- What do they do for a living?
- What books, magazines, and newspapers do they read?
- What are their political beliefs?
- What are their values and beliefs?

EXERCISE INVENTING AUDIENCES FOR DIFFERENT PURPOSES

This exercise will help you gain experience inventing and visualizing unknown audiences. Think about each audience and purpose, and then write an answer to each of the questions.

1. Purpose: Explain why you do or don't smoke cigarettes
   Audience: A nurse in your school's medical office
   a. What does this reader already know about you and about cigarette smoking?

   b. What is this reader's attitude toward smoking?

   c. What might this reader want to know or need to know?

2. Purpose: Explain some of the possible reasons why minorities are rarely shown in television commericals
   Audience: Your Sociology professor
   a. What does this reader already know about television commercials and about minorities?

   b. What are this reader's attitudes toward commercials and toward minorities?

   c. What might this reader want to know or need to know?

3. Purpose: Describe a concert starring your favorite musical group
   Audience:
   (Invent an appropriate group of readers or an appropriate magazine for this description)

a. What do these readers already know about this topic?

b. How do these readers feel about this topic?

c. What might these readers want or need to know?

OPTIONS FOR DEVELOPING DETAILS

Your audience and purpose determine the kinds of details that are appropriate for the focus of any writing that you have to do. For example, suppose you were asked to write a brief essay on "my best friend." As you do some freewriting, brainstorming, and clustering about this topic, you might realize that you have many ideas about it and points that you want to make. You would also begin to see that you have a variety of options for narrowing your focus and for developing your points:

- You could describe the way your best friend looks, sounds, and behaves.
- You could describe an incident or a scene involving your best friend.
- You could compare and contrast your best friend to other types of friends.
- You could discuss different examples of the ways in which best friends act toward one another.
- You could analyze some of the reasons why you (or people in general) chose a best friend.
- You could analyze the effects and the consequences of having a best friend.
- You could use a combination of all the strategies above to support your ideas about people's need for best friends.

How do writers select the best option (or combination of strategies)—describing, relating a story, explaining, illustrating, analyzing, evaluating, or arguing? Successful writers think about their purpose and their audience and ask themselves questions as they write:

- What do I want to convince my readers of?
- Which details will be most convincing to these particular readers?

- Which strategies fit my purpose, ideas, and details?
- What ideas and words are appropriate for this audience?

WRITING ACTIVITY   **CREATING DIFFERENT DETAILS**
FOR DIFFERENT PURPOSES AND AUDIENCES

Who is your best friend? For this activity, you will be writing two different descriptions of this person.

Task 1

Your best friend has asked you to write a letter of recommendation for a part-time job that he or she really wants and needs. Write this letter to an imaginary employer (whose name, business, and address you will have to invent), and convince the employer to hire your friend immediately. (You will also have to invent the job title.)

Task 2

This same friend is depressed because he or she has recently moved to a new city and doesn't have any friends yet. You decide to help your friend by writing and sending a letter to the "People in Our Town" column of the local newsletter. Write a letter to the editor of this newsletter describing your friend in a way that will convince people to call him or her and make plans to get together.

When you finish both tasks, identify the similarities and the differences in your two descriptions of your best friend.

A STUDENT RESPONSE

The paragraph below was written in response to the following assignment: "Describe your best friend and relate an experience that supports your impression of him or her." The audience was "classmates."

```
     My best friend and I look so much alike that we're often

mistaken for sisters.  We are both 5'6" tall and weigh 120

pounds.  And we both have shoulder-length curly red hair.  But

our resemblance is only skin deep.  Emotionally we're very
```

different. Unlike me, my friend Lizette is cool and calm.
She doesn't have many highs and lows whereas I'm always either
really excited and happy or down in the dumps. But even
though Lizette is so easy-going and self-controlled she still
has very passionate feelings. She loves her family and
friends deeply and she would sacrfice her own happiness for
theirs. For example last week she won tickets to see a jazz
group that we both really like and she told me to take the
tickets and go with my boyfriend. She said "You like them
better so you go. You'll enjoy it more." And she wasn't just
saying that. She wouldn't stop pestering me about the tickets
until I finally agreed to take them. She is always doing
things like that. I guess that's why she's such a wonderful
friend and why her friendship is so important to me. She
helps me stay sane and stable and I know that she'll always
care for me, no matter what happens or what I do.

Luisa Lord

TYPES OF SUPPORTING DETAILS

As Luisa Lord's paragraph illustrates, effective writers support their ideas with a variety of different types of details including facts, experiences, and observations.

Facts are details that express "truths"—statements that can be verified (checked for their truth or their accuracy). Facts often refer to specific names, dates, amounts, and statistics, or to actual things, places, and events. Writers often use facts to convince readers of their points or their arguments. Lord included several facts—statements that could be proved true—to support her point.

Experiences are details that tell the story of an incident or an event that the writer has experienced or witnessed. Writers use these kinds of details to let the reader "see" the actions and "hear" the words of the people involved in the incident. There are three kinds of experiences that can be used as supporting details:

- *direct*—experiences that the writer actually had
- *imaginary*—experiences that the writer dreamed, thought or wondered about
- *vicarious*—experiences that the writer heard about from others, read about or saw in a movie or on television

In her narration of a direct experience that she had with her best friend, Lord provides specific details about the way her friend acted and spoke, and these details allow readers to understand how and why she feels as she does.

Observations are sensory details that reveal writers' impressions about their topic. These kinds of details let the reader know how the writer perceives the topic and how the writer feels about it. Lord's paragraph is filled with observations about her friend's physical and emotional characteristics. These sensory images and illustrations enable readers to share the writer's perspective and believe her conclusions.

In Chapter 2, you practiced sharpening your senses and improving your ability to create sensory images for your readers. Observations are often composed of these images, and the more specific they are, the easier it is for your reader to sense them and almost experience them. For example, which of the following details gives you a clearer impression of the writer's observation?

1. The sun shone brightly through the light blue afternoon sky.
2. The sun seemed like a dazzling orange ball shining brightly over the pearl blue sky and the iridescent clouds.

What picture do you "see" from the details in the second sentence? How is this different from the picture that the first sentence communicates to you? In the second sentence, the writer used "pearl blue" to describe the color of the sky. She could have used a different shade of blue. In fact, the *Dictionary of Color Names* lists over 500 different shades of blue. Below is a sample listing of some different blues. Examine this list and decide which of these shades best describes the color of the sky today.

blue ashes	bright bluish violet
blue black	chrome blue
bluebird blue	dark bluish gray green
blue chill	dull blue green black
blue drab	dusky blue green

blue gray	dusky bluish red
blue lavender	dusky dull bluish green
blue olive	violet blue
blue plum	water blue
bluish red	wedgewood blue
bright bluish green	wrought iron blue

DETAILS THAT "SHOW"

When you describe an observation or an experience that you had, try *showing* readers what you saw, heard, and felt instead of *telling* them. Let your readers share your experience; don't simply summarize it for them. Provide your readers with enough details so that they can make their own judgments and reach their own conclusions. For instance, here is a sentence that "tells" about my experience of writing this chapter:

Writing this chapter was a very difficult, draining experience for me.

Here is a revision of this sentence that "shows" you the details and lets you draw your own conclusions:

I sweated through all five versions of this chapter, biting my nails till my fingers were raw, twisting out clumps of hair, and generally being obnoxious to friends and family.

WRITING ACTIVITY SHOWING INSTEAD OF TELLING

Think of a person who is very important in your life now. Do five minutes of freewriting about this person and then do a cluster about him or her. In your cluster, list some of this person's actions and gestures and some of his or her most striking characteristics. Then, use your freewriting and cluster to write a brief description of this person. Try not to "tell" readers why this person is so important to you; instead present details that "show" why he or she is so special.

A PROFESSIONAL RESPONSE

Below is an excerpt from a book by Norman Mailer. This paragraph describes his first impression of Senator Robert Kennedy. Notice that Mailer's observations are composed of very specific sensory details and that these details reveal his subject's personality.

So it had begun well enough, and the reporter had been taken with Kennedy's appearance. He was slimmer even than one would have thought, not strong, not weak, somewhere between a blade of grass and a blade of steel, fine, finely drawn, finely honed, a fine flush of color in his cheeks, two very white front teeth, prominent as the two upper teeth of a rabbit, so his mouth had no hint of the cruelty or calculation of a politician who weighs counties, cities, and states, but was rather a mouth ready to nip at anything which attracted its contempt or endangered its ideas. Then there were his eyes. They were the most unusual. His brother Teddy Kennedy spoke of those who "followed him, honored him, lived in his mild and magnificent eye," and that was fair description for he had very large blue eyes, the iris wide in diameter, near to twice the width of the average eye, and the blue was a milky blue like a marble so that his eyes, while prominent, did not show the separate steps and slopes of light some bright eyes show, but rather were gentle, indeed beautiful—one was tempted to speak of velvety eyes—their surface seemed made of velvet as if one could touch them, and the surface would not be repelled.

WRITING ACTIVITY   DEVELOPING DIFFERENT TYPES OF SUPPORTING DETAILS

Think of one person whom you know very well. Write the person's name on top of a piece of paper, and next to this name, write your dominant impression of the person—the quality that you think of most immediately when you think of this person or when you see him or her. A dominant impression is the characteristic that best describes a person (for example, "gentle," "fierce," "sexy," "aggressive," "bubbly," "depressed").

Next, write the heading "Facts" on your paper, and list as many facts as you can think of that contribute to your dominant impression of this person. These facts can be statements about the person's physical characteristics, gestures, behavior or actions. Make sure that the details you are listing are not merely your opinions—each detail must be one that other people would agree is true. For example, my dominant impression of my son is "active." One fact that I might list to support this impression is "Even when Evan is asleep, he tosses and turns and wriggles around his bed." This is a fact because it can be verified—people can watch him and determine if my statement is true.

When you finish listing facts, write the heading "Observations," and list all the other details that contribute to your dominant impression of the person. What physical characteristics contribute to this impression? List sensory details that show how this person looks, behaves, sounds, smells, and feels. For example, one of my observations of my son's activity is that "Evan seems to be always in motion, eyes darting, mouth jabbering away, hands twitching, and feet tapping."

Then, write the heading "Experiences," and write down the details of one or two experiences in which the person said things or displayed behavior that revealed your dominant impression of him or her. Make the experience "come alive" by including sensory details about the setting, the people involved, their actions, and their exact words. (See Chapter 12 for information on how to punctuate direct speech.)

When you have completed your entire list, exchange it with a classmate. Read the list very carefully to determine whether every fact, observation, and experience supports the dominant impression of the person being described. Put a star next to any detail that seems irrelevant. When you are both finished, return lists to one another and examine the starred details. If you are not sure why any of the starred details are irrelevant, ask your classmate.

A PROFESSIONAL RESPONSE

Below is a description of her sister by the writer Jessamyn West. What is West's dominant impression of her sister? Which words reveal this impression? (Note: When West refers to "Grace" in the following excerpt, she is referring to her mother. Similarly, see calls her father by his name, "Eldo.")

It is easy to recognize the ways in which Carmen and I differed. We no doubt had likenesses less easy for me to detect.

There were first of all the differences that could be seen. I was big-boned, five feet seven, square-jawed, square-shouldered, freckled, bookish, athletic.

Carmen was five feet five, small-boned, with narrow, sloping shoulders; small-waisted, with the full bosom, taut bottom, and rounded calves that made men who saw her at the beach pretend (she believed) to be photographers searching for suitable subjects for a photographic essay entitled "A Sunday at the Beach." Would she pose?

Carmen believed none of this. Men had a line against which Carmen often warned me. "You believe everything that anyone tells you," she said. Well, I wouldn't have believed anyone who said he wanted me as an illustration for an article on "A Sunday at the Beach." But how do I know? For one thing, no one ever asked me.

Grace never achieved what she wanted: a black-haired, bronze-skinned replica of Eldo. But Carmen, at least, had olive skin and big hazel eyes set in her head with a slant reminiscent of those of our ancestors who had first reached this continent from Asia. She was a towhead, but with no hint of Irish red to contradict the slant of her eyes and the color of her skin.

Carmen and I had a long-standing argument about necklines; neither of us realized until we were in our thirties that each had chosen what was most suitable to her build. Carmen, with her sloping shoulders, oval face, and long, slender neck, preferred and wore high, severe, even mannish collars. She urged me to do the same. She considered my U-necks and V-necks and frills and flounces unchic in the extreme. I, wearing anything like her ascots and Arrow collars, would have felt, and no doubt looked, like a lady horse doctor.

It was less a question of chic than of native understanding of the requirements of differing builds. I needed a softening neckline. Bowler hat and bow tie could not have disguised Carmen's femininity.

We didn't have many years at home together. I graduated from high school at sixteen, and was never at home except for visits and vacations. First college, then marriage separated us.

In the years we were at home together, we lived separate lives. My playlife was with my older brother; my worklife was with Grace. Carmen cared as little for hiking and baseball as for housework. She never went on Sunday hikes with my brother and me; never had fancing duels using lathes as sabers; never played burn-out or practiced broad-jumping with orange boxes as incentives for extended effort.

Inside, with two housekeepers already working, she wasn't really needed; and, besides, housework didn't really appeal to her, ever.

So why was it, then, on my visits home, happy as I was to see everyone, that it was Carmen's presence that gilded those occasions?

"Is Carmen here?"

She had for me what is now called "star quality."

1. What is West's focus? What is the main point that she wants to make about her sister Carmen?

2. This excerpt is from West's memoirs, in which she tried to portray all the people who influenced her life. What do you think West imagined her audience to be like?

3. Which words in the description enable you to *see* her sister?

4. What kinds of supporting details—facts, observations, or experiences—did West use most often in this excerpt?

5. Try to describe Carmen in your own words (in a sentence or two).

SUBJECTIVE VERSUS TECHNICAL DESCRIPTION

Description is always influenced by the speaker's or the writer's audience and purpose. For example, think about how you would respond if you walked into your home and discovered that it had been burglarized while you were away. Your room is wrecked: everything has been ripped or broken, and the place is a mess. Imagine that you call the police and then you call your best friend to describe the burglary. How would you describe the scene to the police officers who come to your home? How would you describe the scene to your best friend? Probably, the details that you would give to the police officers would be **technical** ones: the extent of the damage, the location of every item, the ways in which things had been moved or broken. The police officers would need to know specific details about how your room looked before and after the burglary. They would not be too interested in how you feel about what happened. Your best friend, on the other hand, would probably want to know your personal response to the burglary—what it means to you and to your life. The description that you would give your friend would be **subjective;** it would convey your feelings and impressions.

Whenever you write descriptions of people, places, or things, you have to decide whether your purpose and your audience requires technical or subjective details or a mixture of both kinds. Here is an example of a technical description and a subjective description of a place. How do they differ?

Pennsylvania is roughly rectangular in shape and its area of 45,333 square miles, ranks it 33d in size among the States. Situated astride the Appalachian Mountains, it has access to the Atlantic Ocean, the Great Lakes, and the Ohio River Valley.

Altitudes range from sea level in the Philadelphia area to 3,213 at the summit of Mt. Davis in Somerset County. Although there are lowlands near the Atlantic Ocean and the Great Lakes, most of the State's terrain is moutainous. Its mean altitude is about 1,100 feet.

Except for a narrow lowland in the northwest corner of Pennsylvania, the western and northern parts of the State are occupied by a plateau. The Appalachian Mountain Range, averaging about 70 miles in width, trends north and northeast across the central and east-central parts of the State. East and southeast of these mountains, low rolling hills and shallow valleys extend to the Philadelphia area. A narrow lowland in the southeasternmost part of the State is part of the Atlantic Coastal Plain, which fringes the Delaware River and Delaware Bay.

U.S. Department of the Interior

Pennsylvania means many things to different people. To one it means the glow of steel mills along the Monongahela at night or strip mines in Venango County or the milky water of the Clarion at Johnsonburg. To another it means the trout streams of Centre County, duck hunting at Pymatuning, a cabin on the upper Allegheny, maple trees at Myersdale in autumn, the long beach bordered by cottonwoods at Presque Isle, or the ski slopes at Ligionier when the snow lies deep upon the mountains. Or it means an eagle seen from Mt. Davis fighting its way through a thunderstorm, a deer starved and winter-killed in Elk County, acres of trillium along Thorn Creek, or the pink mountains of Bedford County when the wild azaleas bloom. For each of us there is a favorite picture or recollection. Mine takes me back a good many years.

Edwin L. Peterson

WRITING ACTIVITY   EXAMINING SUBJECTIVE AND TECHNICAL DETAILS

Reread the two preceding descriptions of Pennsylvania and answer the questions that follow.

1. How did the first description make you feel? Which details made you feel this way?

2. How did the second description make you feel? Which details made you feel this way?

EXERCISE   DEVELOPING TECHNICAL AND SUBJECTIVE DETAILS

Below is a picture of a family who lost their home in a flood. On a separate piece of paper, make two lists. For the first list, note details that describe exactly what you see in the picture. For the second list, write details about how the picture makes you feel. When you are finished writing both lists, write a paragraph describing the picture based on *one* of your lists.

WRITING ACTIVITY SHAPING SUBJECTIVE AND TECHNICAL DESCRIPTIONS

Do five minutes of freewriting about your home town (your neighborhood or your city). Then do some brainstorming and clustering about your town. You will be using your freewriting, brainstorming, and clustering to write the two different descriptions below. For each one, consider your purpose and your audience, and decide how subjective or how technical your description should be.

Description 1

Write a description of your home town for the real estate newsletter *People and Places*. This newsletter will be distributed to real estate agents across the country. They will be handing it out to their clients—mostly people aged 25–35 who are interested in buying a new home or renting a new apartment. The editor of this newsletter has asked you to write a description that will convince these readers to buy or rent a home in your town.

Description 2

Write a description of your home town for the magazine *Money-Making Opportunities*. The people who subscribe to this magazine are mostly middle-aged business people who have some money to invest and who are looking for investments that will make a lot of money. Several builders are considering building a new shopping center in your town and they want to convince readers of this magazine to invest in their center. They have asked you to write a brief description of your town, convincing readers that it is an excellent place for new buildings and growth.

How do your descriptions differ?

SOME ALTERNATIVES FOR ORDERING DETAILS

As you developed details for the writing activities in this chapter, you probably wrote them down in the order in which they came into your mind. You know how your details are related, but you should try to make the connections among them clear so that your audience can understand these relationships. Examine some of the facts, observations, and experiences that you wrote for an activity in this chapter or in the preceding one. Do you see a logical way of ordering your details? How can you arrange your ideas so that your reader can understand the relationships among them? There are several alternative ways of ordering details:

- from *least important* to *most important*
- from *least personal* to *most personal*
- from *past* to *present* to *future*
- from *top to bottom* or from *left to right*
- from *far to near* or from *outside to inside*

EXERCISE   ORDERING DETAILS

Examine the brainstorming list entitled "My Favorite Place: My Car" on page 31 of Chapter 2. On a separate piece of paper, list all of the different arrangements that this student could have used to order his details.

SOMETHING TO THINK ABOUT

Below is an essay by Karen R. Buchanan about her grandmother. Buchanan was a student at Highline Community College in Washington when she wrote this essay in her composition course. The essay won a Bedford Prize in Student Writing and was published recently in an anthology of essays written by students. As you read the essay, underline the words which enable you to see and hear the writer's grandmother.

DANCING GRANDMOTHER

Grandma celebrated her fifty-third birthday just weeks before Grandpa died of cancer in 1965. Although his passing was tremendously difficult for her, I think their shared struggle to prolong his life taught Grandma that good health was not to be taken for granted, and she vowed to live the remainder of her own life as fully and as long as she could. Although we always suspected Grandma had dutifully subdued a zest for living during the long years of Grandpa's illness, we were hardly prepared for the personality that emerged from within her after he died. When she announced her decision to invest part of Grandpa'a life insurance benefits in lessons at the Fred Astaire Dance Studio in Portland, Oregon, where she lived, we rolled our eyes in embarrassment and helplessly wished she would just stay home and bake cookies as normal grandmothers did. Many years filled with countless dance lessons passed before we learned to appreciate the wonder of having a dancing Grandma.

I suppose Grandma's primary motivation for wanting to learn to dance was social. She had been a shy girl, always very tall and heavy, and had married into Grandpa's quiet lifestyle before developing any grace or confidence in her personal appearance. Dancing, on the other hand, filled her life with glittering lights, wonderful parties, beautiful gowns, dashing young dance instructors, and the challenge of learning. Although the weekly dance lessons did not diminish her ample, two-hundred-pound figure, Grandma surprised everyone with energetic performances on the dance floor that soon gave her as much poise, grace, and confidence as any Miss America contestant.

Never one to lack confidence in her own decisions, Grandma signed up from the beginning for enough weekly dance lessons to last for years. She learned the rumba, the cha-cha, and various waltzes easily and was soon participating in dancing contests all over the Northwest. When I was fourteen, Grandma proudly invited me to watch her compete in one of these contests to be held in the grand ballroom of Seattle's Red Lion Inn. My attitude was still unenthusiastic at that point ("Grandmas aren't supposed to dance," I often grumbled), but to make her happy, my mother and I attended the competition. As if to prove me wrong, Grandma made a spectacular showing in every event she entered. The one dance that I particularly remember was a Spanish dance involving a dizzying amount of spinning, dipping, and fast-paced twirling. Her timing was perfect, her sparkling smile never wavered, and her lovely handmade black and red dress shimmered under the spotlights, swirling in rhythmic complement to every movement. I thought she was truly the belle of the ball during that dance, and my thoughts were echoed by the judges a short time later when she was awarded a glistening gold trophy for her outstanding performance.

Grandma's dance costumes were dazzling, and most were her personal creations. Because she was never conservative in her choice of colors or styles, designing glittering, eye-catching ballroom dance dresses came as naturally for Grandma as baking apple pies comes for ordinary grandmothers. Since a costume was rarely repeated from one dancing event to another, she had huge cardboard boxes of tissue-wrapped dresses in her basement, most of which had been worn only once. I discovered those boxes while helping her move from Portland to Seattle in 1975 and was promptly given my own private showing of the vast collection. As she tenderly unfolded each dress and held it up for me to admire, her eyes glowingly expressed the well-earned pride she felt toward each costume and the vividly remembered moment on the dance floor that it represented. Consequently, I felt warmly honored several months later when Grandma wore one of her favorites to my wedding, although she nearly stole the show when she stepped majestically down the church aisle in the stunning dress of glossy white satin, boldly printed with bright red roses and billowing about her to the floor. Topped with her crown of snow-white hair and wearing her proudest smile, Grandma was an unforgettable picture of diginity and grandeur.

Occasionally, I still long for a grandmother who rocks cozily in a rocking chair next to a warm fireplace, knitting afghans and feeding everyone chocolate chip cookies that she has baked herself. Then I think of my own version of a grandmother and burst with pride for her in spite of myself. Although it took many years for me to appreciate the wonder of having that very unique and talented lady for my grandmother, I will never again begrudge her chosen path in life. In fact, someday I may follow in her dancing footsteps.

WRITING ASSIGNMENT SHAPING A DISCOVERY DRAFT
FOR A SPECIFIC PURPOSE AND AUDIENCE

Your purpose in this writing assignment is to describe your dominant impression of someone you know well. This description can be about the same person whom you described for the activity on pages 52–53, or it can be about someone else. Your goal is to focus on the one characteristic that best describes this person.

Prewriting Guidelines

Your first job is to specify your focus:

• Whom are you describing?

- What is this person's relationship to you?
- What is your dominant impression of him or her?

Next, determine your audience:

- Who might be interested in knowing about the person you are describing?
- What does this reader (or group of readers) already know about the person?
- What do they need to or want to know?

Then, refine your purpose for writing this description and decide exactly what effect you want to have on your reader:

- How do you want your readers to see this person?
- What do you want your reader to think or feel about this person?

Begin by using the prewriting techniques that you learned about in Chapter 2: Write down the person's name and your dominant impression of him or her. Underneath that, write your audience for this description and your purpose (what you want your readers to think and feel). Then develop some supporting details by doing some free-writing, brainstorming, and clustering. Take the most interesting details and include them in a discovery draft of your description. Next, get your classmates' responses to this draft by following the guidelines for "How to Get Feedback About Your Discovery Draft" previously discussed on pages 40–41. Use classmates' feedback and your answers to the questions below to help you revise your draft.

Revising Questions
1. What is the dominant impression that I want to convey about this person?
2. Which words in my description reveal this dominant impression?
3. Who is my audience, and what else does the audience need to know about the person that I am describing?
4. Which words or sentences let the reader see this person?
5. Which words or sentences let the reader hear this person?
6. What facts have I included about this person? What other facts do I know about this person that would support my dominant impression of this person?
7. What observations have I included about this person? What other observations do I have about this person that would support my dominant impression?
8. What experiences have I included about this person? What other experiences could I relate about this person that would support my dominant impression?

9. How do my details seem to be organized? If the logic breaks down, where does it do so and why?
10. What words make my description sound complete or make it sound incomplete?

ADDITIONAL TOPICS TO WRITE ABOUT

Here are some more topics for descriptive paragraphs:

1. Describe your favorite meal or the best meal that you ever ate.
2. Describe the best course that you ever took in school.
3. Describe a person who you think is very beautiful.
4. Describe a person who you think is very ugly.
5. Describe the person (living or fictional) whom you admire most or whom you would most like to be.
6. Describe a teacher whom you really respect.
7. Describe an employer whom you really respect.
8. Describe a place that has special meaning for you.
9. Describe a place where you would like to live (now or in the future).
10. Describe your neighborhood or your city.

Reminders

Specify your focus:

- Whom or what are you describing?
- What is your dominant impression of this person, place, or thing?

Determine your audience:

- Who might be interested in knowing this person, place, or thing you are describing?
- What does this reader (or group of readers) already know about him, her, or it?
- What do they need or want to know?

Refine your purpose:

- What do you want your reader to think or to feel about this person, place, or thing?
- What do you want your reader to see, hear, smell, touch, or taste?

After you finish your discovery draft, get your classmates' responses to this draft by following the guidelines for "How to Get Feedback About Your Discovery Draft."

ISSUES FOR YOUR JOURNAL

1. For most of the writing activities in Chapter 2 and in this chapter, you were asked to describe things, experiences, and people. Which descriptions did you most enjoy writing? Why? Which ones did you dislike writing? Why?
2. Who is the best teacher you ever knew (in *or* out of school)? Who taught you the most about something or about life? What did you learn from this person?
3. What is the most interesting thing that you learned in one of your classes this week? Why do you find it interesting?
4. What would be the ideal career or job for you? If you could have any job in the world, what would you choose? Why?
5. Why are you going to college? How do you think it will help you? What will you gain from the experience?

CHAPTER FOUR

WRITING PARAGRAPHS

Content and form, form and content—which comes first? The answer has to be content. Form is not an empty jug into which the writer pours meaning; form grows out of meaning, so much so that many writers come to believe that form, in a very real sense, is meaning.

DONALD MURRAY

INTRODUCTION: PARAGRAPH DEVELOPMENT

There are as many different types of paragraphs as there are kinds of writing: introductory, body, and concluding paragraphs in academic essays; paragraphs in fictional and non–fictional stories; paragraphs in newspaper articles; paragraphs in lab reports; and paragraphs in business memos. All of these different types of paragraphs vary in structure and in length. For example, here is the second paragraph of a recent newspaper article:

The percentage of young people who own their own homes has declined since 1980 because of stubbornly high interest rates. Yearly earnings for workers younger than 35 have declined 15%, after inflation, since 1973. And the percentage of children who live below the poverty line has jumped 50% since 1980.

And here is the second paragraph of a student's political science essay on the same topic. In what ways do these two paragraphs differ?

During the past decade, the older generation has "passed the buck" to the younger one and to future generations. The federal debt has doubled, causing interest rates to remain high and saddling young taxpayers with heavy financial burdens. The yearly earnings for young workers are declining rather than rising, whereas the proportion of federal spending allocated to the elderly rises every year. In effect, this means young workers are supporting the elderly and will continue to do so for quite a while.

In general, each paragraph in an academic essay focuses on a specific point and provides an explanation of or evidence for the point. The number of sentences needed to explain or to support a point depends on the complexity of the point and on the reader's knowledge about it and attitudes toward it. Teachers frequently tell students to start each paragraph with a sentence that states the main point of that paragraph. This sentence, known as the **topic sentence**, lets readers know what to expect in the paragraph. Writing paragraphs that begin with topic sentences can help writers select and limit the types of examples and reasons that can be included in each paragraph. However, many experienced writers do not write topic sentences. The details of their paragraphs are so closely related that readers can infer the main point of each paragraph. For example, here is a paragraph from a student essay. It does not have an obvious topic sentence but it has a clear main point:

```
    Workers are among the people most effected by technology.

In addition, managers who cannot adjust to computers and

telecommunications systems are losing their jobs every day.

And at the other end, secretaries who don't learn how to use

computers may be fired or their jobs may be taken over by

computers and other forms of technology.
```

What is the main point of the preceding paragraph?

GROUP WRITING TASK **EXAMINING EXPECTATIONS ABOUT**
TOPIC SENTENCES AND PARAGRAPHS

Get into a group with three other students, read the following student paragraph, then discuss the questions. Choose one group member to write down the responses of the entire group.

```
    I really enjoy being a checker at Gristedes Supermarket.

I like being able to go to school and work part-time and I

make enough money to buy the things I need.  Also, everyone

agrees that I'm an excellent checker.  I don't even have to

look at the keys on my register.  The store sells thousands of

different items.  The prices change every month, sometimes

even every day.  I have to be careful to watch for these price
```

changes. I also have to watch for shoplifters. The store
loses hundreds of dollars a day in stolen merchandise.
Usually, this loss means that they have to charge shoppers
more money in order to make a profit. I look at people's
clothing and pocketbooks to see if they have any stolen stuff
in them. In addition, I've made some close friends during the
past five years that I've worked at Gristedes. My co-workers
are nice to me and my boss is terrific. I guess the only
thing I don't like about my job is that if I make a mistake,
they take it out of my pay. Otherwise, it's a good job for me
at this point in my life.

Mike Leung

1. Which sentence is the topic sentence?
2. Which words in this sentence limit what the writer can discuss in the paragraph?
3. After you read the topic sentence, what did you expect the paragraph to be about? What kinds of facts, observations, and experiences did you expect to see in the paragraph?
4. Which details do not seem related to the topic sentence? Why not?

THE TOPIC SENTENCE AS A FOCUSING GUIDE

By clarifying a paragraph's main point, a topic sentence can help readers understand the writer's ideas. And in addition to serving as a guide for readers, a topic sentence can also act as a guide for writers. If writers underline the key words in each topic sentence, then they can check to make sure that every other sentence in the paragraph supports the topic sentence. Mike Leung's paragraph illustrates how frustrating it is for readers when a writer does not stick to the idea stated in his topic sentence. Frequently, writers wander off the main point of their paragraph because they have written a topic sentence that is too narrow. Topic sentences that are too narrow are simply statements of fact that don't require much support. Readers usually react to them by thinking "So what?" Here are some examples:

- I work as a checker in Gristedes Supermarket.
- There are eight Gristedes Supermarkets in Manhattan.
- Supermarkets sell more products than do groceries.

Narrow topic sentences can be revised so that they give the writer's opinion about the topic or they make statements that need further development. Here are revisions of three preceding narrow topic sentences.

- I really enjoy my job as a checker at Gristedes.
- The eight Gristedes Supermarkets are superior to all of the other supermarkets in Manhattan.
- Supermarkets sell an incredible variety of products.

EXERCISE REVISING TOPIC SENTENCES

The topic sentences below are either too narrow or too broad to be developed in a paragraph. Decide why it would difficult to write a paragraph about each one and then write a revised version of it in the space below it. The first one has been done for you.

1. "Police are important to any community."
   What is the problem with this topic sentence?

   It's too broad — it doesn't help the writer limit his or her ideas.

   Your revision:

   The police in my community serve many important functions.

2. "I have been a policewoman for two years."
   What is the problem with this topic sentence?

   Your revision:

3. "Policemen and women often have to work ten hours a day."
   What is the problem with this topic sentence?

   Your revision:

4. "Policemen and women have problems just like the rest of us."
   What is the problem with this topic sentence?

   Your revision:

TOPIC SENTENCES AND SUPPORTING DETAILS

In Chapter 3, you practiced developing different types of supporting details—observations, experiences, and facts—for different purposes and audiences. Most topic sentences can be supported by a combination of facts, observations, and experiences. It is up to you to
balance your purpose against the reader's needs and decide which type
of details or which combination will work best for a particular topic
sentence. One way to make this decision is to consider whether you
should support your topic sentence with **examples** or with **reasons** or
with a combination of examples *and* reasons. An **example** is a detail
that answers the reader's question, "What do you mean by that statement?" Examples provide illustrations of your points—specific cases,
objects, or instances. For instance, if you wanted to support the point
that "being a housewife is a difficult job," you could provide examples
of what you mean by "difficult":

- I cook three meals a day and clean the whole house.
- I also have to do all the laundry and ironing.
- Furthermore, I have to shop for the kids and help them prepare
  for all their daily activities.

A **reason** is a detail that answers the reader's questions, "Why
should I believe you?" Reasons provide explanations and justifications

of your point—evidence that will convince readers that your argument makes sense. For instance, if you wanted to support the point that "housewives are the most unrewarded workers in this country," you could provide reasons for why you think they are "unrewarded":

- They work very hard twenty-four hours a day, but they receive no salaries.
- Their job doesn't give them any sick leave, vacation, pay or medical payments.
- When a housewife grows old, she has no pension to support her.

When you are asked to "describe," "illustrate" or "analyze" a topic, you are actually being asked to present **examples** as evidence that you understand the topic. When you are asked to "argue" or "evaluate" a topic, you are being asked to present **reasons** for your opinion about the topic. When you are asked to "discuss" a topic or to "explain" something, you should present *both* examples and reasons.

WRITING ACTIVITY SUPPORTING TOPIC SENTENCES WITH EXAMPLES AND REASONS

Develop two different paragraphs about the same topic: a job that you had or currently have. This job can be one for which you were paid by an employer or one which you did for relatives or friends (such as babysitting for a younger sibling, mowing the lawn, or painting the apartment). After you have read the following directions, do some freewriting, brainstorming, and clustering about this job.

Paragraph 1
The first paragraph should describe the job. Use facts, experiences, and observations to develop **examples** that will enable your classmates and teacher to get a clear sense of the job. What exactly was (or is) the job? What did you have to do? Where and when did you have to do it? For whom did you work? For how many days, months, or years did you do this job?

Paragraph 2
The second paragraph should evaluate the job. Use facts, experiences, and observations to develop **reasons** that will let your readers understand why you liked or disliked this job. What were (or are) its good points and its bad points? Why did you like or dislike it?

LEVELS OF GENERALITY

Effective paragraphs consist of details that are **accurate** and **specific**. If your details are inaccurate, your reader will probably find it difficult to believe you. And if your details are very vague, then your reader will not be able to understand you. Usually the topic sentence is the most general idea in a paragraph. Each of the details that support it should be specific. However, no detail is completely general or completely specific: ideas are either more general or more specific than other ideas. For example, the idea that "I have a job" is more general than the idea that "I have a job in the health care profession." Here are some ideas arranged according to their levels of generality.

1. I have a good job.
2. I have a good job as a nurse.
3. I have a good job as a baby nurse.
4. I am a baby nurse at Central General Hospital, and it is a good job.
5. I am a baby nurse at Central General Hospital, and I enjoy my job for many reasons.
6. I am a baby nurse at Central General Hospital, and I enjoy my job because I love babies and I make a good salary.
7. I am a baby nurse at Central General Hospital, and I enjoy my job because I love taking care of newborns and because I like making $35,000 a year.

Notice that each detail makes the idea above it more specific by providing more information about a key word or phrase. For example, sentence 5 gives more information about the word "nurse." It lets the reader know what kind of nurse the writer is and where she works. And sentence 7 is even more specific because it lets the reader know what the writer means by a "good" job that she "enjoys." It is important to make your supporting details specific because in school or at work, your readers do not know you well enough to understand exactly what you mean when you use vague terms like "great" or "awful." What is "awful" to you might be wonderful for your readers. If you don't explain exactly what you mean—by giving specific examples—your reader may misunderstand you or get confused. There are several ways to make supporting details more specific:

1. Give the exact names of things rather than writing about them in general terms. For example, how do these two pairs of sentences differ?
   a. She's a college teacher.
   b. Dr. Sanchez is a professor of computer science at Hunter College.

    c. Dr. Sanchez teaches several courses.

    d. Dr. Sanchez teaches Introductory Fortran, Advanced Cobol, and Integrated Systems.

2. Use concrete words that appeal to the readers' five senses—sight, hearing, touch, smell, and taste. How are these two pairs of sentences different?

    a. Dr. Sanchez doesn't look like a college professor.

    b. Dr. Sanchez is a tiny, slim woman with long, tawny red hair. Unlike my other female professors, she wears heavy makeup.

    c. Prof. Sanchez is usually very serious.

    d. Prof. Sanchez rarely smiles or laughs. She never makes jokes during a lesson, and she doesn't chat with students.

Notice that specific concrete details usually require more words or sentences to express them than do general abstract ideas. Also note that you cannot make an abstract idea more concrete or specific by explaining it with another abstract term:

> Dr. Sanchez is very serious. She usually seems quite solemn and earnest.

"Solemn" and "earnest" are just as general as "serious." Neither expresses a sensory image that allows a reader to understand exactly what the writer means by "serious."

WRITING ACTIVITY MAKING GENERAL IDEAS MORE SPECIFIC

Each of the sentences below is too general to communicate a clear idea. Rewrite each sentence so that it has exact names and concrete sensory details (that you invent). You may have to write more than one sentence.

1. My physical education teacher is okay.

2. I'm in one of his gym courses.

3. We do a lot of interesting stuff in his class.

A third way of making your details more specific is to use vivid, descriptive verbs instead of ordinary, unclear ones. For example, compare the two descriptions of a baseball player below. The first is my paragraph, and the second is a poem by Robert Francis.

The runner is on first and he keeps moving off the base toward second. He goes a little way toward second and then gets nervous and runs back to first. He steps off the base again, and the pitcher watches him closely. He moves further and further away from the base. And then, as the pitcher throws the ball toward the batter, the runner runs to second base.

THE BASE STEALER

Poised between going and back, pulled
Both ways taut like a tightrope-walker,
Fingertips pointing the opposites,
Now bouncing tiptoe like a dropped ball
Or a kid skipping rope, come on, come on,
Running a scattering of steps sideways
How he teeters, skitters, tingles, teases
Taunts them, hovers like an ecstatic bird,
He's only flirting, crowd him, crowd him,
Delicate, delicate, delicate, delicate—now!

What impression do you get from the verbs in my paragraph? How is this different from the impression that you get from the verbs in the poem?

EXERCISE **EXPERIENCING DESCRIPTIVE VERBS**

Do this exercise in a group in class or at home with your friends or family. Pick one of the sets of verbs below and act out each of the three verbs in the set. Ask the people watching you to guess each verb that you are performing and to discuss the differences in the set.

1. walk   stroll   strut
2. smile   grin   smirk
3. look   glance   glare

WRITING ACTIVITY **MAKING DETAILS MORE SPECIFIC**

Below is a paragraph that is very vague and general. On a separate piece of paper, rewrite this paragraph by making up specific details to substitute for the underlined words. Try out the methods described earlier: use exact terms, concrete sensory words, and vivid verbs.

I work in a restaurant in my neighborhood. I'm going to quit soon because I don't like this job. The first reason why I don't like it is because I get paid so little. Also, the benefits are terrible. Secondly, the restaurant is really ugly. I want to work in a place that looks nice. Furthermore, the place smells. Sometimes, I get ill from the different smells in the kitchen. The only advantage of the job is that I get some meals there. And the food tastes pretty good. Since I'd like to make a lot of money and get free meals, I'm going to look for a job in a newer, cleaner place.

A STUDENT RESPONSE

Here are two uncorrected paragraphs that a college freshman wrote about her job. In each paragraph, underline the topic sentence and circle every specific word or phrase.

On most afternoons, you can find me working hard at my job as a telephone solicitor for The Daily News. After my classes end, I ride the bus downtown, hop up to my desk on the fifth floor, and grab up the phone. Each day my supervisor hands me a new list of people's names, addresses, and phone numbers and I simply go down the list calling each one. I try to get people to subscribe to the paper by offering them discounts on home delivery or by telling them about the charity that part of their money will go to.

Telephone soliciting pays reasonably well ($3.50 an hour) and I receive some medical benefits. And the job is interesting. I don't have to worry about what to say because my speech is written down on a little card that I've almost

memorized. Most of the people I call are happy to talk to me
and many of them are willing to buy the subscriptions,
especially if they know the money is going to a decent charity
like Care or the March of Dimes. However, sometimes I get
depressed when people hang up on me or when they get very
nasty. The worst ones are the people who curse me. They make
me feel like crying. Despite these ups and downs though, I
enjoy my job and I'm lucky to have it.

                                                    Lisa Grant

---

EXERCISE **MAKING WRITING MORE SPECIFIC**

Reread Lisa Grant's paragraphs and write answers to these questions on a separate piece of paper.

1. Which examples or reasons help you to understand Grant's main points?
2. How could Grant's first paragraph be improved?
3. How could Grant's second paragraph be improved?

OPTIONS FOR DEVELOPING PARAGRAPHS

The strategies that you can use to develop a paragraph grow out of your details. Depending upon your purpose, your audience, and your examples and reasons, you can use one or more of the following strategies:

- **narrate** a story or an experience that reflects your ideas or feelings about the topic.
- **describe** a person, place, thing or process as it relates to the topic.
- **define** the topic by explaining its distinguishing characteristics and by illustrating it with examples of what you mean by it.
- **classify** people, things, processes, events, or concepts into groups according to a characteristic that is shared by all members of the group.
- **compare** or **contrast** two or more people, things, processes, events, or concepts by noting points of similarity and differences between them.

- **analyze** the parts or categories of a complex object, idea, or event *or* explain the causes or the effects of an event, or a behavior.
- **evaluate** the worth or the value of an object or an idea according to criteria or values that you specify.
- **argue** your point of view by using some or all of the strategies above.

Not only do your examples and reasons determine the most appropriate strategy for developing a paragraph, but they also determine the ordering of details. For example, when a writer narrates a story of an experience, the most natural order is a **chronological** one. In a chronological sequence, details are arranged in the order in which they actually happened in time. Here is a student paragraph that illustrates this order.

I will always remember the morning that I had my first job interview. I woke up early because I was so nervous. My fingers shook as I was shaving, and I cut myself in several places. This made me even more nervous because I worried that the interviewer would think I was careless or clumsy. I dressed up in my best grey pin-stripe suit and I shined my wing-tip shoes till they gleamed. Then I became concerned that I was going to be late, so I ran to the bus. The bus ride seemed to stretch on forever. Finally, I arrived at the company office and gave the receptionist my name. My stomach was grumbling and I was sweating all over. I tried doing yoga breathing to calm down and finally my name was called and I walked in to the first interview of my life.

Paul Brasili

WRITING ACTIVITY DEVELOPING DETAILS CHRONOLOGICALLY

On a separate piece of paper, do some freewriting and some clustering for a discovery draft of a paragraph that describes the morning of your first job interview, or your first day on a new job, or your first day at a new school. Invent an appropriate audience and purpose. After you finish your discovery draft, circle the topic sentence. Underline every specific detail and circle every descriptive verb.

Academic paragraphs often begin with a generalization—a topic sentence—that is followed by increasingly specific examples or reasons that clarify or explain the generalization. Lisa Grant's first paragraph (on page 75) illustrates this kind of ordering of details. Another typical pattern for organizing a paragraph is to develop specific details that lead up to a generalization. This method is illustrated by Grant's second paragraph. Sometimes, the order of details will be specified in the assignment. Here is an example:

> Write a one-paragraph description of a clutch pencil that will enable a novice draftsman or draftswoman to recognize it and use it. Your paragraph should identify and define the object, provide an overall description of its major components, and discuss its functional uses.

If the order is not specified and if you are not narrating an experience, you can organize your details **spatially** or **climactically**. In a spatial sequence, details are presented in an order that allows readers to see the physical relationship of different objects or parts of objects. The details can be organized from right to left, top to bottom, front to back, near to far, outside to inside, and so forth. The student paragraph that follows illustrates spatial order.

Last summer I drove a cab for a taxi company, and I never want to do that job again. Many of the cabs that are assigned to part-time drivers are wrecks that are falling apart. The outside of the cab that I was given to drive was all dented and rusted. Its windshield wipers were falling off, and its tires were dangerously bald. The old scratchy seats were falling apart with stuffing streaming out of every opening. And I always had trouble breathing in the cab. Since the ventilation openings were in the back of the cab, I was constantly breathing in fumes from my own engine.

Furthermore, the brakes were low and most of the engine valves

were leaky. Driving that cab made me really nervous.

Sal Beninotti

WRITING ACTIVITY   DEVELOPING DETAILS SPATIALLY

Do some freewriting, brainstorming, and clustering for a discovery draft of a paragraph that describes one of the following things spatially: a classroom, a room at work, or a tool or instrument that you use at work or school. Invent an appropriate audience and purpose. After you finish your discovery draft, circle the topic sentence and underline every descriptive verb.

The most typical order for presenting details in academic paragraphs is climactic. A climactic sequence organizes details in a progression from the least important to the most important: the writer saves the most important examples or reasons for the end of the paragraph. Here is an example:

I've had several jobs during the past four years, but

being my daughter's mother has to be the best job in the

world. My precious Celia is four years old now and she makes

me happy and proud in so many ways. People are always coming

up to me to tell me how beautiful she is with her sweet oval

face, black button eyes, and curling onyx hair. Not only is

she lovely on the outside, she also has a sweet gentle

personality that everyone falls in love with. Even more

importantly, she is quite smart and we have hours of fun

together reading books and playing word games. And the very

best thing about Celia is that she teaches me how to look at

the world in a new way so that I am growing and learning

almost as much as she is.

Rosaria Rogers

WRITING ACTIVITY DEVELOPING DETAILS CLIMACTICALLY

Begin with some freewriting, brainstorming, and clustering for a draft of a paragraph that describes your values. Think about what matters most to you in life: satisfying family relationships, rewarding friendships, good health, financial stability, professional success, athletic success, and so forth. Write a paragraph describing your values in specific detail, and arrange your ideas climactically.

STUDENT RESPONSES

Here are two paragraphs that use different strategies but that are both developed climactically.

EVALUATIVE PARAGRAPH ABOUT A

CAREER IN PHARMACEUTICALS

After weighing all the factors relating to choosing a career, I have decided to go into the pharmaceuticals industry. I like doctors and nurses and these are the people whom I would be meeting each day. Pharmaceutical sales involves weekly travel, and the pressure is high but I think I would enjoy it. The starting income for a pharmaceuticals salesman is average ($18,000), and this salary is reviewed semi-annually (with raises of $1,000-$3,000 possible at each review). The job also has terrific benefits including pension, medical, and dental policies and usually a free car. But the best thing about the job is that it offers excellent opportunities for promotion. A salesman or woman can become a sales manager after only five years and can make more than $30,000 a year. Thus, I think pharmaceutical sales is a good career for me.

Ken Morris

ARGUMENTATIVE PARAGRAPH

ABOUT WORKING WOMEN

Working women, especially married working women, get
rewarded in many ways. All of my girlfriends work, and
although some of our husbands have had trouble adjusting, we
wouldn't give up our jobs for anything. Working outside the
home makes us more interesting people and more stimulating
wives. We have something to talk about beside shopping and
cleaning. We can share the struggles and the joys of trying
to achieve success and happiness. This makes many of us
better companions because we can be sympathetic to our
husband's problems. Also, working outside the home lets women
meet all kinds of interesting people and go to different
places. This lets us make many more friends and business
acquaintances than if we just stayed home. But the best
reason for working is that women can earn a lot of money and
that makes a real difference to their families.

Jackie Nathanson

WRITING ACTIVITY ORDERING DETAILS FOR A DEFINITION
AND A COMPARISON PARAGRAPH

For this activity, write two separate paragraphs. For each one, do
some freewriting, brainstorming, and clustering. Then decide on the
most appropriate order for developing the details in each paragraph.

Paragraph 1
Write a paragraph in which you define the term "profession."
Your audience is fellow classmates. Begin developing your details by
looking up the term in a dictionary. However, remember that a dictionary definition cannot let your reader know what the term means to
you. Given your experiences and your knowledge, what does a "profession" mean to you? You have many options for developing a definition

paragraph: you can illustrate the term by providing several specific examples; you can narrate an experience that illustrates a profession; you can compare several different professions to show what they all have in common; or you can explain the process of achieving a profession.

Paragraph 2

Write a paragraph that compares and contrasts a "profession" with a "job." In what specific ways are a profession and a job similar? In what ways are they different? Your audience is a group of high school students who are thinking about whether they want to go college. Use your experiences, your observations, and any facts you know in order to illustrate the ways in which a job and a profession are similar *and* different. For both of these paragraphs, think about what your audience already knows about the topic and what else they might need or want to know. Also, decide exactly what you want to make your audience feel or think or do after they read each paragraph.

A STUDENT RESPONSE

Here is a comparison/contrast paragraph by a student who was considering what kind of company he wanted to work for after he graduated.

Ever since the day I took apart and reassembled my parent's television set, I knew I wished to be an electronics engineer. Like doctors and lawyers, electronics engineers specialize in one of many areas, and I want to do aerospace research and rocket design. I have been thinking about the company that I want to eventually work for, and I'm having trouble making up my mind. Do I work for a giant corporation like Rockwell International in California or a small company like Rocket Research in Washington? They both design rocket engines and conduct applied aerospace research. But Rockwell is huge: it employs 95,000 people and offers many career opportunities. Rocket Research on the other hand has only 300

people and there isn't much room for advancement. But at

Rocket, engineers are involved with all parts of systems

design and application. At Rockwell, they only get to work on

one small part of the project. I think I have to visit

several more types of rocket research firms before I can make

up my mind about the kind of place that's right for me.

Isaac Stein

1. Which details are particularly concrete or specific, enabling you to understand what Stein means?

2. Which verbs were particularly descriptive or interesting?

3. What order did Stein use to develop his details?

WRITING ACTIVITY ORDERING DETAILS FOR VARIED AUDIENCES AND PURPOSES

For this activity, write two different paragraphs about the best teacher you ever had (in school *or* out of school). For each paragraph, do some prewriting and develop a discovery draft on a separate piece of paper. Decide on an appropriate order for developing your details. Use sensory language to let the reader see and hear this person in action.

Paragraph 1

The first paragraph should begin with a topic sentence that is followed by specific examples and reasons. The audience for this paragraph is a friend who is considering taking this teacher for a course next semester (or working with this person on a job next year). Your purpose is to convince this reader to study with this teacher.

Paragraph 2

The second paragraph should be composed of specifc details leading up to your topic sentence. Develop your details climactically. The audience for this paragraph is a supervisor who is deciding whether to rehire this teacher for the next three years. Your purpose is to convince this reader to rehire the teacher.

SOMETHING TO THINK ABOUT

Below are two charts that present the results of a survey of American workers. The survey, entitled "Work in the 1980s and 1990s," was conducted by the Public Agenda Foundation. The first chart shows the ten job qualities that workers rated most important in terms of "motivation"—the qualities that would make them work harder. The second chart shows the ten job qualities that workers rated most important in terms of "satisfaction"—the qualities that would make them feel better at work.

1. What do the men and women surveyed need most to be satisfied with their jobs?

2. What job qualities most motivate these men and women to work hard at their jobs?

3. Why do you think the top "motivator" is so different from the top "satisfier"?

4. Which qualities on the list would motivate you most? Why?

5. Which qualities on the list would satisfy you most? Why?

The Top Ten Motivators

Managers and Professionals		Blue-Collar Workers		Clerical Workers
Men	Women	Men	Women	Women
A good chance for advancement (48%/29%)*	A good chance for advancement (47%/22%)*	Good pay (50%/22%)*	Good pay (44%/28%)*	A good chance for advancement (56%/19%)*
A great deal of responsibility (45/28)	A job that enables me to develop my abilities (44/18)*	A good chance for advancement (47/23)*	A good chance for advancement (42/17)*	A job that enables me to develop my abilities (52/24)
Recognition for good work (44/32)*	Recognition for good work (43/30)*	Pay tied to performance (47/28)*	Pay tied to performance (41/30)*	A challenging job (47/23)
A job where I can think for myself (44/29)	A great deal of responsibility (40/22)	Recognition for good work (42/37)*	A challenging job (37/23)	A job where I can think for myself (45/21)
A job that enables me to develop my abilities (42/28)*	A job where I can think for myself (38/33)	Interesting work (38/34)*	A job where I can think for myself (35/29)	A job that allows me to be creative (45/25)
A challenging job (42/29)	Good pay (37/30)*	See end results of my efforts (38/22)	Interesting work (35/28)*	See the end results of my efforts (45/30)
A job that allows me to be creative (41/29)	Pay tied to performance (37/33)	A job that enables me to develop my abilities (36/29)	A job that enables me to develop my abilities (34/27)	Good pay (42/35)*
A job with pay tied to performance (40/39)*	A challenging job (35/25)	A challenging job (34/38)	See end results of my efforts (34/31)	A great deal of responsibility (42/37)
A say in important decisions (39/33)	A say in important decisions (32/33)	A job that allows me to be creative (34/34)	A job that allows me to be creative (33/33)	Recognition for good work (39/32)*
A place that does quality work (39/29)	A place that does quality work (32/32)	A job where I can think for myself (33/39)*	Recognition for good work (32/39)*	Interesting work (37/41)*

The first figure in parentheses is the percentage in the group that rated this factor a motivator; the second shows those who called it a satisfier.

*Items marked with an asterisk were on the list of the top-ten job features this group of workers most wanted more of (WORKING WOMAN, June 1983).

The Top Ten Satisfiers

Managers and Professionals		Blue-Collar Workers		Clerical Workers
Men	*Women*	*Men*	*Women*	*Women*
Job without too much rush and stress (71%/6%)	Job without too much rush and stress (57%/15%)	Job without too much rush and stress (57%/20%)	Job without too much rush and stress (55%/20%)	Convenient location (69%/13%)
Good working conditions (67/9)	People really care about me as a person (57/12)	Good working conditions (57/13)	Being informed about what goes on (55/10)	Working with people I like (69/8)
Convenient location (65/9)	Working with people I like (56/14)	Convenient location (53/10)	Getting along well with supervisor (51/17)	Job without too much rush and stress (66/12)
Being able to control work pace (61/9)	Convenient location (55/12)	Working with people I like (52/22)	Working with people I like (48/16)	Being able to control work pace (62/8)
Flexible working hours (61/15)	Getting along well with supervisor (54/17)	Getting along well with supervisor (52/20)	Flexible working hours (48/11)	Good working conditions (60/14)
Working with people I like (56/15)	Good fringe benefits (52/21)*	Being informed about what goes on (50/19)	Being able to control work pace (45/19)	Informal work environment (59/16)
Good fringe benefits (53/25)*	Job security, little chance of being laid off (52/27)	People who listen to your ideas (50/28)	People treat me with respect (45/17)*	All the tools I need to do my job (59/21)
Never asked to do anything improper or immoral (53/11)	Good working conditions (51/11)	Informal work environment (49/7)	Convenient location (44/14)	Efficient, effective managers (58/20)
Place I'm so proud of I want everyone to know I work there (53/20)	Never asked to do anything improper or immoral (50/15)	Being able to control work pace (47/29)	Good working conditions (44/14)	Fair treatment (54/15)*
Employer with good reputation (52/21)	Flexible working hours (48/19)	Fair treatment (46/26)	People who listen to your ideas (44/17)	Getting along well with supervisor (54/27)

The first figure in parentheses is the percentage of the group that rated this factor a satisfier; the second is the percentage that rated it a motivator.

*Items marked with an asterisk were on the list of the top-ten job features this group of workers most wanted more of (WORKING WOMAN, June 1983).

The following is a cartoon about one woman's ideal job.

"I'm hoping to find something in a meaningful, humanist, outreach kind of bag, with flexible hours, non-sexist bosses, and fabulous fringes."

1. What do think her chances of finding this job are?

2. What kinds of jobs might fulfill her needs?

WRITING ASSIGNMENT   **DEVELOPING TWO PARAGRAPHS ABOUT AN IDEAL JOB**

For this writing assignment, you will be developing two paragraphs about a job that you would consider ideal. Even if you have already chosen a career for which to prepare, speculate on the kind of job you would most like to do if you could have your choice of any job in the world. Is there a job that you always dreamed of doing when you were younger? Imagine that you didn't have to worry about family responsibilities, or money, or location—what job would make you feel truly satisfied? Write a discovery draft of a paragraph that describes this ideal job in detail. Then write a discovery draft of a second paragraph that gives specific reasons why this job would be ideal for you.

Prewriting Guidelines

Your first job is to specify your focus:

- What exactly are you describing?
- How much do you already know about this job?
- What else do you need to find out about it?

Next, determine your audience:

- Who might be interested in your ideal job?
- What do these readers know about the job?
- What do they need to know about it or about you?

Then, refine your purpose for writing this description. While your goal is to describe your ideal job and the reasons for your choice, you need to consider exactly what effect you want to have on your reader:

- How do you want your readers to see you?
- What do you want your reader to think about you?

Begin by using the techniques that you learned about in Chapter 2 to do some prewriting: on a separate piece of paper, write down the job title and do some freewriting, brainstorming, and clustering about it. Turn these ideas into a discovery draft of each paragraph. When you are finished with each paragraph, circle the topic sentence in each, and underline all of the specific words and phrases and all of the vivid verbs. In the margin, next to each paragraph, write down the order that you used to develop your details. Then, get your classmates' responses to these drafts by following the guidelines on "How to Get Feedback About Your Discovery Draft" on pages 40–41. After you have received some responses to your discovery draft, use the following questions to determine whether it needs more specific supporting details.

Revising Questions

1. Which words in each paragraph are examples of sensory language? Where do I need more of these examples?
2. Which details in each paragraph are very specific? Which ones are too vague or general?
3. Who is my audience, and what else do they need to know about the job that I am describing?

4. What facts have I included about the job? What other facts could I state about this job that would reveal why it is ideal for me?
5. What observations have I included about this job? What other observations could I tell about this job that would reveal why it is ideal for me?
6. What experiences have I included about this job? What other experiences could I relate about this job that would reveal why it is ideal for me?
7. How are the details in each paragraph organized? If the logic breaks down, where does it do so and why?
8. What words make each paragraph complete or make it sound incomplete?

Revise your discovery draft based on your classmates' comments and on your answers to the Revising Questions above.

ADDITIONAL TOPICS TO WRITE ABOUT

Here are some more topics for you to write paragraphs about and practice the skills that you learned in this chapter.

1. Narrate an experience at school or at work that taught you a lesson.
2. Narrate an experience that you had with a classmate or with a coworker that made you feel very pleased with yourself.
3. Describe your academic or professional goals and dreams.
4. Describe the nature of the work that people do in the job or profession for which you are preparing.
5. Define success: What does success mean to you (emotionally, socially, professionally, financially, athletically, or in other ways)?
6. Classify the different fields or specializations in the job or profession for which you are preparing.
7. Compare or contrast going to school and working at a job or profession: How are these two activities similar and/or different?
8. Analyze the steps or processes required to prepare for and to get a position in the job or profession in which you are interested.
9. Evaluate the job or profession for which you are preparing: What are its negative and positive characteristics?
10. Argue your viewpoint about sex discrimination in the workplace: Should women have equal opportunities to work at any job or profession that currently employs only men?

Reminders

Specify your focus:

- What points do you want to explain or describe?
- How much do you already know about your topic?
- What else do you need to find out about it?

Determine your audience:

- Who might be interested in reading your paragraph?
- What does this reader (or group of readers) already know about your topic?
- What else do they need or want to know about it or about you?

Refine your purpose:

- How do you want your reader to see you?
- What do you want your reader to think, feel, or do?

After you finish your discovery draft, get your classmates' responses by following the guidelines for "How to Get Feedback About Your Discovery Draft" previously discussed on pages 40–41.

ISSUES FOR YOUR JOURNAL

1. What did you learn from this chapter that you had not known before?
2. Reread your journal entries for the past month. Which ones had you forgotten? How does it make you feel to recover thoughts, observations, and feelings that you had forgotten about?
3. What does it mean to be a "man" or a "woman"? How does a child learn his or her sex role? How did you learn your sex role? Who or what taught you what it means to be a man or a woman?
4. Does pollution bother you? If so, what kind bothers you the most? Why? Do you think we are destroying our air and water? If so, what can the average citizen do about this environmental destruction?
5. How you feel about space exploration? Our government spends millions of dollars on the research and development of space shuttles, space satellites, and space weapons. What is your opinion of this expenditure?

WRITING ESSAYS

Because there is no neat gradual way to learn to write and because progress seems so unpredictable and just plain slow, a major part of learning to write is learning to put up with this frustrating process itself.

PETER ELBOW

INTRODUCTION: ESSAY DEVELOPMENT

Up to this point, most of the writing that you have been doing for this book has taken the form of several long paragraphs. Often, however, your teachers or employers may ask you to write about topics that require you to develop your ideas in more detail than you could in one or two paragraphs. For these assignments, you need to write multi-paragraph essays or reports. Although an essay is longer and more detailed than a paragraph, the method for developing both types of writing is essentially the same. Both forms—the paragraph and the essay—require writers to go through the following processes:

- focusing on a central idea for a clearly defined purpose and audience
- developing a main point with specific facts, observations, and experiences that can serve as convincing examples and reasons
- arranging details in a logical order
- writing an effective introduction and a conclusion

In an essay, the main point that the writer wants to make is his or her "thesis statement." The **thesis statement** of an essay, like the **topic sentence** of a paragraph, limits what can be discussed in the essay and acts as a focusing guide for the writer *and* for the reader. A thesis statement is usually more general than a topic sentence is because it expresses the main point of the whole essay. Each paragraph within the essay may have its own specific topic sentence. Since you have already practiced all the skills necessary for writing effective paragraphs, you should feel confident about writing effective essays.

GROUP WRITING TASK **LISTING THE DIFFERENCES BETWEEN PARAGRAPHS AND ESSAYS**

This writing task will help you explore some of the differences between a paragraph and an essay. Read the uncorrected paragraph and essay below and answer the questions that follow. Choose one person to record the group's answers.

DISCOVERY DRAFT OF A PARAGRAPH

ON THE EFFECTS OF TECHNOLOGY

America is slowly becoming a high-tech society. New

technologies like computers and chemicals have changed the way

most of us live and work. While many people like the results
of these changes, many of us are suffering the consequences of
these changes. And the worst consequence is unemployment.
The millions of people out of work today think that it is due
to the recession. But it isn't. People have been put out of
work by robots, computers, and other kinds of machines that
can do the work that people used to do. These machines can do
work faster and more efficiently so many industries have fired
people and put in machines. And not only workers but managers
have also been affected by technology. Managers who cannot
adjust to computers are losing their jobs every day.
Technology may be improving our life but it is also taking
away our livelihood!

Robert Mason

DISCOVERY DRAFT OF AN ESSAY

BASED ON THE PARAGRAPH ABOVE

America is slowly becoming a high-tech society. New
technologies like computers, robotics and chemical engineering
have changed the way most of us live and work. Life is
certainly easier now that we have new foods and drugs,
microwave ovens to cook in, computers to work on and new forms
of energy. However, while life has gotten easier in some
ways, technology has had terrible consequences for many, many
Americans.

Many people are suffering the consequences of the changes
brought by technology. In my opinion, the worst consequence

of the new scientific technologies is unemployment. Millions of people are out of work in America today, and many of them think that it is due to the recession. But it isn't. Many people have been put out of work by robots, computers, and other kinds of machines that can do the work that people used to do. The clearest example of this is the automotive industry, where robots have replaced human workers. These machines can do work faster and more efficiently, they can work twenty-four hours a day and they don't get sick or drunk. Thus hundreds of thousands of people who used to work on building cars no longer have jobs and may never get new ones.

In addition, workers are not the only people who are affected by technology. Managers who cannot adjust to computers and telecommunications systems are losing their jobs every day. And at the other end, secretaries who don't learn how to use computers may be fired or their jobs may be taken over by computers.

Thus we may have more food, better drugs, cheaper energy, and better communications. But we may lose our ability to pay for or use these things. Technology may be improving our lives, but it is also taking away our livelihoods!

Robert Mason

1. Underline the topic sentence in the paragraph and the thesis statement in the essay. How do they differ?
2. Circle the introductory sentence in the paragraph and the introduction in the essay. In what ways do they differ?

3. In what ways do the examples and the reasons in the paragraph differ from those in the essay?

4. Mark off the concluding sentence in the paragraph and the conclusion in the essay. In what ways do they differ?

TITLE AND THESIS STATEMENT

An essay's title and thesis statement focus the writer and the reader on the main points that will be developed in the paragraphs that follow. Since it is important that your title and thesis statement reflect exactly what your essay will discuss, you may want to write them both *after* you have written a discovery draft of your essay. For example, the first draft of Robert Mason's essay did not have a clear thesis statement because he was not sure whether he wanted to prove a point about the effects of technology or just relate his observations about the topic. When he did some more brainstorming, he came up with more details and then he wrote another draft. Only then did he write a thesis statement: "While life has gotten easier in some ways, technology has had terrible consequences for many, many Americans."

WRITING ACTIVITY **PREDICTING THE CONTENT OF ESSAYS FROM TITLES AND THESIS STATEMENTS**

This activity is designed to show you how much readers rely on a clear, accurate title and thesis statement to get an overview of an essay. For each title and thesis statement below, write a brief description of the ideas that could be developed in an essay based on that title and thesis statement. The first one has been done for you as an example.

1. Title: "The Benefits of Science"

Thesis Statement: "During the past century, scientists and their practical partners—engineers—have worked together to solve some of humanity's worst problems and have improved the daily life of millions of people."

Ideas that this essay will probably develop:

The essay will probably give examples of the problems that scientists and engineers have worked together to solve.

2. Title: "The Case Against Nuclear Energy"

Thesis Statement: "Those people who see nuclear energy as the clean, cheap, cost-efficient answer to America's ongoing energy crisis have somehow managed to ignore all of its hazards and dangerous problems."

Ideas that this essay will probably develop:

3. Title: "Chemical Technology: Our Answer or Our Annihilation?"

Thesis Statement: "While we have all come to be dependent on the products produced by modern chemical technology, many people wonder whether accidents like the 1984 Bhopal tragedy will increase and destroy whole populations."

Ideas that this essay will probably develop:

4. Title: "Knowing Little About How Things Work"

Thesis Statement: "At a time when television broadcasts, newspapers, magazines, advertisements, and political speeches are regularly sprinkled with technical terms, the U.S. public often has very little idea of what the terms mean."

Ideas that this essay will probably develop:

A PROFESSIONAL RESPONSE

Below is an essay that has the same title and thesis statement as does #4 in the writing activity above. How accurate were your predictions of the ideas that would be developed in an essay with this title and thesis statement?

KNOWING LITTLE ABOUT HOW THINGS WORK

At a time when television broadcasts, newspapers, magazines, advertisements and political speeches are regularly sprinkled with technical terms, the U.S. public often has little idea what the terms mean. A recent probe of the technological literacy conducted for the National Science Foundation (NSF) shows that only 31 percent of about 2,000 people surveyed by telephone have a clear understanding of radiation, 27 percent understand what gross national product (GNP) means and 24 percent understand what computer software is. Just one in five think they know how a telephone works.

The same poll, conducted late last year by Jon D. Miller, director of the public opinion laboratory at Northern Illinois University in DeKalb, shows that about two in five people believe that rocket launchings have affected the weather, that space vehicles from other civilizations have visited the earth and that lucky numbers exist. Overall, on a rough index of technological literacy, people from 18 to 24 years old—those most recently in high school— had a significantly *lower* rating than all other age groups except those over 65.

"It is clear that young Americans just emerging from their formal education are not as likely to be technologically literate as somewhat older adults," says Miller. He presented his preliminary survey results last week in Baltimore at a conference on technological literacy.

"The technologically literate person should understand how basic technologies work, which aspects are changeable and which are not, and some of the impacts and implications of major technologies," Miller says. "Increasingly the issues on the public agenda are going to be issues that involve some aspect of technology."

Ironically, these results come at a time when public interest in science is relatively high. In another recently published NSF survey, almost half of the respondents report great interest in new inventions and scientific discoveries. Young people, regardless of grade level, are particularly interested.

Nevertheless, "interest is not the same as literacy or competence," says Erich Bloch, NSF director. About three quarters of those interested in science and technology admit they don't know very much about either one, he adds.

"What we have," says Miller, "is a large number of people who believe in science, who have unrestrained faith in it, but who haven't the foggiest notion why it happens." The biggest problem is not hostility to science, but that people deal with it as if it were magic, he says. Moreover, people tend to confuse real or likely technologies and fictional ones.

"Our concern," says Rustum Roy, who chaired the meeting and directs the NSF-funded "Science through Science, Technology and Society" project at Pennsylvania State University in University Park, "is that we have not been able to educate 99 percent of the public to appreciate technological issues." A larger segment of the population should understand the choices and values inherent in today's and future technologies, he says. "We must insist that school systems teach it."

"What we're talking about is a redefinition of what's fundamental for learning," says Cecily C. Selby of New York University. Technology studies are generally not part of school curricula. Too much emphasis is put on the theoretical, she says, and too little on how things work.

However, notes F. James Rutherford, education officer for the American Association for the Advancement of Science, based in Washington, D.C., "It's not clear at all what we need to know collectively across the whole range of science, technology and social behavior . . . in order to lead rich, full lives."

"You don't have to be a scientist or a technician to vote," says Gov. Richard D. Lamm of Colorado. But, he adds, "we have to make sure that we are making our science and technology decisions correctly."

I. Peterson

1. In the essay above, what do you think was the writer's purpose?

2. The essay appeared in a newsweekly called *Science News*. Whom do you think the writer imagined as his audience?

3. Reread the essay and underline the facts and observations that support the writer's thesis statement most convincingly.

4. How has the writer organized his supporting details?

OPTIONS FOR DEVELOPING ESSAYS

Writing an essay is very similar to writing paragraphs. First you have to choose a topic that you feel comfortable writing about. If the topic has been assigned, you have to decide on a **focus** that is neither too broad or too narrow. Next, you have to figure out what is your **purpose** and who is your actual or imaginary **audience**. Then, you should do some freewriting or brainstorming or clustering to develop the facts, observations, and experiences that will accomplish your purpose for these readers. The strategies for developing these details are the same ones that you practiced in Chapter 4 when you were developing different types of paragraphs: narrating, describing, defining, comparing, contrasting, analyzing, evaluating, and persuading. These are simply the patterns of thinking that people use to sort out the events and experiences of their daily lives. A writer may use only one of these patterns to develop an essay or he or she may use a combination of these strategies. For example, if you were asked to write an essay on technology and science, you might decide to write an essay that is purely descriptive, with each supporting paragraph describing a different form of current technology. An outline of a draft of this essay might look like this:

- Paragraph 1—Introduction (with a "working" thesis statement)
- Paragraph 2—Description of one form of technology that has proven very valuable or useful
- Paragraph 3—Description of another form of helpful technology
- Paragraph 4—Description of the results of a study of the impact of technology on human progress
- Paragraph 5—Conclusion

Depending on your purpose and audience, you could also have developed different details and used them to write an essay contrasting the advantages and the disadvantages of modern technology. Here is an outline of this essay:

- Paragraph 1—Introduction (including a "working" thesis statement about the impact of technology on the human condition)
- Paragraph 2—Description of the most important recent technological breakthroughs
- Paragraph 3—Description of some of the advantages of these breakthroughs
- Paragraph 4—Description of some of the disadvantages of these breakthroughs
- Paragraph 5—Analysis of whether the benefits of the breakthroughs outweigh their disadvantages and problems
- Paragraph 6—Conclusion about the impact of technology

Notice that although the essay outlined above is a **comparison-contrast** essay, three of its body paragraphs are **descriptive** and one is **analytical**. For a different purpose and audience, one could use a different combination of strategies:

- Paragraph 1—Introduction (including a definition of modern technology and a "working" thesis statement)
- Paragraph 2—Description of one problem created by modern technology
- Paragraph 3—Description of another problem
- Paragraph 4—Analysis of some of the causes of these problems
- Paragraph 5—Analysis of some reasons why it is important to re-think our attitude toward the uses of technology
- Paragraph 6—Conclusion

The strategies of the overall form of an essay develop naturally from one's purpose, thesis, and audience. Sometimes, thinking about the purpose and the audience helps writers realize that they need to do more brainstorming and clustering in order to generate new facts, observations, and experiences about the topic. These new details may suggest a pattern for a particular paragraph or for the entire essay, and this pattern may in turn suggest specific strategies.

A STUDENT RESPONSE

Below is a draft of an essay that a student wrote for her school newspaper. Her purpose was to convince other students that the chemical industry does not have adequate safety procedures. This essay is a persuasive one, but the writer used a combination of several types of paragraph patterns to make her point. Try to identify the strategy (or strategies) that the writer used in each paragraph.

THIRD REVISION OF AN ESSAY

ON THE SAFETY OF CHEMICAL TECHNOLOGY

1)   Recently, I was thinking about how "chemically dependent" all of us are. For example, each morning, I wake up and eat a breakfast composed of chemical preservatives and additives. Then I dress myself in clothes woven from chemical fibers and drive to school in a car that is built from chemical compounds and that runs on other chemicals. I eat my chemical lunch and drink a totally synthetic soda. If I'm not feeling well, I take chemically-created pills or tablets. I don't know how we would exist without all of these chemicals, but I wonder if we are paying too high a price.

2)   When I say "too high a price," I'm not talking about their cost in money. What I mean is that chemical engineering is a dangerous industry, and I think we are all vulnerable to chemical accidents. Everyone knows about the worst chemical accident in history, the release of toxic gas in Bhopal, India that killed almost 10,000 people and injured another 100,000. The chemical company responsible for this accident was Union Carbide, the same company that manufactures many of the additives in my food and the synthetics in my clothes.

3)   When the Bhopal accident occurred, everybody said that it was an isolated incident that could never occur in America with all of its safety standards and checks. But it happened

again, this time in West Virginia, when another deadly
chemical seeped out of a Union Carbide plant. This accident
was similar to the one in Bhopal. Somehow aldicarb oxide, a
toxic chemical, leaked out of the plant. It was a miracle
that nobody died. Unlike in Bhopal, no one was killed, and
only 100 people were injured by the fumes. Clearly, however,
these kinds of accidents are happening more frequently than
anyone would have believed.

4)   What causes these kinds of chemical accidents? Union
Carbide hasn't answered this question, but it seems that
safety procedures in many different chemical engineering
companies are unbelievably loose. People working in some
factories don't even know that they are working with toxic
chemicals nor do the people who live in the neighboring
communities. Safety drills aren't practiced regularly and
neighborhood evacuation plans don't exist or do not really
work. A repeat of the Bhopal nightmare could happen just
about anywhere near you or near me.

5)   I know that many of the chemical manufacturers are now
developing policies about chemical accidents and are trying to
establish warning systems and evacuation plans. But I think
their efforts are too little and too late.

                                          Marla McWilliams

How do you feel about McWilliams's assertions?

A PROFESSIONAL RESPONSE

Below is an excerpt from a book on bioengineering by David Lygre. Read it carefully and underline the main point in each paragraph.

Reverence for life. Everyone I know believes in that. There's a mystery and wonder in life that fills us with awe and humility; it seems impossible that we could ever understand it all.

And yet, as we learn more about the mechanics of life, some of its secrets are disappearing. We're discovering how living creatures obey the same laws of nature as the rest of creation. Just as we are seizing control over our physical world, we are learning how to manipulate our biological world—to make "test-tube babies," to change our genetic makeup, to invent artificial body parts, to alter our brains, and to live longer. Indeed, we may even discover we can make life itself.

The revolution in biology could change not only our physical selves, but also the way we think of ourselves and others. The implications are truly stunning. As we put life under the microscope, carefully dissecting and analyzing each of its parts in the most exquisite detail, we may come to view life as a material, a lump of clay we can mold to our design. No longer will we accept the notion that a disease is incurable; no longer will we believe our bodies must eventually wear out and die; no longer will we accept whatever genetic features we happen to be born with. Indeed, we will no longer accept nature's way as inevitable, for we will wrest that power—and responsibility—from her.

Our technology promises to sweep us into a golden age, an age where we will control the mechanics of life. But our glittering new tools are only part of the story, for they are intertwined with the whole fabric of our society. Indeed, they create social, ethical, and legal dilemmas we have not faced before, problems we must resolve if our new age is to be a better one. For example, we have learned how to separate procreation from intercourse; now we can consider them separate matters as we seek moral guidelines for our behavior. With artificial insemination and "test-tube babies" at our disposal, we no longer must accept infertility as nature's final verdict; now we must decide how and when we should take matters into our own hands. When human cloning becomes a reality, we will have to decide when, if ever, to use it. As we learn how to diagnose more genetic diseases early in pregnancy, we will increasingly base our abortion decisions on the quality of our fetuses, including their sex. And as we learn how to control our genetic makeup directly, we will have even more power to choose what kinds of people we want. Who will we accept as "healthy" and "normal"? And since we will be able to keep people mechanically alive almost indefinitely, we will also have to decide when to let them die.

These and other issues we will explore spring directly from our growing ability to manipulate life. The intrusion of this technology on our most intimate activities—having children, growing old, dying—forces us to respond. But what should we say? Should we say we will use these tools to benefit the largest number of people, or should our first priority be the dignity of each person? Whose rights are paramount—those of society as a whole, the prospective parents, the individual?

As the biorevolution speeds ahead, we find our legal, ethical, and social values lagging behind. It is hardly surprising. We pass new laws, for example, because of real problems, not hypothetical, pie-in-the-sky ones. The trouble is that some of these problems are not just hypothetical anymore. Our moral and social values also take time to change. Yet some of the questions we again face (What is life? When does life begin? When does it end? What is "meaningful" life? When should we "play God"?) are timeless, and it may be too much to expect that we will reach a consensus. Moreover, it is not at all clear how much our values should change just to accommodate our advancing technology. Indeed, science tells us what we *can* do; it does not tell us what we *should* do.

In the space below, summarize this excerpt by writing the author's main idea and most important details *in your own words*. Your summary should be brief—no longer than five sentences.

WRITING ACTIVITY   **COMBINING PATTERNS TO DEVELOP AN ESSAY**

How do you feel about bioengineering? Today scientists are using technology to develop new drugs, new sources of fuel, and new kinds of food. Bioengineers have also developed techniques for overcoming infertility (through artificial insemination and "test-tube" fertilization) and have also produced many artificial organs including hearts, heart pacemakers, kidneys, veins, and hip joints. Moreover, bioengineers are currently working on drugs to enable humans to live longer and to allow the transplantation and even regeneration of body parts. Read the directions that follow and then write a discovery draft of an essay about your reactions to these uses of technology.

1. Begin by doing ten minutes of freewriting on this topic. Write down any experiences that you have had with bioengineering and observations that you have about it or facts that you know about it.
2. Narrow down your focus on this essay. What point do you want to make about bioengineering?
3. Decide for whom you are writing. What is this audience like? How familiar are they with the topic? How do they feel about it? Make a list of all the things that they will need or want to know about this topic.
4. Decide on your purpose. What exactly do you want to explain, describe, or prove? What do you want your audience to feel, think, or do?
5. On a separate piece of paper, do five minutes of brainstorming your focus. Circle the words or phrases that seem most important or useful and draw lines between the circle that seem related.
6. Take two of your circles from your brainstorming and do five minutes of clustering about them. Then, write a sentence that explains what your clustering is about.
7. Write a thesis statement about your focus.
8. Write four paragraphs that will support this thesis statement. For each paragraph, choose one of the following strategies. (Do *not* write nine paragraphs.)

   - Define "bioengineering" and illustrate your definition with examples of what you mean by this term.
   - Narrate an experience that you have had with the products of bioengineering (and explain how that experience reflects your opinions about it).
   - Describe some consequences of bioengineering and describe your reactions to them.
   - Describe the reactions of your friends or relatives to results of bioengineering.
   - Classify different types of bioengineering (and let the reader know how you feel about each type).
   - Compare and contrast the results of one type of bioengineering to another (and let the reader know how you feel about each type).

- Compare and contrast the responses of different groups of people to bioengineering and try to explain why these groups feel differently.
- Compare and contrast current bioengineering efforts to the bioengineering efforts that existed ten years ago.
- Analyze the effects of bioengineering on our society or on particular groups of people in our society.

When you are finished writing your discovery draft of these four paragraphs, follow the guidelines for "How to Get Feedback About Your Discovery Draft" discussed on pages 40–41.

A STUDENT RESPONSE

Here is an uncorrected student response to the preceding writing activity.

DISCOVERY DRAFT OF AN ESSAY ON BIOENGINEERING

I think that bacteria are the horses and cattle of the future. Scientists will breed them and harness them to provide us with food and energy just like horses and cattle used to. And one day thanks to technology and the bioengineering of bacteria, people on this planet will not go hungry any more.

Millions of people around the world do not have enough to eat and are malnourished. They don't eat a balanced diet and they often get sick. Bioengineering can solve this problem. Biochemists are now creating techniques for growing bacteria that produce food. They can stimulate bacteria to act like green plants and produce starch from carbon dioxide and sunlight. If large quantities of this starch could be

produced cheaply then nobody would ever have to go hungry
again.

Also bioengineers are splicing genes in different
bacteria to make them produce things like vitamins and
antibiotics. If these things could be produced cheaply they
could be distributed all over the world. This would mean the
end of malnourishment and the diseases associated with it.
For example enough synthetic vitamins C and D are now
available to wipe out scurvy and pellegra. If other countries
could buy or develop these synthetic vitamins, these terrible
diseases would be wiped out.

Some people say that people should not tinker with nature
and that changing genes or bacteria is dangerous or has the
potential to be dangerous. But I think that anything we can
do to end the misery of hunger and starvation in this world
ought to be done. The benefits are worth the risk.

                                             David McMahon

What is McMahon's thesis and what is your response to it?

WRITING ACTIVITY DEVELOPING AN ESSAY

Here is another activity that will help you feel more confident
about your ability to use different strategies to develop essays. For this

activity, focus on another use of technology—space exploration. Currently, our country is exploring outer space for many purposes including the building of space colonies to solve the problem of overpopulation and the development of space weapons to protect us against nuclear attacks. America currently spends millions of dollars on research and development of space satellites, space shuttles, and space stations. How do you feel about space exploration and about all of the money that is spent on it? Develop a discovery draft of an essay on this topic by following these directions:

1. After completing ten minutes of freewriting, write down your feelings about space exploration, space colonies, or space weapons. Write down any experiences that you have had relating to this topic and any facts that you know or observations that you have.
2. Narrow down your focus on this essay. What point do you want to make?
3. Decide for whom you are writing. What is this audience like? How familiar are they with the topic? How do they feel about it? Make a list of all of the things that they might need or want to know about it.
4. Decide on your purpose. What do you want to explain, describe, or prove? What do you want your readers to think, feel, or do?
5. On a separate piece of paper, do five minutes of brainstorming on the focus that you have chosen for this essay. Then, circle the words or phrases that seem most important and draw lines between circles that seem to be related to one another.
6. Take two of your circles from your brainstorming and do five minutes of clustering about them. When you are finished, write a sentence that explains what your clustering is mainly about.
7. Review your freewriting, brainstorming, and clustering, and decide if you have enough ideas to start writing a draft of an essay. If you think that you do not have enough details, think of more facts, observations, and experiences that can serve as examples and reasons. When you think you have enough details, write a working thesis statement.
8. Examine your thesis statement and the details that you have developed and decide what types of paragraphs you should write to support your thesis.

   - Should you define your key terms and examples of what you mean by them?
   - Should you narrate an experience that supports your point?
   - Should you describe specific examples of people, things, or places (and your observations about them)?
   - Should you give several specific examples that illustrate your points?

- Should you explain the similarities and the differences in things that you are discussing?
- Should you analyze causes or effects?
- Should you try to persuade your readers with facts, observations, and experiences?

INTRODUCTIONS

The first paragraph of an essay is the most crucial one because it makes the reader decide whether or not to continue reading. In addition, the introductory paragraph usually states the writer's thesis and point of view so that the reader knows what to expect from the essay. Many experienced writers often write their introduction *after* they have finished writing a draft of their body paragraphs and have a clear idea of what they wanted to show or to prove. In other words, they may write a one-sentence introduction and a one-sentence conclusion. Then, after they finish the first draft of the whole essay, they expand and revise their introductory and concluding sentences. Here are some possible approaches for capturing your reader's attention in your introduction.

1. Refer to a common condition that your thesis will discuss. For example:

    Everyone is a born writer. Young children love to tell stories and young storytellers are thrilled when someone else can read their artful squiggles. But some of us lose our natural spontaneity as we grow up, and writing becomes more and more difficult to do.

2. Start with a direct quote that illustrates your thesis. For example:

    "I can't write. I'm trying to begin, I can't think of anything to say," wrote Patricia Cumming in her essay on writing. Many students in our schools today feel similarly.

3. Use a brief story that illustrates your thesis. For example:

    When my little brother Tommy was born, my life changed. When I first saw him, I knew something was wrong with him, but I didn't know how much that something was going to affect me.

4. Ask a question that will lead to your thesis. For example:

    Everyone knows that women and men in America are not treated as equals. Women have less power and make less money. Why is this so?

Remember, the approach that you select for your introduction must be appropriate for your topic, your purpose, and your audience.

WRITING ACTIVITY **WRITING INTRODUCTIONS**

Examine the four paragraphs on bioengineering that you wrote for the writing activity on pages 104–106. On a separate piece of paper, write *two* different introductions for an essay that would incorporate these four paragraphs. Use a different approach for each introduction.

Special Introductions

If you are writing an extended essay for a term paper, a research paper, or a lab report, you will have to use a different approach to writing an introduction than the general approaches described on page 109. To get a better idea of what these special introductions look like, examine some essays in the professional journals in the social and physical sciences. The introduction to a paper in the social sciences usually states the question or issue that the paper will explore and explains its significance.

Every society has some system of ranking or stratifying its members. Since societies differ greatly in the criteria by which members are stratified, it is important to examine the factors that determine one's position in any given society. There are a variety of overlapping factors that affect the social stratification system of America today.

The introductory paragraph of a paper in the *natural sciences* is slightly different. Generally, a research report or a lab report begins with a brief discussion of the background of the paper (including the nature, purpose, and scope of the research or experiment). The introduction in science papers should also include a clear statement of the problem.

Several recent studies have shown that cell division is affected by cell polarity at fertilization (Childs and Graves, 1980; Anderson and Beedle, 1981). Other researchers have concluded that cell polarity is not a critical factor in determining differentiation (Roberts, 1979; Passmore and Gunther, 1982). Thus, the importance of cell polarity remains unresolved. This review of the literature on the effects of cell polarity was undertaken to clarify the issues concerning cell division and differentiation.

CONCLUSIONS

The closing paragraph of an essay is just as important as the opening one. If a conclusion is effectively written, it lets the reader know that the writer has supported his or her thesis, and it gives the essay an ending so the reader isn't left hanging. Just as there are several approaches to writing effective introductions, there are a variety of ways of writing interesting conclusions:

1. Briefly summarize the essay's main points. For example:
   Despite these ups and downs, though, I enjoy my job and I'm lucky to have it.
2. Make an interesting analogy or comparison. For example:
   Producing writing, then, is not so much like filling a basin or a pool once, but rather getting water to keep flowing *through* till it finally runs clear.
3. Suggest specific actions that the reader should take in light of your information. For example:
   Thus, you can get ideas for writing simply by opening your eyes and your ears to what is going on inside of you and all around you.
4. Speculate about what your thesis implies for the future. For example:
   Although it took many years for me to appreciate the wonder of having that very unique and talented lady for my grandmother, I will never again begrudge her chosen path in life. In fact, someday I may follow in her footsteps.
5. Make a brief remark that sums up your feelings. For example:
   I wish that I could write as well as I run.

WRITING ACTIVITY WRITING CONCLUSIONS

Read the following brief essay. It is an uncorrected revision of an essay written by a college freshman in response to the topic "space exploration." The concluding paragraph of this essay has been left off. Write *two* different conclusions for this essay, using different methods.

Why do the mightiest nations of the world spend so much energy and money on space exploration? Why are American taxpayers willing to pay billions of dollars each year for the construction of satellites and spaceships that explore barren planets where nothing lives? Where and when is the pay-off? I have wondered about these questions for the past decade.

Space enthusiasts say that our solar system has more value for us than we can predict now. The different planets and their moons may have chemicals that will improve our lives and the weightlessness of space may allow us to create new and valuable substances. And one day the planets and their moons may serve as home to pioneers from the earth who can no longer stand the overcrowded conditions on our planet. I don't agree with people who say this. I think it's more important to use what we have here on earth (including the millions of dollars we spend on space flight) to feed, clothe and house all the poor and the homeless.

Other people say that although we may not see immediate benefits from space exploration, it satisfies our need to explore. Humans have a craving to explore and they have examined every inch of the earth. Space is the next frontier. I don't know how to answer this defense of space except to say that I think it's cruel and selfish to satisfy our need to explore while we allow men, women and children to die from exposure and hunger.

People in **NASA** and in the White House see space exploration as a kind of steppingstone to future achievements such as permanent space stations that could monitor our weather and provide new sources of energy. They also see space as the battlefield for World War III. The Star Wars

project that President Reagan asked our scientists to develop
is supposed to intercept and destroy nuclear weapons while
they are still in outer space. However, everything I have
read about this project leads me to believe that it is
impossible to build a protective shield against nuclear
missiles.

Your first conclusion:

Your second conclusion:

PROBLEMS IN INTRODUCTIONS AND CONCLUSIONS

Writing becomes ineffective when introductions and conclusions
contain the following problems:

1. apologies for lack of knowledge or information:
   "I really don't know much about this area."
   "Although I am not too sure about this, ..."

When I read apologies, I feel like the writer doesn't know what he or she is talking about. If you genuinely do not know what you are discussing, find out more information! Don't advertise your ignorance to your readers.

2. announcements about the content of the paragraph or essay to follow:

    "This essay will discuss . . ."

    "Now I will summarize the . . ."

    If your writing is clear and logically developed, then the reader doesn't need announcements about what you are going to say. Announcements imply that the writer isn't clear about where he or she is going.

3. overused beginnings or endings (such as dictionary definitions, familiar quotations, and cliches):

    "My dictionary describes 'sexism' as . . ."

    "Thus, you can really see that 'if you've got it, flaunt it.'"

Dictionary definitions and overworked expressions are boring. They make readers feel that the writer didn't care enough about his or her readers to think up something original to say.

WRITING ACTIVITY   **WRITING INTRODUCTIONS AND CONCLUSIONS FOR ESSAYS**

Take out the discovery draft of the essay on bioengineering or space exploration that you wrote for the writing activities in this chapter. On a separate piece of paper, write an introduction and a conclusion for your essay. Then answer the following questions in the space provided.

1. Which approach did you use for your introduction? Why?

2. Which approach did you use for your conclusion? Why?

SOMETHING TO THINK ABOUT

Below is an excerpt from a book entitled *Science and Survival* by Barry Commoner, a biologist who chairs the Board of Directors of the

Scientists' Institute for Public Information. Read this excerpt and answer the questions that follows it.

There is considerable scientific disagreement about the medical hazards of the new pollutants: about the effects of DDT now found in human bodies, about the diseases due to smog, or about the long-range effects of fallout. But the crucial point is that disagreements exist, for they reveal that we risked these hazards before we knew what harm they might do. Unwittingly we have loaded the air with chemicals that damage the lungs, and the water with substances that interfere with the functioning of the blood. Because we wanted to build nuclear bombs and kill mosquitoes, we have burdened our bodies with strontium-90 and DDT, with consequences that no one can now predict. We have been massively intervening in the environment without being aware of many of the harmful consequences of our acts until they have been performed and the effects—which are difficult to understand and sometimes irreversible—are upon us. Like the sorcerer's apprentice, we are acting upon dangerously incomplete knowledge. We are, in effect, conducting a huge experiment on *ourselves*. A generation hence—too late to help—public health statistics may reveal what hazards are associated with these pollutants.

To those of us who are concerned with the growing risk of unintended damage to the environment, some would reply that it is the grand purpose of science to move into unknown territory, to explore, and to discover. They would remind us that similar hazards have been risked before, and that science and technology cannot make progress without taking some risks. But the size and persistence of possible errors has also grown with the power of science and the expansion of technology. In the past, the risks taken in the name of technological progress—boiler explosions on the first steamboats, or the early injuries from radium—were restricted to a small place and a short time. The new hazards are neither local nor brief. Air pollution covers vast areas. Fallout is worldwide. Synthetic chemicals may remain in the soil for years. Radioactive pollutants now on the earth's surface will be found there for generations, and, in the case of carbon–14, for thousands of years. Excess carbon dioxide from fuel combustion eventually might cause floods that could cover much of the earth's present land surface for centuries. At the same time the permissible margin for error has become very much reduced. In the development of steam engines a certain number of boiler explosions were tolerated as the art was improved. If a single comparable disaster were to occur in a nuclear power plant or in a reactor-driven ship near a large city, thousands of people might die and a whole region be rendered uninhabitable—a price that the public might be unwilling to pay for nuclear power. The risk is one that private insurance companies have refused to underwrite. Modern science and technology are simply too powerful to permit a trial-and-error approach.

It can be argued that the hazards of modern pollutants are small compared to the dangers associated with other human enterprises. For us, today, the fallout hazard is, for example, much smaller than the risks we take on the highway or in the air. But what of the risks we inflict on future generations? No estimate of the actual harm that may be done by fallout, smog, or chemical pollutants can obscure the sober realization that in each case the risk was undertaken before it was fully understood. The importance of these issues to science, and to the citizen, lies not only in the associated hazards, but in the warning of an incipient abdication of one of the major duties of science—prediction and control of human interventions into nature. The true measure of the danger is not represented by the present hazards, but by the disasters that will surely be visited upon us if we dare to enter the new age before us without correcting this basic fault in the scientific enterprise. And if we are to correct this fault, we must first discover why it has developed.

What is Commoner's main point? What is he trying to prove to readers?

WRITING ASSIGNMENT   DEVELOPING AN ESSAY ABOUT TECHNOLOGY

For this writing assignment, you will be developing an essay about the topic that you read and wrote about for this chapter: the uses and abuses of technology. You may be wondering, "How many paragraphs should this essay be composed of?" My answer is: as many as it takes for you to illustrate or support your point. (If you're really concerned about the length of this particular essay, try to write a minimum of four paragraphs and a maximum of eight.) Begin with ten minutes of freewriting about technology. Select a focus in your freewriting and do ten more minutes of brainstorming on this focus. Next, do five minutes of clustering about your focus to see if you have enough ideas to begin writing a discovery draft.

Prewriting Guidelines
   Specify your focus:

- Which aspect, part, or characteristic of your topic are you going to discuss?
- How much do you already know about this focus?
- What else do you need to find out about it, and where will you look for this information?

   Determine your audience:

- Who might be interested in knowing about the topic and focus that you have selected?
- What does this reader (or group of readers) already know about your topic and focus?
- What else might they need or want to know about this topic and focus about you?

   Refine your purpose for writing this essay:

- What do you want your readers to understand about the topic and the focus that you have selected?
- What do you want your readers to think or to feel or to do when they are finished reading your essay?

   Write a sentence that can serve as your working thesis statement. Then, reread your freewriting, brainstorming, and clustering and consider the way in which your details relate to your focus, audience, purpose, and working thesis statement. If you think you have enough examples or reasons to start writing a discovery draft, then start. If not, do some more thinking, brainstorming, and clustering. Then decide on the strategies that seem most appropriate for your purpose, your reader, and your details:

- Should you narrate a story or a sequence of events?
- Should you describe your observations about specific people, places, or things?
- Should you define your key terms and offer some examples of what you mean by them?
- Should you explain the similarities or differences between the things that you are discussing?
- Should you analyze the categories, the types, or the causes and results of specific events or behaviors?
- Should you evaluate the worth or importance of specific ideas or behaviors?

   When you finish writing the discovery draft, write a title that sums up your topic or focus in a few words. Get responses to your discovery draft by following the guidelines for "How to Get Feedback About Your Discovery Draft" on pages 40–41. After you have received some responses to your discovery draft, answer the following questions to determine whether it needs more specific supporting details.

Revising Questions

1. What approach did I use for my introduction? How could I make my introduction more interesting?
2. How can I make my thesis statement clearer?
3. Who is my audience and what else do they need to know about my thesis?
4. What experiences have I included to support my point? What other experiences should I include?
5. What observations have I included to support my thesis and are there other observations I should include?
6. What facts have I included to support my thesis? What other facts should I consider?
7. Which words in each paragraph are examples of sensory language?
8. Which details in each paragraph are very specific? Which are too general?
9. How are the details in each paragraph organized? If the logic breaks down, where does it do so and why?
10. Which approach did I use in my conclusion? How could I make my conclusion more effective?

Revise your discovery draft based on your classmates' comments and on your answers to these Revising Questions.

ADDITIONAL TOPICS TO WRITE ABOUT

Here are some more topics for you to write essays about using the various strategies that you practiced in this chapter.

1. A 1985 National Science Foundation poll found that "only one in fourteen Americans meets a minimal definition of scientific literacy" and that "40% of those polled believe in flying saucers, lucky numbers, and that rockets change the weather." In response to these findings, several scientists have proposed that elementary and secondary schools should have required courses in scientific and technological literacy. How do you feel about this proposal?

2. One of the worst side effects of recent advances in technology is pollution: Our air and water are being destroyed by pesticides, herbicides, synthetic plastics, aluminum, glass, and radioactive wastes. Barry Commoner feels that we are "destroying this planet as a suitable place for human habitation." What is your response to Commoner's assertion? What can or should American citizens do about technological pollution?

3. On January 28, 1986, six American astronauts and one civilian—teacher Christa McAuliffe—died in the explosion of the space shuttle *Challenger*. Polls taken after the tragedy (by the Roper Organization) indicated that most of the public felt that these deaths were "a price we must be willing to pay for the exploration and mastery of space." Do you agree or disagree? Why?

4. Statements made by President Reagan and by several of his predecessors indicate they think that a nuclear war could be limited and controlled. However, statements made by leaders of the Soviet Union make it clear that they intend to respond totally in the event of a nuclear attack. Should the United States continue to build offensive nuclear weapons or should it work toward negotiating an arms control agreement with the Soviet Union, or should it do both?

5. Chuck Yaeger, the first person to break the sound barrier in an airplane, was recently asked what America's goals in space travel should be. His answer was, "We've got to compete with the rest of the world. There are a lot of resources out there—strategic material and minerals that we will come up short with on the earth's surface in the next fifty to one hundred years." What is your reaction to Yaeger's answer? And what do you think America's goals in space exploration should be?

Reminders

Specify your focus:

- What points do you want to explain, describe, or defend?
- How much do you already know about your topic?
- What else do you need to find out about it?

Determine your audience:

- Who might be interested in reading your essay?
- What does this reader (or readers) already know about your topic? How do they feel about it?
- What else do they need or want to know about it?

Refine your purpose:

- What do you want your readers to think or feel or do?
- Which strategies will best accomplish this purpose (or these purposes)?

After you finish your discovery draft, get your classmates' responses by following the directions for "How to Get Feedback About Your Discovery Draft."

ISSUES FOR YOUR JOURNAL

1. What did the readings in this chapter make you think about?
2. What have you been writing about for your other courses? What topics—in your reading and writing—have been particularly interesting?
3. How do you feel about the school you are currently attending? What are its good points? What are its bad points? How could it be improved?
4. Do you have a favorite television program? If so, what is it and why do you enjoy watching it? What do you learn about people or about life from it? How realistic is it? What kinds of stereotypes does it portray?
5. Look over your journal entries for the past two weeks. Which ones are particularly interesting? Why? Which ones might you want to develop into essays?

PART TWO

REVISING

CHAPTER SIX

REVISING IDEAS AND DETAILS

*Writing and rewriting are a constant search
for what it is one is saying.*

JOHN UPDIKE

*I have rewritten—often several times—every
word I have ever published. My pencils
outlast their erasers.*

VLADIMIR NABOKOV

INTRODUCTION: THE IMPORTANCE OF REVISING

All writers need to revise. As they write a draft, they discover their ideas, making personal associations and private connections. Their ideas and logic may not make much sense to readers, so, like sculptors, they need to chisel and cut their material into a clearer, more precise form. Experienced writers know that revision is the *most important part* of the writing process: they write, then they revise, then write, then revise over and over again, producing numerous revised drafts. They do not stop revising until they feel that they have produced a piece of writing that is worth editing. But what exactly is revision? It is not editing, nor is it copying over a draft and fixing up the mistakes. Revising *is* rethinking, reseeing, and reshaping—making a draft fit the writer's purposes and the intended reader's needs.

What should you revise first? Surveys of teachers and employers reveal that they consider problems in ideas and clarity the most serious flaws in papers. When teachers and employers are asked what they mean by "ideas" and "clarity," they usually take out essays and make comments like these:

"I don't understand what he's trying to prove in this essay."
"I read this report three times and I'm still not sure what her points are."
"I just can't follow his line of thought."
"This paper is so vague that I don't believe one word."

You have already worked on revising the ideas and clarity in your discovery drafts using the Revising Questions at the end of each chapter. This chapter and the two chapters that follow expand these revising activities by presenting strategies that you can incorporate into your own writing processes.

PAIRED WRITING TASK DETERMINING REVISIONS IN EACH OTHER'S ESSAYS

Do this writing task with another classmate. Take out a discovery draft of a piece of writing that you wrote for one of the assignments in this book (or for your teacher). Exchange papers with your classmate. After you have read your classmate's paper, write answers to the following questions (on a separate piece of paper). Do *not* discuss each other's papers until you are both finished writing your comments.

Your classmate's name:

1. What do you think was the writer's purpose here? What was he or she trying to say or to show?

2. Whom do you think the writer envisioned as the audience for this piece?
3. Which examples or reasons best support this main point?
4. Were there any places where you got confused? Why? Where did you need more information?
5. What else do you want to know about the topic that the writer is discussing? What else should the writer have included to make the piece more interesting?

HOW TO ACHIEVE SOME DISTANCE FROM YOUR WRITING

Whenever you write something, your first reader should always be *you*. When you reread a draft in order to revise it, you are doing a very special kind of reading: you are reading your writing in order to determine its strengths and its problems. This kind of evaluative reading is quite difficult to do, especially when the text that you are evaluating consists of your own thoughts and feelings. However, you must get in the habit of reading your writing carefully and judging it honestly in order to make revisions. In order to do this, you have to gain some distance from your writing and read it from the perspective of your intended audience. How do experienced writers gain the distance from their own writing that is needed to evaluate it honestly and critically? In other words, how do writers stop themselves from seeing details and connections that may be in their minds but that are *not* on the pages? Here are several methods:

- Put the draft away for at least twenty-four hours. When you reread a draft after several hours or days, you may not remember everything that you were thinking when you wrote the draft. This makes it easier for you to read and evaluate what is actually on the page. Putting a draft aside for a while allows you to see where your ideas don't make sense and where the connections between the ideas are unclear.
- Pretend to be a reader who knows absolutely nothing about your topic. Think about what this reader would act like and think like; then read your draft from this reader's perspective and see if this reader would be confused by any parts of your draft.
- Read the draft out loud so that you can hear where it sounds strong or weak. Reading aloud also enables you to notice problems that you might not have noticed when you were reading silently. If you can, tape record yourself reading the draft aloud and then

take notes on the problems in the draft as you play back the oral version.

- Ask classmates, friends, or relatives to read your draft and to tell you what they liked about it and what they thought was confusing or unclear.

EXERCISE   **TAKING SOMEONE ELSE'S PERSPECTIVE**

Most of the time, readers will see things a bit differently than the writer does because their backgrounds and their experiences are different. This exercise asks you to consider the various responses that different people might bring to the same piece. The piece in this exercise is not a written text—it is a picture of a painting of Dwight Gooden, a pitcher on the New York Mets baseball team, by the artist LeRoy Neiman. Examine the picture and then answer the questions that follow it.

How might different people respond to this painting? Take the perspective of each of the following people and write a few sentences about what you think each might see when he or she looks at Neiman's painting:

1. an artist:

2. a Mets fan:

TECHNIQUES FOR REVISING DISCOVERY DRAFTS

Before you start revising, remind yourself again that the ideas and details in your discovery draft are merely your initial thoughts. Don't feel committed to your first thoughts—new and better ideas will occur to you as you try to figure out exactly what it is that you want to say. Keep an open mind and be willing to cross out or change what you have already written. In addition, try using the following techniques to help you identify and revise problems in the content of *each* paragraph in your draft:

- Pinpoint the parts that sound good or that are particularly effective in order to get some clues about how to revise the weaker, confusing parts. Which of your details or words are particularly clear or interesting? Which sentences let your meaning come through loudly and clearly? Where is your voice especially strong and convincing?
- In the margin next to each paragraph, write one sentence explaining what the paragraph should make the reader think, feel, or do. Make sure that every paragraph actually does what your marginal sentence says it should do. If it doesn't, rewrite it.
- Check to see if one of your supporting sentences is actually the main point that you want to make. If it is, rewrite the paragraph so it focuses on and supports this main point.
- Consider whether you have enough observations, experiences, and

facts to convince the specific reader for whom you are writing. If you don't, add more.

● Make sure that your details are specific enough. Do they contain sensory details that let your reader see, hear, touch, and smell the subject of the paragraph? If not, cross out the general or vague words, and add descriptive words and lively, active verbs.

● Make sure that each observation, experience, or fact supports the main idea of the paragraph. If you are not sure whether one does, cross it out or rewrite it so that it is clearly related to the main point.

If a paragraph does not have enough specific supporting details that will convince your reader that you know the topic, then do some more freewriting, brainstorming, and clustering.

WRITING ACTIVITY   ANALYZING PROBLEMS IN SUPPORTING DETAILS

Identify the problems in the supporting details of this uncorrected paragraph by answering the six questions that follow it.

```
      I remember my first job interview.  I got up early and
got myself ready so that I would look good for the interview.
Then I got dressed in my best suit and shoes.  I ate a good
breakfast and talked to my mom.  I did everything I knew to
try to calm myself down.  Then I ran to the bus.  The ride was
very long.  On the way, I saw many of my friends going to
work.  When I got to the company, my stomach was making noises
and I was really nervous.  I tried to calm down because I
didn't want the interviewer to see how nervous I was.  Boy was
that a tough morning!
```

1. What is this paragraph supposed to make the reader think, feel, or do? (Write a one-sentence answer in the space below.)

2. Does the paragraph accomplish this purpose? If not, what kinds of details should be added or changed?

3. Is one of the supporting sentences actually the main point? If so, underline it.
4. Does this paragraph have enough observations, experiences, and facts to be convincing? If not, what kinds of details does it need?

5. Does each observation, experience, or fact support the main idea of the paragraph? If any supporting detail does not do this, cross it out.
6. Are the observations and direct experiences believable? If not, which ones aren't and why aren't they believable?

7. Are the details specific enough? Do they contain sensory images that enable a reader to see, hear, smell, and almost touch the subject of the paragraph? If not, where are more specific details needed?

The paragraph in this writing activity is actually the discovery draft of Paul Brasili's paragraph on page 77 of Chapter 4. What are some of the differences between the discovery draft (in this writing activity) and the revised version (in Chapter 4)?

A PROFESSIONAL RESPONSE

Below is a copy of the first draft of the beginning of Chapter 1. The comments and questions were written by one of the composition teachers who reviewed this book. (Before a textbook gets published, each chapter is reviewed seven or eight times by several expert teachers.) The handwritten revisions are mine. Compare the draft below to page 4 in this book. Note that the actual page of this text is different from the revised version below. This is because I revised almost every page in this book four or five additional times before my reviewers, my editor, and I were satisfied with it.

a born writer

Everybody is born with a desire to communicate. ~~As they learn to speak,~~ young children love to tell stories, and they are ~~so pleased~~ *thrilled* when other people understand these stories.

Do you mean and "communicate" or "write"? Clarify your meaning and strengthen this sentence.

~~When they begin to write, they are just as thrilled when people~~ read their writing. Some of us continue to ~~be thrilled~~ *preserve this sense of the magic of the written word as we* ~~as we grow up.~~ Others of us ~~stop writing--or stop enjoying it--~~ *lose touch with the magic of the criticisms that we receive* because no one takes delight in our writing. *or because*

these details seem connected. Can you make them more so?

Why?

~~Some of us also stop writing for other reasons: parents or teachers criticize us or make us follow rules that don't make sense to us.~~ *lose our spontaneity and we* *How do you feel about writing?* Gradually, we develop negative attitudes toward writing. Attitudes are very important: They ~~determine~~ *influence* ~~our desire~~ *a writer's habits and processes* ~~and our ability to do anything.~~ *so* ~~Thus,~~ writers ought to understand their attitudes toward writing. One attitude that many people have is that writing is easy and *can create perfect prose* that professional writers ~~write well~~ every time they write.

Too vague. What do you mean here?

These ideas are related; they should be in the same paragraph.

This is not true! ~~Another attitude that interferes with people's ability to write effectively is a belief that good writers can write a piece of polished perfect prose in one sitting. This is also untrue.~~

~~Most successful writers go through a complex process when they write and they have many problems.~~

These ideas seem unrelated to the ones above. Maybe you should put them in a different paragraph.

(moved to another section)

What strikes you as being the most important revisions that I made in my discovery draft of the opening page of this book?

HOW TO GENERATE ADDITIONAL DETAILS
AND A NEW THESIS STATEMENT

Much of the writing done in school and at work requires writers to present information beyond their personal experience, knowledge, and observations. Teachers and employers expect you to be able to broaden your perspective and examine other people's viewpoints about a topic or a problem. This means that you will have to gather information about your topic from public sources, even if your assignment is not a research paper. These sources include the following:

- people who know about the topic and can speak about it intelligently (including relatives, friends, classmates, teachers, employers, and other people who have information about your topic)
- articles in newspapers, magazines, and journals
- books, encyclopedias, and other reference works
- television and radio programs and movies

Public sources can provide you with additional observations and facts to include in your essays. They can also provide statistical information and visual material (charts, graphs, and tables) that you can use to illustrate particular points. When you consult people or read materials or watch programs about your topic, use the following techniques to help you record important information.

1. Write down all questions that interest you about your topic. What else do you want or need to find out about it? Use these questions to guide your readings.
2. If you are consulting a person, prepare specific questions in advance. Make sure that your questions are not "yes/no" questions but are ones that elicit the information that you need to know.
3. Take notes (when you talk to a person, when you consult reading material, and when you watch a program). Taking notes helps you keep track of and remember information, and it enables you to record the ideas and questions that occur to you as you are listening, reading, or watching.
4. Identify the source at the top of the note. If the source is a person, write down her or his name, title, and relationship to you. If the source is reading material, give the author's name, the title, the publisher, the date published, the page numbers and the library call number. Use a separate note card for each different source.
5. If you write down the exact words that the source uses, make sure you surround them with quotation marks. (See Chapter 13 for further information on taking notes and working with sources.)

A STUDENT RESPONSE

Most writers use 3″ by 5″ index cards for their notes. Here are examples of note cards that a student wrote as he conducted interviews and as he read an article about an essay that he was trying to revise.

As you consult public sources of information, you learn new ideas and facts that can increase your understanding of your topic and that can serve as the basis of new examples and reasons in your revisions. In addition, these sources may help you discover a new and more interesting focus for your paper; this may lead you to write an entirely new discovery draft. After examining several sources of information about your topic and considering the viewpoints of other people, you may want to revise the thesis statement of your draft. If this is the case, rewrite your thesis statement so that it expresses your new main point. Similarly, after you revise each paragraph, you may want to rewrite the topic sentence so that it states the main point of the paragraph more accurately.

When you are finished consulting sources and taking notes, you may have so many new ideas that you may want to expand a paragraph in your draft into two or more paragraphs. For example, here is Isaac

---

Call #   p 177 ("Employer Profiles")

Rocket Research Company, Redmont, WA
Hires 1 business and 2 engineering majors
per year. Starting Salary : $18,000
Tuition and fees reimbursed up to $200.
Summer Employment for College students

Rockwell International, El Secundo, CA

Hires 200 business and 700 engineering
majors per year.
              Starting Salary : "competitive"

Interview with Jack Irving (next door neighbor), Senior Electronics Engineer at Royal Research, Inc, Eugene, Oregon.

Dr. Irving does the kind of work I want to do: he designs airborne electronics systems for use in rockets and space shuttles. He wanted to be in a small firm because he wanted to be in charge of the projects he designs. Also he wants to work near his home and not have a big commute. He said small companies offer more opportunities for promotion and

Interview with Chana Stein (cousin), Electronics Technician at Rockwell International El Segundo, California.

Mrs. Stein doesn't mind the long commute to Rockwell because the work is so interesting — she gets to work on automotive, aerospace, and telecommunications projects. Also Rockwell is paying 100% of her education for a Ph D in electronics engineering. And it offers her medical and dental plans, a pension program, and a recreational fitness program. She

Stein's original uncorrected comparison/constrast paragraph that he wrote for the writing activity on page 81 of Chapter 4. Below it is his first uncorrected revision, based on the information that he recorded from the source he consulted.

DISCOVERY DRAFT

Ever since the day I took apart and reassembled my parent's television set, I knew I wished to be an electronics engineer. Like doctors and lawyers, electronics engineers specialize in one of many areas and I want to do aerospace research and rocket design. I have been thinking about the company that I want to eventually work for and I'm having trouble making up my mind. Do I work for a giant corporation like Rockwell International in California or a small company like Rocket Research in Washington? Rockwell and Rocket design rocket engines and conduct applied aerospace research. Rockwell is huge: it employs 95,000 people and offers many career opportunities. Rocket Research has only 300 people and there isn't much room for advancement. At Rocket, engineers are involved with all parts of systems design and application. At Rockwell, they only get to work on one small part of a project. I think I have to visit several more types of rocket research firms before I can make up my mind about the kind of place that's right for me.

FIRST REVISION

Ever since the day I took apart and reassembled my parent's television set, I knew I wished to be an electronics engineer. Like doctors and lawyers, electronics engineers specialize in one of many areas and I want to do aerospace research and rocket design. I may have difficulty deciding on the kind of company that I want to work for. Do I work for a giant corporation like Rockwell International in California or

a small company like Rocket Research in Washington? Rockwell
and Rocket design rocket engines and conduct applied aerospace
research. And they offer competitive entry level salaries and
medical, dental, and pension plans.

They do have differences. Rockwell is huge: it employs
95,000 people and it hires 700 each year. Rocket has only 300
people and hires only two or three engineering majors each
year. Rockwell pays for 100% of its employee's education
expenses. Rocket only pays for $250. At Rocket, engineers
are involved with all phases of systems design and
application. At Rockwell, they only get to work on one small
part of a project. Rocket is closer to my home. If I worked
at Rockwell, I would have to move or have a big commute. My
neighbor, Dr. Jack Irving who works at a small engineering
company said that small firms like Rocket offer many more
opportunities for promotion. I think I have to visit several
more types of rocket research firms before I can make up my
mind about the kind of place that's right for me.

A STUDENT RESPONSE

Here is the uncorrected discovery draft of two paragraphs that a
student wrote in response to the writing assignment at the end of Chapter 4: "Write a paragraph that describes your ideal job, and write another paragraph explaining why you think this job would be ideal for
you." The handwritten comments were written by the writer's classmates.

DISCOVERY DRAFT

Ever since I was twelve years old, I wanted to be a *What's the job?*
lawyer. My uncle is a lawyer and he's terrific. He works for *What do lawyers do?*

The 2nd and 3rd sentences don't seem to belong here. the District Attorney and he is the person I want to model myself on. My whole family has deep social concerns and I want to do something about this. Law is the answer. I want to be a civil liberties lawyer and handle discrimination cases. I know that being a lawyer involves a lot of hard work *Like what?*

Why? but I am looking forward to it.

I want to become a lawyer because it is the perfect *Why?* career for me. I enjoy helping people. And I think I have *What other skills do you have? What experiences have you had?* the right skills for this job. I like to have a lot of responsibilities and I don't mind working long hours. Money *What's okay?* doesn't mean that much to me but the salary is okay. I just have to be able to support myself. (I don't want to have to *What does this have to do with being a lawyer?* depend on my family and I don't want my future wife to work.) Thus, I think that being a lawyer will be a challenging and rewarding job.

Dear Shawn— I'm not clear about the main point of your first paragraph. And you need to provide more details Shaun Morrissey *about what civil liberties lawyers actually do. I like the second paragraph. It has more details. But you need to say more about why you want this career. —Irene*

After the writer read his classmates' comments and questions, he realized that he needed to consult other sources of information. He spoke to several relatives and teachers and read some magazine articles and books about his topic. His first uncorrected revision incorporates his new details.

FIRST REVISION

Ever since I was twelve years old, I wanted to be a lawyer. My whole family has deep social concerns and I want to do something about the injustice in our city and our

community. Law is the answer, especially civil liberties law.
A civil liberties lawyer protects the constitutional rights of
minorities and of the poor and works on discrimination cases.
They also interpret legal rulings and regulations for
individuals and businesses who cannot afford their own private
lawyers. This kind of work involves much reading, researching
and writing but I am looking forward to doing these things. I
want to be prepared so that I can win cases and help my
clients.

Civil liberties law is the perfect career for me. I
enjoy helping people and I despise discrimination. Also I
think I have the right skills for this job. I am a volunteer
worker at the Main Street Legal Aid Society and I help the
lawyers conduct research and write briefs. I like to have a
lot of different responsibilities and I don't mind working
long hours. I know that civil liberties lawyers don't make as
much money as other types of lawyers, but the $20,000-$30,000
a year is quite enough for me. And lawyers have good working
conditions: offices and courtrooms are comfortable places to
work. Thus, I think that being a civil liberties lawyer will
make me very happy.

What are the most important differences between this writer's
discovery draft and first revision?

WRITING ACTIVITY **REVISING IDEAS AND DETAILS IN A STUDENT'S ESSAY**

This activity will help you broaden your perspective and practice the revising skills that you have learned so far in this chapter. Do this activity in a group. Select one person to record your group's comments, questions, and suggestions about the following draft of an essay on an ideal job. Consider what additional information should be added to make the essay clearer and more specific, and use the revising techniques discussed on page 127 of this chapter to suggest revisions in this essay. It is double-spaced so that your group's suggested revisions can be written directly on the draft.

DISCOVERY DRAFT: INDUSTRIAL ENGINEERING

Very few engineers are women, but the opportunities for women engineers are terrific. There are more jobs at higher salaries available for women than in almost any other profession. However, because most engineers are traditionally men, most young women don't even consider a career in engineering.

I have wanted to be an engineer for a long time. In high school, I did well in science and math and my teachers encouraged me to think about a career in science. Most of them suggested that I go into nursing or become a science teacher. But I wanted to be able to design and to develop things. Now I am majoring in engineering and I think I want to be a mechanical engineer because I was always good with my hands and good at constructing things.

A mechancial engineer designs and develops machines that produce and that use power. She can change water and air power into electrical power. The specific work varies according to the field that you specialize in. But all mechanical engineers do research, design, and test work products. And not only do mechanical engineers design machines and tools, but they also design the factories that make this equipment.

The thing that excites me most about being a mechanical engineer is that I will be designing and building machines that make life easier for people. Also I will be designing systems that can convert natural energy into electricity. Both of these activities will help our country in many ways. I will be making a contribution--as an engineer and as a woman.

May Chang

HOW TO MAKE YOUR SUPPORTING DETAILS MORE CONVINCING

If you or some classmates read one of your discovery drafts and decide that it isn't believable, then you will have to add additional details and make your details more convincing. The previous section helped you learn how to develop new details, and this section will help you revise your details to make them more appropriate and more convincing. First, practice identifying problems in faulty reasoning. Here are eight details taken from different essays. Each illustrates a different type of unconvincing evidence, and each is followed by a suggestion for revision.

1. "Being a teacher isn't rewarding. My best friend makes only $15,000 and spends most of his time disciplining the children instead of teaching them."

   Problem: This writer provided **insufficient evidence**. One example doesn't prove anything. Readers might know many teachers who make much more money and who truly enjoy teaching.
   Solution: The writer should narrow his assertion and present more examples.

2. "I dream of becoming the president but I know I never will. There has never been a Jewish president and there never will be one."

Problem: This writer has made a **hasty conclusion** that didn't follow from her evidence. Readers may think that there is an excellent possibility that a Jew will become president in the future. Moreover, just because a pattern has existed in the past doesn't mean that it will go on forever.
Solution: The writer should think more carefully about the main point and examine the possibilities for change in American politics.

3. "I conducted an interview with my English professor, and he noted that the job outlook is best for computer systems analysts and technical engineers."

Problem: This writer has cited a **false authority**. Why should readers believe that this English teacher is an expert on career options? Also, why should readers be convinced that this teacher's opinion is valid?
Solution: The writer should interview experts on the topic and consult other sources of public information for new evidence.

4. "Racism and sexism are very injurious to our society. These attitudes are damaging because they hurt people."

Problem: This writer has used **circular reasoning**—she has tried to prove her point by repeating it in different words. Readers often get bored or annoyed reading the same unsubstantiated assertions over and over again.
Solution: The writer should provide specific facts, observations, and experiences that support the point.

5. "I doubt whether women will make it to the top executive levels of American corporations because most of them aren't ambitious or aggressive enough."

Problem: This writer offered a **stereotype** that appeals to people's prejudices. This may antagonize readers who believe that women are just as qualified and as capable as men are. Furthermore, readers who know successful female corporate executives will find this stereotype unconvincing.
Solution: The writer should examine the details to determine whether they are factual or simply reflect prejudices. Then, the writer should look for examples that can serve as convincing evidence.

6. "If a woman is going to have a family, then she doesn't need a long-term career. She can work until she has children and then give up her job and stay home."

Problem: In addition to presenting a stereotype about women, this writer is using **either-or reasoning**. There are many alternatives that the writer has not considered. Readers may know women who have successful careers and happy families or women who work part-time and spend the remaining time with their children.

Solution: The writer should interview people who are knowledgeable about the topic and consult sources of public information about it.

7. "More and more college graduates are preparing for careers in the computer field. Thus, I think it is the most promising field today."

Problem: This writer is using **majority rule reasoning**. She assumes that if most people are doing something, then it must be valid or right. However, readers may feel that an action or an idea is wrong or silly despite what the majority feels about it.

Solution: The writer should explore other reasons for the assertion. In this case, she should think of other reasons why the computer field seems promising.

8. "I have always wanted to be a surgeon because they have the most challenging jobs and they make much more money than other doctors do."

Problem: The writer has **overgeneralized**—he has turned one point into a broad conclusion about *all* surgeons. Readers might know surgeons who make less money than do other types of doctors or readers may know surgeons who are dissatisfied with their jobs.

Solution: The writer should qualify the assertions by using words like "most," "many," and "some" or by prefacing assertions with phrases like "In my experience" or "According to the doctors I know well."

Overgeneralizing is one of the most common problems that inexperienced writers make. One simple technique for narrowing down generalizations is to find the indefinite pronouns in a discovery draft and substitute qualifiers for them. Here is a list of some indefinite pronouns and of qualifiers that can be substituted for them:

Indefinite Pronouns	Qualifier Substitutes
all, every, everybody	most, many, several, some
none, no one, noboby	almost none, almost nobody, very few
always	frequently, often, usually
never	almost, never

EXERCISE IDENTIFYING AND REVISING FAULTY REASONING

Each sentence in the following paragraph is numbered, and these numbers correspond to the list below the paragraph. Read the paragraph. Then reread each sentence. If you think the reasoning is logical and convincing, write "OK" next to the corresponding number. If the reasoning is not logical or convincing, write a revision of it next to the corresponding number. The first one has been done for you as an example.

(1) Part-time work—working between fifteen and thirty hours a week—is better than working full-time. (2) Everybody I know works part-time and they think it's a terrific arrangement. (3) Part-time work is particularly good for women because once they have a family, they don't want to work full-time. (4) It's also good for senior citizens who do not want to work every day but who want the stimulation and the money they get from working. (5) Part-time employment is excellent; it really helps many people. (6) I work part-time at an art gallery and my employer thinks that part-time work is the answer to our city's unemployment problem. (7) In addition, part-time employment gives people experience and money while also allowing them to fulfill other needs in their lives or try out other career possibilities. (8) My best friend is a part-time waitress while she is studying acting, and she says that part-time employment is terrific. (9) I just might become a permanent part-timer!

1. Part-time work has several advantages over full-time work. _____

2. _____

3. _____

4. _____

5. _____

6. _____

7. _____

8. _____

9. _____

TECHNIQUES FOR REVISING INTRODUCTIONS AND CONCLUSIONS

After rereading and revising a draft several times, you may find that the introduction or conclusion no longer makes the point that the revision develops. Also, if a classmate or teacher tells you that your introduction is not clear or your conclusion is too abrupt, you should reshape them. Make sure that the introduction introduces your main point clearly and accurately so that readers know what to expect from the essay that follows. Also, ask yourself if it is interesting enough to make a reader want to continue reading. If not, use a different technique described on page 109 of Chapter 5. In addition, check your conclusion to make sure that it reminds your reader of your main point without repeating it word for word. If it doesn't, use one of the other techniques for developing a conclusion.

WRITING ACTIVITY REVISING INTRODUCTIONS AND CONCLUSIONS

Take out the essay that you wrote for the Writing Assignment in Chapter 5 on page 116, and examine your introduction carefully. Use different techniques (from the ones described on pages 109–110) to revise this introduction to make it more interesting or more forceful. Then examine the conclusion of your essay and try to revise it so it will make your readers continue to think about your points.

WRITING ASSIGNMENT WRITING AND REVISING AN ESSAY ABOUT SCHOOL

Every educational institution has its unique strengths and weaknesses. Write a discovery draft of an essay that describes and evaluates the school that you are currently attending. Why did you choose this school? What are its best features? What are its worst? Do you like it, dislike it, or have mixed feelings about it? Why? Would you recommend it to students interested in attending it? Why or why not? Remember to begin by prewriting—freewriting, brainstorming, and clustering—in order to explore your feelings and ideas and in order to clarify your focus, purpose, and audience. When you are finished prewriting, write a draft of the essay and revise it using the techniques discussed in this chapter. These techniques are rephrased as the Revising Questions that follow.

Revising Questions

1. What are the strengths of this essay? Which parts sound particularly forceful and convincing?
2. What is the point of each paragraph? In the margin next to each paragraph, write a sentence explaining what it should make the reader think, feel, or do. If the paragraph does not do what you intended it to do, add new ideas or rewrite the original ones.
3. Is one of your supporting sentences actually the main point that you want to make? If so, rewrite the essay so it focuses on and supports its new main point.
4. Are your details specific enough? Do they contain sensory details that let your reader see, hear, touch, smell, or taste the subject of each paragraph? Do the details convey clear pictures of how your subject looks and sounds to you? If not, cross out vague words and add descriptive words and active verbs.
5. How does each observation, experience, or fact support the main idea of each paragraph? If you are not sure whether it does, cross it out or rewrite it so that it is clearly related to the main point.
6. Do you think your reader will believe your observations and direct experiences? If not, consult public sources and add more vicarious experiences—and cite their sources (see pages 131–133 about how to cite references) or add more facts and statistics (and cite their sources too).
7. Does the introduction make your point(s) clear? Is it interesting? If not, use a different technique to develop a new introduction or make the original one clearer and more interesting.
8. Does the conclusion remind the reader of the main point(s) without using the same words you used in the introduction? Does it stick to the point without bringing up new ideas? If not, make the conclusion clearer and more to the point or develop a new one using a different technique.

ISSUES FOR YOUR JOURNAL

1. Look over your journal entries for the past month. Are there any entries that you might want to "revise" so that they are more accurate or reflect your feelings more honestly? Revise them.
2. Complete this sentence: At this point in my life, I should be . . . What should you be now and why? What should your life be like now? Why?
3. According to statistics released by the Bureau of Census in 1985, the median duration of marriage in America during the past half

century was seven years. Why do you think this was so? What happens to a married couple after seven years of marriage? Why do so many couples get divorced?

4. Have you ever been discriminated against? What happened? Why did it happen? How did it make you feel? What did you do about it? What could you have done about it? What will you do if it happens again in the future?

5. How do you feel about the proliferation of nuclear arms? Do nuclear weapons serve as a deterrent to war? What will happen if a country uses its nuclear weapons?

CHAPTER SEVEN

REVISING ORGANIZATION AND IMPROVING COHERENCE

*To be a writer is to throw away a great deal,
not to be satisfied, to type again, and then
again, and once more, and over and over.*

JOHN HERSEY

INTRODUCTION: METHODS OF REVISING ORGANIZATION AND COHERENCE

Organization refers to the arrangement of a series of ideas; **coherence** refers to the relationships between these ideas. Writers who don't revise often have serious problems with the organization and the coherence of their material. This happens because of the nature of the writing process: writing stimulates thinking—new ideas occur to us as we write—and we have to rush to get these ideas down before they fade from memory. Frequently, the connections among these new ideas are in our heads but *not* on our papers. Thus, the organization of our discovery drafts may not be recognizable to our readers or may be inappropriate to the overall piece of writing. Most readers—except English teachers—simply are not willing to struggle to see connections that are not on the page.

In the previous chapter, you practiced revising the ideas and details in discovery drafts by adding and deleting material, expanding and elaborating on generalizations, spelling out the implications of ideas, and crossing out irrelevant details. When one revises organization and coherence, however, instead of adding and deleting, one tries to rearrange ideas and make them flow smoothly. The goals of this type of revision are to make sure that one's essential points get enough attention and to make certain that each sentence is related in a recognizable way to the sentences that come before and after it. Thus, revising organization often consists of "cutting and pasting": literally scissoring out each sentence and rearranging it in a new order with the other details in the draft. If your school has microcomputers and word-processing programs, now is the time to use them. A word-processing program allows you to move, reorder, add, and delete sentences almost magically!

PAIRED WRITING TASK   DETERMINING REVISIONS IN ORGANIZATION AND COHERENCE

Work with another classmate. Take out a discovery draft of a piece of writing that you wrote for one of your assignments in this book or for your teacher. Exchange papers with your classmate. After you have read your classmate's paper, write answers to the questions below. Do *not* discuss each other's papers until you are both finished writing your comments.

Your classmate's name:

1. Is the essay or paragraph developed with a logical order? If so, what is this order?

2. How else might this essay have been organized?

3. What is the most important information in this essay? Does this information get highlighted—does it get enough attention? If not, where should this information be moved to?

4. Is there any place in the essay where you get lost or confused? Point out this place (or these places) to the writer and explain why the ideas do not seem to develop logically or clearly.
5. Put a star (*) next to each sentence that does not seem clearly related to the one before it or to the one that comes after it. Be prepared to discuss these sentences with the writer.

TECHNIQUES FOR REVISING ORGANIZATION

Before you examine the organization of your drafts, try to get some distance from your writing by using the techniques recommended on page 125 of Chapter 6. Then, look at the order you used to develop your details and think about whether readers will be able to follow the development of your ideas. Ask yourself the following questions:

- Is the order that I used recognizable to the readers for whom I am writing? Can they follow the development of my ideas without getting lost or confused?
- Is the order that I used the most appropriate and effective order for my details? Will my order help readers remember my most important points?

If you arranged the details in a discovery draft **chronologically,** check to see that each detail is described as it occurred in time. Make sure that you didn't jump back and forth in time, confusing your readers. Also, reread your writing and decide if there is a different order that might be more appropriate for your points. If you arranged your details **spatially,** check to make sure that you used an obvious pattern of movement which a reader can follow (left to right, top to bottom, far to near, whole to parts). Also, think about whether you should use a different pattern that might be clearer or more appropriate. Finally, if you arranged your details **climactically,** check to make sure that you used a pattern that a reader can follow (least important to most important, least personal to most personal).

WRITING ACTIVITY **IDENTIFYING AND REVISING PROBLEMS IN ORGANIZATION**

Here is the uncorrected discovery draft of two paragraphs that a student wrote based on the brainstorming list that was shown on page 31 of Chapter 2. He has already revised this essay for ideas and details—these changes are incorporated in the "first revision" below. Read the paragraphs and answer the questions that follow them.

```
        FIRST REVISION: MY FAVORITE PLACE

    My favorite place in the world is my car.  It's the first

car that I have ever owned and I really enjoy being in it.  I

like to sit inside and breathe the smell of leather and oil.

The car is a 1979 Camaro and its previous owner took care of

it.  The blue paint gleams and the chrome sparkles.  It's

really smooth.  The blue leather is worn but clean.  And the

stripes on the sides of the car really look fierce.  Also

there's an stereo radio and cassette with four speakers that

can blast me to heaven.

    I feel like this car is my real home.  It's private.  No

one bothers me when I'm driving around or even sitting in the

car.  I can use it to go places that buses and trains just

can't go.  It's a terrific place to think and dream.  Also, I

like to race friends in the local drag strip.  Even when I'm
```

doing this, I feel alone and I love the feeling of space and
privacy. I zoom along feeling powerful and free. I also use
my car simply as a place to hang out, cruising the streets
with my girlfriend. And I enjoy being alone in the car. It's
my own space and my own machine and I love it.

Allen Brower

1. How is Brower's first paragraph organized? If you do not see a recognizable order or pattern, how would you suggest that he rearrange his details?

2. How is Brower's second paragraph organized? If you do not see a recognizable order or pattern, how would you suggest that he rearrange his details?

Here is the way that the writer revised these paragraphs after his classmates commented on the problems in their organization:

SECOND REVISION: MY FAVORITE PLACE

My favorite place in the world is my car. It's the first
car that I have ever owned and I really enjoy it. The car is
a 1979 Camaro and its previous owner took good care of it.
The blue paint gleams and the chrome sparkles. And the
stripes on the sides of the car really look fierce. It is
sleek and smooth like a jet plane. The blue leather inside is
worn but clean. I like to sit inside and breathe the smell of
leather and oil. I also like to listen to the stereo radio

```
and cassette deck with four speakers that can blast me to
heaven.

     Besides making me feel proud, my car has given me my
freedom.  I can use it to go to places that buses and trains
just can't go.  Also, I like to get in it and race friends in
the local drag strip.  I zoom along feeling powerful and free.
Or I can use my car simply as a place to hang out, cruising
the streets with my girlfriend.  But most of all, I enjoy
being alone in the car.  It's private.  No one bothers me when
I'm driving or sitting in it.  It's a terrific place to
think and dream.  It's my own space and my own machine and I
love it.

                                               Allen Brower
```

What are the most important differences between these two versions of Brower's piece?

EXERCISE REORGANIZING SUPPORTING DETAILS

Here is a magazine article about the most promising careers for the next century. Read the article carefully.

CAREERS THAT PROMISE BIG PAYOFFS

The best preparation for a job in the year 2000 will be to master the tools required for advancement in almost any field: conceptual, reasoning and communication skills, as well as the ability to use a computer. But finding a promising career will also require an understanding of the future labor market. For example, accountants, doctors and lawyers will continue to thrive, but their fields won't grow as fast as those of, say, gerontologists or executive chefs.

Money's selections are based on forecasts by the Bureau of Labor Statistics and private experts on occupational trends. While the number of openings over the next 15 years can be projected for some careers, other jobs are too new for reliable estimates. Advanced degrees are important in research and academic jobs but often won't pay off as well as practical skills in other careers. The salaries listed are those currently earned by jobholders.

Artificial-intelligence specialist. Software experts who can program machines to mimic human thinking will be in the forefront of computer research and applications. Openings: at least 50,000. Salary: $40,000 to $100,000 for corporate system developers. Master's and Ph.D. programs in artificial intelligence, helpful for top jobs, are offered by Carnegie-Mellon University in Pittsburgh and Massachusettes Institute of Technology in Cambridge.

Data-base manager. A combination of computer expert, executive and librarian, this specialist will occupy a pivotal position at many corporations, controlling the creation and flow of information. Openings: 30,000 to 100,000 or more. Salary: $29,000 to $90,000. Graduate degree: computer science or business administration—or both—or library science. Two top library science schools: UCLA and the University of Michigan.

Environmental engineer. The federal government's toxic- and hazardous-waste cleanup program—the so-called superfund—is likely to be renewed, providing an additional $7.5 billion for environmental projects by 1990. Corporate spending for waste disposal and recycling should also rise. The best jobs will go to engineers with environmental specialties. Openings: 20,000 immediately. Salary: $26,000 to $75,000 for a high-level manager. Schools with undergraduate programs include the University of Alabama, Michigan State University and Tulane University.

Executive chef. Jobs for all restaurant cooks will increase 42% by 2000, and executive chefs—graduates of well-known culinary schools with management skills—will be at the top of their trade. Openings: 50,000. Salary: $17,000 to $100,000. Among the best schools: Baltimore Institute of Culinary Arts, the Culinary Institute of America in Hyde Park, N.Y. and Johnson and Wales College in Providence, R.I.

Fiber-optics researcher. Optical fibers that transmit large amounts of information very quickly will be used in many industries. Openings: some 40,000 for fiber-optics researchers and technicians. Salary for researchers with master's degrees: $30,000 to

$40,000. Graduate degrees in optics are offered at the University of Arizona and the University of Rochester.

Gerontologist. Specializing in the study of aging, these experts will find jobs ranging from managers of retirement facilities to researchers. Openings: 500,000 for nurses with geriatric training, 50,000 for researchers and therapists and 10,000 for physicians. Salary: $23,000 to $40,000 for specially trained nurse practitioners, $20,000 to $80,000 for researchers and as much as $125,000 for doctors. Schools with gerontology programs include Brandeis University, the University of Michigan and the University of Southern California.

Industrial psychologist. Specialists who study issues of the workplace are already being hired before they can complete their doctoral studies. Key areas range from personnel testing to redesigning corporate management hierarchies. Demand is expected to rise steeply over the next 15 years. Salary: holders of master's degrees earn $45,000 to $85,000. Some of the best programs are offered by the University of Maryland, Michigan State University and the University of Minnesota.

Skilled repairer. Computers still haven't learned how to fix themselves, and there will be no slackening in demand for mechanics, repairers and installers in other specialties ranging from air-conditioner installation to electronics. Openings: more than 1 million. The fastest growth will be in repair of desktop computers; some 55,000 technicians will be needed. Salary: $13,000 for newly minted vocational school graduates to $30,000 for experienced workers. Education required: high school, vocational school or junior college.

Teacher. A million more instructors will be needed, but the highest salaries will probably go to those who teach professional skills to corporate employees. Salary: $35,000 to $75,000. Premiums will be paid for teachers with specialties in computers and business management. Demand will also be strong for teachers of kindergarten through 12th grade, as well as vocational instructors at junior colleges. Top teaching programs include those at Columbia, Ohio State and Stanford universities.

Writer or entertainer. Expansion in the movie and television industries is expected to result in more than 100,000 new jobs for actors, musicians, scriptwriters and other artists. Salary: zero up to $350,000 a week for, say, a headliner in Las Vegas. Top acting schools include the Yale University School of Drama and the Julliard School in New York City; universities with respected writing programs are the University of Iowa and Stanford University.

Writer: William C. Banks

Reporter associate: Kay Williams

Next, read an uncorrected revision of a paragraph that a student wrote summarizing this article. Then answer the questions that follow the paragraph.

PROMISING CAREERS (FIRST REVISION)

Recently, Money magazine surveyed private experts and government sources to find out which careers will promise the biggest payoffs in the year 2000. Careers in the computer field seem to be thriving best particularly artificial-intelligence specialists and data-base managers. Money implied that a "promising career" is one that is growing quickly and one that offers high salaries. I want to be a marketing researcher even though Money didn't list this career as one of the most promising ones. Fiber-optics research and environmental engineering are promising careers. The careers that most people think of as the best and the highest-paying (careers in law, medicine, and accounting) are not growing as fast as some other fields. Other promising careers, according to Money, include gerontologists, executive chefs, and skilled repairers. Money notes that teaching is a promising career, but most teachers make very low salaries.

Elliot Carson

1. Can you recognize a logical order or development of ideas in this student's summary? If so, what is it? If not, where do you get lost or confused?

2. Which sentences don't seem to belong? Why not? Cross them out or draw an arrow pointing to the place where they might fit more logically.

WRITING ACTIVITY   WRITING AND REVISING A BRIEF ESSAY

Reread the magazine article about promising careers on page 151. What is your reaction to the information presented in it? Here are some questions for you to consider:

- Does one of the careers strike you as particularly promising? Why?
- What do the nine careers all seem to have in common, if anything, (besides their salaries)?
- The writer calls these careers "promising" because they have high salaries and large numbers of job openings. Do you consider these the most important factors in selecting a career or are there other factors that are just as important (or even more important)?

Write a discovery draft of an essay about the career(s) that you consider most promising. You do *not* have to respond to any of the questions above. Begin by doing some freewriting, brainstorming, and clustering to find a purpose and an audience and to develop your examples and reasons. Write a discovery draft of an essay and revise the ideas and details in it using the techniques that you practiced in Chapter 6. Then, examine and revise the organization of your paragraph by answering the following questions:

1. Whom did I imagine as my audience when I wrote this paragraph? Will these readers recognize the order that I used? Can they follow the development of my ideas without getting lost or confused? If not, how can I rearrange my ideas so that they develop more logically?
2. Is the order that I used the most appropriate and effective order for my details? Will my order help readers remember my most important points? If not, how can I reorder my details so that they will develop my ideas logically and clearly?
3. Do my details fit together smoothly? Will my readers understand the relationships among my ideas? If not, how can I make these connections clearer?

Revise the organization of your draft based on your responses to these three questions.

A PROFESSIONAL RESPONSE

Donald Murray is a famous English teacher who has written many books about teaching and learning writing. Here are two revisions of the opening paragraph of the preface to one of his books. Note that he uses the word "title" instead of the book's actual title (*A Writer Teaches Writing*) because he did not write a title until after he had finished the book.

How do Murray's two revisions differ? (See the next two pages.)

RETROSPECTIVE OUTLINES

Many teachers and textbook authors recommend that writers prepare outlines of their ideas and details as a way of logically organizing their material. While some writers use "scratch" outlines to see the logical relationships among their ideas, many others are uncomfortable preparing an outline before they have written a discovery draft. The reason for this is that in order to outline a piece of writing, a writer has to know, in some detail, what he or she wants to write about and how he or she plans to develop the ideas. Because almost all writers discover their ideas *as* they try to write about a topic, they may find it impossible to do any outlining until they are finished writing a draft. Another problem that can result from outlining ideas before exploring them in a discovery draft is that writers may feel that they have to stick to the outline and may not consider other more interesting or important ideas that aren't on their original outlines. If you do want to prepare an outline in advance, make sure that you don't get stuck on it. Be willing to include details that occur to you as you are writing.

Outlining can be a very useful way of checking the logic and organization of a piece of writing, if the outline is prepared *after* the discovery draft is written. Outlining a first draft can give a writer a sense of the places where supporting details are missing or are not logically organized. Page 159 presents my discovery draft of the first paragraph in this chapter, followed by my **retrospective outline** of the paragraph. I call this kind of outline retrospective because retrospection means a review or a reexamination of things that have passed. As you can see, my retrospective outline of this paragraph also includes notes to myself about problems revealed by the outline.

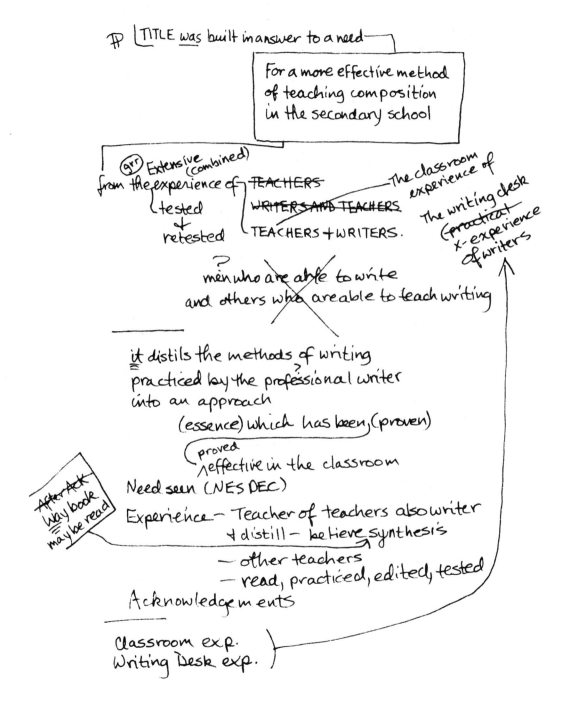

¶ [TITLE <u>was</u> built in answer to a need⌐

For a more effective method
of teaching composition
in the secondary school

(gr) Extensive (combined)
from the experience of ~TEACHERS~ ——The classroom experience of
⌐tested   ~WRITERS AND TEACHERS~   The writing desk
⌐retested   ⌐TEACHERS + WRITERS.   (~practical~ x-experience of writers

?
men who are able to write
and others who are able to teach writing

it distills the methods of writing
practiced by the professional writer
into an approach
      (essence) which has been (proven)
         ⌐proved
      ∧effective in the classroom
Need seen (NES DEC)
Experience — Teacher of teachers also writer
            & distill — believe synthesis
            — other teachers
            — read, practiced, edited, tested
Acknowledgements

After Ack
Way book
may be read

Classroom exp.
Writing Desk exp.

Preface

¶ TITLE was ~~built~~ *written to give* (~~from the experience of publishing writers and practicing teachers~~) ~~so that~~ (~~secondary school~~) English teachers ~~would have a~~ *will* ~~more~~ *an* effective method of teaching composition *based on* ~~The book reveals how~~ the ∧ professional writer ~~works and~~ *experience of* the ∧ ~~shows~~ how the steps ~~he~~ follows can be applied in ~~the~~ classroom.

book was tested by experienced teachers in 100's of classrooms to ~~the writer~~ *publishing writer*

⌐This does ~~not~~ mean that students will be trained to be professional writers. ~~It does mean that writing is a skill~~

~~It does mean that~~ students will be ~~taught~~ *encouraged* *motivated* *to teach themselves* the lessons that professional writers have taught themselves.

~~The professional writer is not just the poet or journalist~~

it does mean ≠ *[add transition]*

~~for~~ writing is ~~not a gift~~ *more* but (a skill), it is not (given) so *(than a gift)* much as it is developed. This book will show the teacher how to help the student develop the ability to communicate in writing with others -- in a business letter, a poem, an engineering report, a news story, [etc.] -- whatever his ability and need.

— in school
test
scholarly
essay
paper
— afterschool

Need
Experience (method book written)
How to use - variety
Acknowledgements

DISCOVERY DRAFT OF PARAGRAPH 1 IN CHAPTER 7

After you have revised the ideas in a discovery draft and developed new details, it's time to reexamine the organization and coherence of your draft. You should do this because your new thesis and details may suggest a totally new pattern for ordering your paragraphs and sentences. Revising the organization of a draft usually consists of "cutting and pasting": literally scissoring out each paragraph or each sentence and rearranging it in a new order with the other details in the draft. Revising coherence involves making the connections among your ideas and details clear and logical.

RETROSPECTIVE OUTLINE OF PARAGRAPH 1 IN CHAPTER 7

(Each Roman Numeral below summarizes a sentence in the paragraph above.)

I. *Topic Sentence*: After you revise ideas and details, revise organization and coherence.

II. *Reason Why:* New thesis and details may suggest a new order.

III. *How To Revise Organization:* "Cut and paste"—scissor out and rearrange each paragraph or sentence.

IV. *How To Revise Coherence:* Check relationships among ideas and details.

Turn to page 147 of this chapter to see the final revision of this paragraph. How is this revision different from the draft?

TECHNIQUES FOR IMPROVING COHERENCE

Deciding on a logical organization for the details in paragraphs is the first step toward communicating these ideas clearly and effectively to readers. The next step is making sure that these ideas develop smoothly—that they are not "choppy" or "jerky." The sentences and paragraphs in an essay should be revised so that they are linked to one another in ways that help readers follow them easily. Each detail must be **coherent**: it must be related in a recognizable way to the detail before and to the one after it. There are a variety of ways of achieving coherence. All of them require writers to make the connections among their ideas clear to a reader. Experienced writers often link details together in four ways:

1. by deleting irrelevant details
2. by using transitions

3. by repeating key words
4. by using pronouns to refer back to key words

Deletion of Irrelevant Details

Details that do not clearly develop the main idea of a paragraph should be deleted—crossed or cut out. As a writer, I know how difficult it is to delete ideas and details in a discovery draft. After struggling, sometimes for hours, to get one's thoughts and feelings on the page, no one really wants to delete a single word. However, if writers want readers to follow their ideas, they must examine every sentence to see if it might lead readers astray. If a detail isn't clearly related to the ones before and after it, it must be deleted.

EXERCISE   **DELETING IDEAS FOR BETTER COHERENCE**

Here is an uncorrected paragraph from a discovery draft of a student's essay on the law of public education. Cross out any sentence that is not clearly related to the main point of the paragraph or that is not clearly related to the sentence before it.

FIRST REVISION: PRAYERS IN PUBLIC SCHOOL

(1) In 1963, the Supreme Court of the United States decided that the reciting of prayers in public school violated students' First Amendment right to freedom of religious beliefs. (2) The First Amendment states, in part, that "Congress shall make no law respecting an establishment of religion, or prohibiting the free exercise thereof." (3) There have been a number of cases involving church-state-education relationships. (4) The Supreme Court has looked at cases involving payments for children in parochial schools. (5) Before 1963, the issue of the legality of prayers in public schools was argued in many state and city courts with differing results. (6) However, the 1963 Supreme Court

decision (which is still in effect) made it illegal for public school teachers to refer to God or a supreme being and to read from the Bible in religious exercises in class. (7) It also made it illegal for public school teachers to wear religious clothes in public school. (8) Currently, many religious groups are questioning the 1963 ruling and trying to get the Supreme Court to reconsider its decision.

Ruth Albert

Transitions

Transitions are words and phrases that show the connections between the ideas or between sentences. Experienced writers use transitional words and phrases to bridge the gaps between ideas that may seem unconnected to readers. Here are some commonly used transitions grouped according to the signal that they give and followed by examples of their use:

1. Transitions that signal an **additional** or a **similar** detail:
   furthermore   in addition   moreover
   also   similarly   likewise

   In 1963, the Supreme Court of the United States decided that the recitation of prayers in public schools violated students' First Amendment right to freedom of religious beliefs. **Furthermore,** the Court prohibited public school teachers from discussing God as part of a class' opening exercise.

2. Transitions that signal a **contrasting** detail:
   however   conversely   nevertheless
   although   even though   on the other hand

   In 1963, the Supreme Court of the United States decided that the recitation of prayers in public schools violated students' First Amendment right to freedom of religious beliefs. **However,** the Court allowed study of the Bible or religion when presented objectively as part of a program of literature or social studies.

3. Transitions that signal a **cause** or an **effect**:

consequently   in conclusion   therefore
thus   because   since

In 1963, the Supreme Court of the United States decided that the recitation of prayers in public schools violated students' First Amendment right to freedom of religious beliefs. **Consequently,** public school teachers have had to restrict most of their references to God while they are teaching.

4. Transitions that signal a **time-related** detail:

first   next   meanwhile
then   while   finally

In 1963, the Supreme Court of the United States decided that the recitation of prayers in public schools violated students' First Amendment right to freedom of religious beliefs. **Before** this decision, many public school students were required to recite the Lord's Prayer as part of every class' opening exercise.

5. Transitions that signal an **illustration:**

for example   such as   for instance
thus   in particular   in other words

In 1963, the Supreme Court of the United States decided that the recitation of prayers in public schools violated students' First Amendment right to freedom of religious beliefs. **In other words,** public school teachers were prohibited from requiring students to profess faith in God or to read the Bible in religious exercises in class.

6. Transitions that signal an **emphasis:**

indeed   in fact   most importantly
to repeat   again   truly

In 1963, the Supreme Court of the United States decided that the recitation of prayers in public schools violated students' First Amendment right to freedom of religious beliefs. **In fact,** public school teachers were prohibited from even referring to God or to a supreme being in a religious manner in class.

EXERCISE USING TRANSITIONS

Here is a paragraph that a student wrote in response to one of the writing activites in Chapter 4. Examine each blank space and decide if a transition is necessary to help readers understand the relationship between the ideas. If a transition is needed, fill in an appropriate one.

Try not to repeat the same transition twice. If you do not think a transition is necessary, leave the space blank.

SECOND REVISION: NEGOTIATING A RAISE

There are several important steps that people have to consider when they try to negotiate a raise with their employers. _____ they have to decide how much they think their work is worth. _____ they have to decide exactly what they want in terms of money, benefits, and vacations. _____ they have to think about what their employers might be willing to pay and what they can realistically afford. _____ they have considered all of these things, people can sit down with their employers and reach agreements. _____ people have to realize that sometimes their employers cannot agree to the kind of raise that they want. _____ they have to be willing to compromise on some other things. _____ they might have to give up some fringe benefits or expense accounts. _____ the more they can understand their employers, the more successful people will be in negotiating raises.

Michael Fontaine

Repetition

Another way to achieve coherence is to repeat key words and phrases so that the main points keep echoing throughout a paragraph. If you don't want to repeat the exact word, you can use a synonym (a word or a phrase that has a similar meaning). For example, here is a paragraph that I wrote for page 159 of this section on coherence. Note that instead of simply repeating the words "coherent" and "coherently," I used other words and phrases to refer back to these key terms.

Deciding on a logical order for the details in paragraphs is the first step toward communicating these ideas clearly and effectively to readers. The next step is making sure that these ideas *develop smoothly*—that they are not "choppy" or "jerky." The sentences and paragraphs in an essay should be revised so that they are *linked to one another* in ways that help readers follow them easily. Each detail must be **coherent:** it must be *related in a recognizable way* to the detail before and to the one after it.

EXERCISE   **REPEATING KEY WORDS AND USING SYNONYMS**

Below is an uncorrected student paragraph from an essay about "sexism." Every time you see the word "sexism" or "sexist" in the paragraph below, underline it. In addition, circle each synonym for "sexism" and for "sexist" that you find in the paragraph below.

(Sexual discrimination) is rampant at City College.
(Discrimination) means "the showing of partiality or of
prejudice" and I think that many of the teachers at our
school are partial to male students and are prejudiced against
female students. Sexism (discrimination on the basis of sex)
is obvious in most classes. Most of my teachers call on men
more often then they call on women and praise men more than
they praise women for similar answers. This discriminatory
behavior seems obvious but very few students are really aware
of it.

What is the effect of all of the repetition in this paragraph?

Pronouns

Pronouns are words that can be substituted for other words or phrases. Some examples of pronouns include *it, she, he, they, you, me, my, his, her, your, their, this, that, these, those, all, some, most, few, other, another.* Pronouns link details or sentences together by pointing the reader's attention back to the words which they are replacing in previous sentences.

> Sexual discrimination is rampant at City College. *It* goes on in almost every class, and most students consider it a serious problem.

EXERCISE **IDENTIFYING PRONOUNS**

Below is Yvette Gardner's uncorrected revision of her comparison paragraph. Circle each pronoun in the paragraph and draw an arrow back to the word it is replacing or referring to. The first one has been done as an example.

An "au pair" is a girl or woman who lives with a family and takes care of (its) children and its housekeeping in exchange for room and board and a small salary. I have been one here in America and in Denmark, and I have seen enormous differences between the workload of American and foreign au pairs. In America, the au pairs that I know are really babysitters. They take care of the children all day. They are also expected to do some cleaning and cook some meals. But after dinner, they usually have their evenings to themselves, and they can go out with their friends. Foreign au pairs, on the other hand, seem to have it much harder. They are babysitters <u>and</u> housekeepers <u>and</u> maids. Most of the foreign au pairs I knew were expected to care for the children, cook all of the meals, clean the house, iron and shop. And in the evenings, they were expected to babysit. I will never work overseas as an au pair again!

A STUDENT RESPONSE

Here is the second uncorrected revision of the comparison/contrast paragraph that Isaac Stein wrote after he consulted several public sources of information. Note his revisions in the organization and coherence of his paper.

SECOND REVISION

Ever since the day I took apart and re-assembled my parent's television set, I knew I wished to be an electronics engineer. Like doctors and lawyers, electronics engineers, *also* specialize in one of many areas and I want to do aerospace research and rocket design. *However* I am having difficulty deciding on the kind of company that I want to work for. Do I work for a giant corporation like Rockwell International in California or a small company like Rocket Research in Washington? *They both* ~~Rockwell and Rocket~~ design rocket engines and conduct applied aerospace research. And, *both of them* ~~they~~ offer competitve entry level salaries and medical, dental, and pension plans. *However* ~~They~~ *are very different* ~~do have differences.~~ Rockwell is huge: it employs 95,000 people and it hires 700 each year. Rocket *on the other hand* has only 300 people and hires only two or three engineering majors each year. Rockwell pays for 100% of its employee's education expenses, *but* Rocket only pays for $250. *However* ~~At~~ Rocket, engineers are involved with all phases of systems design and application. At Rockwell, they only get to work on one small part of a project. *Also* Rocket is closer to my home, *but* ~~If I work at~~ Rockwell *is not.* I would have to move or have a big commute. My neighbor, Dr. Jack Irving who works at a small engineering company said that

```
small firms like Rocket offer many more opportunities for
                    He may be right but
promotion. ∧I think I have to visit several more types of

rocket research firms before I can make up my mind about the

kind of place that's right for me.
```

In order to understand how Stein improved the coherence of his essay, follow the directions below:

1. Circle every transition in Stein's revision (the ones in the typed version *and* the handwritten ones).
2. Underline the key terms in each revised paragraph. Every time a key term is repeated, underline it. Also, underline every synonym that is used to replace these key terms.
3. Use a different color ink to circle every pronoun in the revision and to draw an arrow back to the word that it is replacing or referring to.

WRITING ACTIVITY IDENTIFYING AND REVISING PROBLEMS IN COHERENCE

Below is the uncorrected discovery draft of a paragraph that a student wrote for one of the writing activities in Chapter 4. Read it carefully. Then, follow these directions:

1. Delete any irrelevant sentences.
2. Add appropriate transitions wherever they seem necessary.
3. Repeat the key words or use synonyms to make the connections between the sentences clearer.
4. Substitute or add pronouns wherever they might be appropriate.

```
                        DISCOVERY DRAFT

     After weighing all the factors relating to choosing a

career, I have decided to go into the pharmaceuticals

industry.  The starting income for a salesman in the

pharmaceuticals industry is $18,000.  This salary is much

better than the salary my brother makes as a teacher.  This

salary is reviewed semi-annually (with raises of $1,000-
```

```
$3,000 possible at each review).  The job has terrific

benefits including pension, medical and dental policies and

usually a free car.  This job does involve a lot of traveling

and the pressure is high.  I cope well with pressure.  The job

offers excellent opportunities for promotion.  A salesman or

woman can become a sales manager after only five years and can

make more than $30,000 a year.  Woman can be pharmaceutical

salespeople too.  I think pharmaceutical sales is a good

career for me because I like doctors and nurses and these are

the people who I would be meeting each day.
```
Ken Morris

When you complete this activity, turn to page 80 in Chapter 4 to see Ken Morris's revision of the preceding paragraph.

WRITING ASSIGNMENT   WRITING AND REVISING AN ESSAY ABOUT A JOURNAL TOPIC

For this assignment, you will be writing a discovery draft of an essay and revising it twice: once for ideas and details and another time for organization and coherence. Begin by following the directions below:

1. Pick a topic that you have written about in your journal. Do ten minutes of freewriting about it. Then, do five minutes of brainstorming and five minutes of clustering to find a focus for a discovery draft of an essay about this topic.
2. Imagine that you know nothing about this topic and focus. Write down every question relating to this focus that you can think of. Then write down answers to each of your questions.
3. Narrow down your purpose for writing and write a brief description of the audience for whom you are writing.
4. Write a discovery draft of your essay.
5. Exchange discovery drafts with a classmate. Read your classmate's draft and write down questions about the information that you still need to know in order to understand your classmate's

ideas. Also indicate any problems in the believability or the logic of your classmate's supporting details.

6. Outline your classmate's essay. Then, note any problems in organization and coherence. When you are finished, give the draft and your notes, outline, and comments back to the writer.
7. Revise the ideas and the details in your draft using your partner's comments and the techniques that you practiced in Chapter 6.
8. Use your partner's comments and the techniques that you practiced in this unit to revise the organization and coherence of your draft.

ISSUES FOR YOUR JOURNAL

1. Did you enjoy reading the student writing in this chapter (or in the previous chapters)? Why or why not?
2. What are you writing about in your other courses? Are you revising these pieces of writing? Why or why not?
3. How do you feel about marriage? If you are married, do you enjoy being married? Why or why not? If you aren't married, do you want to be? Why or why not?
4. What kind of music do you like best? Why? What does your preference for this type of music reveal about you?
5. Why is illegal drug use becoming an epidemic in our country? Do you know anyone who uses illicit drugs? Why do they do it? What needs does it fulfill? What are drugs doing to the people who take them?

CHAPTER EIGHT

REVISING SENTENCE STRUCTURE

To shift the structure of a sentence alters the meaning of that sentence, as definitely and as inflexibly as the position of a camera alters the meaning of the object being photographed. Many people know about camera angles now, but not so many know about sentences. The arrangement of the words matters, and the arrangement you want can be found in the picture in your mind.

JOAN DIDION

INTRODUCTION: METHODS OF REVISING
SENTENCE STRUCTURE

In the epigraph to this chapter, Joan Didion notes that shifting the structure of a sentence's parts alters the meaning of that sentence. Didion's point is that English sentences are very flexible—writers can move sentence parts around to express different ideas or emphases. However, as Didion warns, the arrangement of words in a sentence matters, and writers need to play with sentences until they find the arrangement that reflects the exact "picture in their mind." For instance, here are some ideas that I have in my mind right now as I am writing this chapter:

- I am struggling with this chapter.
- I am anxious.
- I hope that my revisions will improve this chapter.

Here are various arrangements of these ideas:

1. I am anxious while I am struggling with this chapter and hoping that my revisions will improve it.
2. Anxiously, I am struggling with this chapter, hoping my revisions will improve it.
3. I am struggling with this chapter anxiously, hoping that my revisions will improve it.
4. As I struggle anxiously with this chapter, I hope that my revisions will improve it.
5. Hoping my revisions will improve this chapter, I struggle anxiously with it.

Which arrangement is "best"? The answer depends on the exact meaning that I want to express: Do I want to emphasize my anxiety (as sentences 1 and 2 do)? Do I want to focus on my struggle with this chapter (as 3 and 4 do)? Or do I want to point out my hope about my revisions (as 5 does)? As Didion says, I have to know the exact "picture in my mind"—my focus and my purpose—before I can decide which sentence structure conveys my precise meaning most accurately and most effectively. In other words, revising sentence structure involves adjusting words and sentences to make them more appropriate for one's purpose and audience. Usually, it is a waste of time for writers to revise sentence structure before they have revised their details, organization, and coherence. Too many students worry about changing sentences or words in a discovery draft, only to realize later that the whole sentence or paragraph is irrelevant and should be deleted.

PAIRED WRITING TASK REVISIONS IN SENTENCE STRUCTURE AND VOCABULARY

Work on this task with another classmate. Take out the discovery draft that you used for the Paired Writing Task on pages 147–148 of Chapter 7. Exchange papers with your classmate, and write answers to the questions below. Do *not* discuss each other's papers until you are both finished writing your comments.

Your classmate's name:

1. How does your partner's sentence structure make him or her "sound"? (For example, does he or she sound uptight, formal, scientific, scholarly, informal, funny, or poetical?)
2. Which sentences are particularly interesting or sound particularly effective? Put a star next to them, and be prepared to tell your partner why you liked them.
3. Which sentences seem too short and simple?
4. Which sentences seem too long and confusing?
5. Point out the sentences that seem unclear and that need more details.

PROBLEMS IN SENTENCE STRUCTURE

One common problem in sentence structure is a lack of variety—a series of short, simple sentences that all begin with the same word or pattern. Some student writers tend to "play it safe" and write simple sentences so that they won't have to worry about whether their sentences have errors in them. Sometimes, short simple sentences are perfectly appropriate. Often, however, a paragraph composed entirely of short simple sentences sounds abrupt or choppy and is boring to read. Also, a series of simple sentences may not convey the relationships and connections among a writer's ideas. Read the following paragraph. What is your reaction to it, and what impression of the writer does it give you?

I am struggling with this essay. I am anxious. I hope my revisions will improve this essay. I will keep revising. I want to express my ideas clearly. I want to be satisfied. I want my teacher to be satisfied.

As writers struggle to find the words and patterns that best express the relationships among their ideas, they may create confusing sentences that disorient their readers. This may occur when writers experiment with formal vocabulary and academic sentence structures that they have read but that they are not yet comfortable using. For example, which sentences in the following paragraph seem confusing?

> Depending on the extent of my anxiety over this essay will determine the amount of struggle with which I will have with it. Since it is imperative that I express my ideas clearly, this essay will be improved by my continuous revisions so as that my teacher and I will be satisfied.

The confusing sentences in the preceding paragraph are a positive sign: they indicate that the writer is attempting to express complex ideas and relationships that cannot be presented in short simple sentences or in informal vocabulary. This writer, and other writers who write similar confusing sentences, need to reread and revise her sentences to make them express her intended meaning and to make them communicate clearly to her readers. There are two techniques that experienced writers use to revise sentence structure: "sentence modification" and "sentence combination." Both are explained in detail in the sections that follow.

TECHNIQUES FOR REVISING SENTENCE STRUCTURE: MODIFICATION

To "modify" means to change or to alter, and writers can modify their sentence in three different ways:

1. by **adding details** to clarify their meaning and attitude toward the topic
2. by **substituting precise details** (concrete, sensory language) for vague or abstract terms
3. by **deleting unnecessary details** that distract the reader because they are irrelevant or confusing

Addition

Addition involves adding descriptive words to sentences. When you revise your writing, examine each sentence and ask yourself if it needs more descriptive details. Use the following questions to help you identify problems in your sentences:

- Who or what is this sentence about? What details can I add to describe this subject more clearly or fully?

- What is this subject doing in this sentence? What details can I add to describe this action more specifically?
- What details can I add to describe where and when (or how long) the action in the sentence is taking place?
- What other words or phrases can I add to make this sentence clearer and more interesting?

As Joan Didion pointed out in the epigraph, English sentences are flexible: there are many different places in a sentence where descriptive words may be added. For example, you can add descriptive words before each of the nouns in a sentence. A **noun** is a word that names a person, object, place, quality, or idea. The technical term for a word that describes a noun is an **adjective**. Adjectives make sentences more precise by specifying the qualities of nouns. For example, here is a sentence without and with adjectives:

This teacher is struggling with this chapter.

This *experienced* teacher is struggling with this *difficult* chapter.

Another place to add descriptive words and phrases is before or after the verbs in a sentence. A **verb** is a word that expresses the action of the sentence. The technical term for a word that describes a verb is an **adverb**. Adverbs make sentences more precise by telling the reader when or where or how the action occurs. Here is a sentence without and with adverbs:

This experienced English teacher has been struggling with this difficult chapter.

For the past four days, this experienced English teacher has been struggling *anxiously* with this difficult chapter.

EXERCISE ADDING ADJECTIVE AND ADVERBS

The sentences below were taken from the discovery draft of Allen Brower's paragraph on "My Favorite Place." As you read *each* sentence, ask yourself "What might this subject look like?" "How, where, and when might this action happen?" Your answers to these questions will provide you with adjectives and adverbs to add to the sentences. In the space below each sentence, rewrite it, adding as many adjectives and adverbs as you can. (You may have to rewrite some of the sentences as two new sentences.) The first one has been done as an example.

1. My favorite place is my car.

Currently, my favorite place to relax is my terrific car.

2. The car is a 1979 Camaro.

3. It has blue paint and silver chrome and stripes.

4. It is sleek and smooth.

5. The blue leather is worn but clean.

6. I like to sit inside my car and smell it.

7. I also like to listen to the car's stereo.

Adding descriptive modifiers can also help you vary your sentence structures. Sentence variety is important for two reasons: (1) writers who consider several options for arranging the parts of a sentence have control over their writing and use language to express their exact meaning; and (2) varied sentence patterns are more interesting to read than a series of sentences that all have the same structure. One simple way to achieve sentence variety is to add adjectives or adverbs to a sentence and then move them to the beginning or the end of the sentence. For example, look at the way the writer of the sentences below achieved some variety in his sentences:

The blue leather inside is worn but clean.
Inside, the blue leather is worn but clean.

The car, a real beauty, is sleek and smooth.
The car is sleek and smooth, a real beauty.

WRITING ACTIVITY ADDING AND MOVING
DESCRIPTIVE MODIFIERS

Go back to the exercise that you did on page 174. On a separate piece of paper, number from 1 to 7, and rewrite *each of your revised sentences*, moving some of the modifiers to the front of the sentences. Examples of possible revisions of the first sentence are below.

1. My favorite place is my car.

a. My terrific car is currently my favorite place to relax.
b. My favorite current place to relax is my terrific car.

A STUDENT RESPONSE

Here is Allen Brower's partially corrected revision of his first paragraph that was discussed in Chapter 7 and in the exercises above. Note his additional revisions in sentence structure.

SECOND REVISION: MY FAVORITE PLACE

My favorite place in the world is my car. It's the first

car that I have ever owned and I really enjoy it. The car is

a *used* 1979 Camaro and its previous owner took good care of it.

The *midnite* blue paint gleams *like new* and the *shiny* chrome sparkles. *With silver* And the

stripes on the sides of *it,* the car ~~really~~ look*s* ~~fierce~~ *like a racer*. It is

sleek and smooth like a jet plane. ✓The blue leather ⓘnside is

Sometimes worn but clean. ∧ I like to sit inside and breathe the *heavy* smell of leather and oil. I also like to listen to the *first-Rate Akai* stereo radio and cassette deck with four speakers that can blast me to heaven.

Allen Brower

Which particular adjectives and adverbs make Brower's sentences varied and interesting?

Substitution

Substitution is another modification technique that you can use to make your sentences more interesting and more informative. When you revise your writing, examine each sentence for vague or abstract terms and substitute more specific concrete or sensory words for the vague ones. For example, look at how the substitutions in the second sentence below clarify the first sentence:

The chrome on my car is shiny.

The chrome on my 1979 Camaro really sparkles.

If you are not sure how to substitute specific details for vague or general ones, reread the section on "Levels of Generality" on pages 72–73 in Chapter 4. It describes several ways of making details more specific, such as:

- Give the exact names of things rather than writing about them in general terms.
- Replace general or absract words with concrete sensory details. A concrete detail is one that can be perceived though the senses (it can be seen, heard, smelled, tasted, and/or touched).
- Use vivid, descriptive verbs instead of ordinary, vague ones.

EXERCISE SUBSTITUTING MORE SPECIFIC DETAILS

The sentences below were taken from a student's discovery draft. Revise each sentence by substituting descriptive concrete details for the vague, abstract words. Cross out the vague words and make up details that make sense. Try to use all three methods: use exact terms, concrete sensory words, and vivid verbs. The first sentence has been done as an example.

1. Researchers have studied television and young people.

During the past decade, many researchers have studied the effects of television programming on children aged three to fifteen.

2. Children start to watch TV when they are young.

3. These young kids have preferences based on their sex.

4. However, TV affects them all in many ways.

5. For example, children learn how to act by watching TV.

6. Some researchers believe that TV violence makes children violent.

7. Others believe it decreases violence.

8. It's hard to be sure because real-life violence is caused by many factors.

PROFESSIONAL RESPONSES

Here are some paragraphs written by people whose writing I admire. As you read each one, underline the descriptive adjectives and adverbs that these writers use.

Far out along the autumn plain, beneath the sloping light, an immense drove of cattle moved eastward. They went at a walk, not very fast, but faster than they could imaginably enjoy. Those in front were compelled by those behind; those at the rear, with few exceptions, did their best to keep up; those who were locked within the herd could no more help moving than the particles inside a falling rock.

James Agee
"A Mother's Tale"

I lay down on a solitary rock that was like an island in the bottom of the valley, and looked up. The grey sage-brush and the blue-grey rock around me were already in shadow, but high above me the canyon walls were dyed flame-colour with the sunset, and the Cliff City lay in a gold haze against its dark cavern. In a few minutes, it, too, was grey, and only the rim rock at the top held the red light. When that was gone, I could still see the copper glow in the piñions along the edge of the top ledges. The arc of sky over the canyon was silvery blue, with its pale yellow moon, and presently, stars shivered into it, like crystals dropped into perfectly clear water.

Willa Cather
The Professor's House

So Elvis Presley came, strumming a weird guitar and wagging his tail across the continent, ripping off fame and fortune as he scrunched his way, and, like a latter-day Johnny Appleseed, sowing seeds of a new rhythm and style in the white souls of the white youth of America, whose inner hunger and need was no longer satisfied with the antiseptic white shoes and whiter songs of Pat Boone. "You can do anything," sang Elvis to Pat Boone's white shoes, "but don't you step on my Blue Suede Shoes!"

Eldridge Cleaver
Soul on Ice

Deletion

Deletion—or crossing out—is the third sentence modification technique. Many inexperienced writers think that sentence length is an absolute virtue: the longer the better. But as the writer James Moffett has pointed out, in the famous example below, a short simple sentence is often more interesting and stylistically better than a long complex one:

I don't want what is left in your cup after you finish drinking.

I don't want the dregs.

Sentence length is less important than sentence **economy**—the degree to which each word in a sentence contributes to the overall meaning of the sentence. Any word that isn't essential or that repeats the sense of another word in the sentence should be deleted. When experienced writers revise, they frequently add adjectives and adverbs to their sentences and then, on a later rereading, decide to delete these modifiers. At this point, you may be asking yourself, "What's the point of adding a lot of modifiers if I'm going to have to cross them out?" The answer is that revising is actually a form of experimentation: it's a process of adding and changing and deleting until each sentence says exactly what you want it to say. Most writers have to add words before they can delete them. Here is an example of this process:

These women will kill their attackers.

Fiercely, these women kill their attackers.

These women slaughter their attackers.

First the writer added the adverb "fiercely" to clarify her meaning. Then she decided to use a more vivid verb, and since the verb "slaughter" implies "kill fiercely," she had to delete the adverb. As you revise your sentence structure, add and substitute words. Then, try to delete all of the "padding"—words and phrases that aren't essential to your meaning—in your sentences to make them clearer and stronger.

EXERCISE   **DELETING ADVERBS AND SUBSTITUTING VIVID VERBS**

Look at the underlined verbs and adverbs in each of the sentences in the following paragraph. For each underlined phrase, substitute a stonger, more vivid verb that will express the meaning more effectively. The first one has been done as an example.

The woman was sitting by herself and was <u>deliberately not</u>
<u>*ignoring*</u>
<u>paying much attention</u> to her companions. She raised her head

and <u>slowly looked steadily</u> about her. Then, she got up and

<u>began to walk very slowly and carelessly</u> toward the river.

She saw one of her friends lying half asleep by the river's

edge, and something caused her to <u>turn her head rapidly toward</u> him. She started <u>running as fast as a leopard</u> toward him. When she reached him, she abruptly took his arm and <u>pulled</u> <u>with a great effort on</u> it. She <u>moved him slowly</u> away from the alligator's jaws just in time.

EXERCISE DELETING UNNECESSARY WORDS AND PHRASES

The uncorrected paragraph below was taken from a student's revision. Cross out all the words and phrases that you think are not essential to the meaning of each sentence. The first one has been done as an example.

~~There are~~ Many myths *exist* about women warriors, ~~and women who fight fiercely. However,~~ *but* most primitive and modern societies do not arm their women and do not send them to armed combat. In my opinion, women can be drafted. They can do non-combat service. They don't take part in any combat that might be dangerous or that might hurt them or kill them. However, Konrad Lorenz has noted that among animals, it is the males not the female animals that fight. When female animals do end up fighting, they fight to the death. It seems that women don't know the many different rituals and the rules of fighting. Thus, women probably should not be allowed to fight.

A STUDENT RESPONSE

Here is the student essay on which the preceding exercise was based. It was revised with the three modification techniques of addition, substitution, and deletion.

THIRD REVISION: WOMEN WARRIORS

Margaret Mead *,the famous anthropologist,* was asked whether women should be permitted

to be combat soldiers. She answered that they shouldn't. She

said that they are "too fierce." I *was intrigued by her answer,* ~~am an anthropology major~~

so I decided to do ~~here at Hunter College and I did~~ some reading. I wanted to

try and figure out what Mead meant. ~~by her answer.~~

I discovered that there are many *historical and modern* myths about women

warriors. However, *in reality* most primitive and modern societies do not

arm their women. Women can be drafted. They can do non-

combat service *in offices. However*, They ~~don't~~ *rarely* take part in any real combat *or fight in* wars

still ~~T~~this doesn't prove that they are "too fierce" to do combat.

Another notable anthropologist, Konrad Lorenz has pointed out that among animals, it is

the males that fight. ~~Not the females.~~ He also stated that

when female animals *do* fight, they *usually fight in defense of their babies* fight to the death. This may *and they*

be a clue into Mead's comment. In addition, Lorenz noted that

throughout history, men and boys are the only ones who learn

the rituals and the rules of fighting. Maybe Mead means that

women don't know these rituals and rules. ~~Women don't know~~

~~how to play fair.~~ What would happen if women were ~~allowed to~~ *armed?*

~~carry deadly weapons?~~ Maybe they would ~~blow up the world.~~

~~They might~~ be too fierce. *Maybe* they ~~might~~ *would* fight to the death of

the world.

Sonja Rossini

How do Rossini's handwritten revisions improve her essay?

TECHNIQUES FOR REVISING SENTENCE STRUCTURE: COMBINATION

The other technique that experienced writers use to improve their sentences is "sentence combination." Writer can combine sentences or parts of sentences to clarify the relationships among their ideas and to highlight specific details. Combining sentences also enables writers to express ideas more clearly in fewer words. There are two basic ways to combine sentences:

1. by **coordinating** two or more complete sentences
2. by **subordinating** parts of sentences and joining these parts to other sentences

Coordination

The most common way to combine sentences is to coordinate them—to join them together with a comma and a **coordinator**. English has seven coordinators:

- **and** indicates that the second idea is in addition to the first idea: "I am writing Chapter 8, *and* I am also trying to revise Chapter 7.
- **but** and **yet** indicate that the second idea is in constrast to the first idea: "I am writing Chapter 8, *but (yet)* I know that I still have to revise Chapter 7."
- **for** indicates that the second idea explains the reason for the event in the first idea: "I can't stop working now, *for* I have two more chapters to finish by next month."
- **so** indicates that the events in the second idea are caused by the events in the first idea: "I must finish two more chapters soon, *so* I can't stop working now."
- **or** indicates that the second idea is an alternative to the first idea: "I can try to write Chapter 8, *or* I can work on revising Chapter 7."
- **nor** indicates that the second idea continues a negative statement begun in the first idea: "I am too tired to work on Chapter 8, *nor* do I feel like revising Chapter 7."

These coordinators are familiar to you: people use them all the time to connect their ideas in speaking and in writing. And I am also sure that at one point in your education, an English teacher told you never to do what I just did—begin a sentence with **and** or **but**. Technically, the coordinators are supposed to join two or more ideas into one complete sentence. But coordinators can be used to join ideas, even when the ideas that they link are separated by a period (as in the two ideas that I just wrote).

EXERCISE   **EXAMINING COORDINATORS**

Advertisers often use coordinators at the beginning of sentences to link an idea to the one that came before it. Read the ad below and circle each coordinator. Why do you think the person who wrote this ad used coordinators to begin sentences instead of using them to combine two sentences into one?

It's the perfect marriage. Sony's new 8mm video phenomenon and your hand.

We call it the Handycam™ camera/recorder. It's so tiny it fits in one hand.

So anyone can use it anywhere, anytime.

Just point and shoot. And capture all the memories as they happen.

Then, with its handy companion deck, you can play your pictures back in full color and vivid sound, on any television.

Up to two hours of good times on a video tape no bigger than an audio cassette.

So bring your hand in to your local Sony dealer.

And try the Handycam on for size.

SONY.
THE ONE AND ONLY®

EXERCISE   **COORDINATING IDEAS**

Read the uncorrected student paragraph below, and decide which sentences might sound better if they were combined. Add a comma and a coordinator in the space between any sentences that you think ought to be joined, and delete any unnecessary words.

(1) Anthropology can be defined as the study of human behavior and culture. (2) Anthropologists can study biological objects. (3) They can study social patterns. (4) Their goal is to understand changes in people's physical

and social development over time. (5) Anthropologists achieve
this goal by examining the changes that have occurred as
people adapted to new environments. (6) They dig up bone
fossils. (7) They can compare the fossil forms to living
ones. (8) Anthropologists make hypotheses about life in
primitive cultures. (9) They cannot prove these hypotheses
because the remains of these cultures are rare and in
fragments. (10) Anthropologists cannot study early human
life. (11) They can do research on ancient documents.
(12) They can also study prehistoric artifacts. (13) These
artifacts reveal how our human ancestors lived.

Subordination

To subordinate something means to treat it as less important than or
dependent on something else. Writers can combine related ideas by
subordinating one of them to the other with a **subordinator.** Here are
two ideas that are joined first with a coordinator and then with a subordinator:

Idea 1: Anthropologists can make hypotheses.
Idea 2: Anthropologists cannot prove their hypotheses

Coordination: Anthropologists can make hypotheses, *but* they cannot prove them.
Subordination: *Although* anthropologists can make hypotheses, they
cannot prove them.

In the first sentence, the coordinator "but" joins two complete
ideas, each of which receives equal emphasis. In the second sentence,
the subordinator "although" indicates that the first idea is less important to the writer than the second idea. The subordinator also makes
the first idea into an incomplete or dependent thought. The second idea
("they cannot prove them") does express a complete thought and, thus,

gets more emphasis. If the writer had wanted to emphasize the *first* idea, he could have subordinated it:

> *Although* they cannot prove their hypotheses, anthropologists can make them.

Subordinators are wonderful tools for revising sentences because they enable writers to show the relationships among their ideas and to emphasize different details. Here is a list of the most common subordinators, included in a chart that shows the three different ways of joining ideas in English:

Methods of Joining Related Ideas			
Purpose	*Coordinators*	*Subordinators*	*Transitions*
To add an additional or similar idea	and		in addition furthermore moreover also
To add a contrasting idea, whereas	but yet	although even though unless	however nevertheless conversely
To add a cause or an effect	for so	because since if so that	therefore as a result consequently thus
To add a time-related idea or an alternative	or nor	once before during after when where	first today meanwhile then next last

Note that English does not have subordinators that can be used to add on an additional or a similar idea. The transitions in the third column of the chart should be familiar to you. In Chapter 7, you practiced using them at the beginning of sentences to bridge the gap between two sentences that might seem unconnected to readers. Take another look at examples of each of these three ways of joining related ideas:

a. Anthropologists can make hypotheses, *but* they cannot prove them.
b. *Although* anthropologists can make hypotheses, they cannot prove them.

c. Anthropologists can make hypotheses. *However*, they cannot prove them.

How are the three sentences above different? All three indicate the same relationship between the same two ideas. However, the three statements differ in emphasis and pausing. The coordinator in sentence a and the subordinator in sentence b signal a close relationship between the two ideas in each sentence. (In sentence a, the related ideas are of equal importance. In sentence b, the second idea is more important.) The period and the transition in sentence c stop the reader and indicate that the relationship between the two ideas is not close enough to justify combining them into one sentence. Remember that these three different methods of joining related ideas create different types of sentences. A coodinator combines two complete sentences into one longer sentence. A subordinator also does this, but it makes one of the sentences into an incomplete idea. If you punctuate this incomplete idea as a sentence, you are making a sentence error called a "fragment":

After they have dug up a fossil. Anthropologists can compare it to a living form.

Don't punctuate the subordinated idea as a complete sentence. Combine it with the other idea to make one sentence:

After they have dug up a fossil, anthropologists can compare it to a living form.

Furthermore, remember that a transition *cannot* be used to combine two sentences into one. Even though a transition sounds like a coordinator, it should not be punctuated like one. If you use a transition to combine two sentences into one, you are making a sentence error called a "run-on":

Anthropologists have found that cultures vary independently, thus they know that no "race" can be better than any other.

If you want to combine two ideas into one sentence, use a coordinator or a subordinator:

Anthropologists have found that cultures vary independently, *so* they know that no "race" can be better that any other.

Since anthropologists have found that cultures vary independently of one another, they know that no "race" can be better than any other.

If you want to keep the ideas in separate sentences, use a transition at the beginning of the second sentence to show the relationship between the two ideas:

Anthropologists have found that cultures vary independently. *Thus*, they know that no "race" can be better than any other.

EXERCISE **USING DIFFERENT METHODS TO JOIN IDEAS**

Here are five sets of related ideas taken from a student paragraph. In the space below, try joining each pair using *all three* methods discussed above. Use the chart on page 186 to help you select an appropriate coordinator, subordinator, and transition. The first one has been done as an example.

1. Anthropological research has shown that human behavior is very diverse. Human habits can vary endlessly.

Combined with a coordinator:

Anthropological research has shown that human behavior is very diverse, and human habits can vary endlessly.

Combined with a subordinator:

(This can't be done.)

Linked with a transition:

Anthropological research has shown that human behavior is very diverse. In addition, human habits can vary endlessly.

2. Most animals reveal the same patterns of behavior within any given species. The human species has very few patterns that are shared by all people.

   Combined with a coordinator:

   Combined with a subordinator:

   Linked with a transition:

3. All humans have similar physical and mental structures. One might expect all human behavior to be similar.

   Combined with a coordinator:

   Combined with a subordinator:

   Linked with a transition:

4. Different societies differ in almost every aspect of their behavior. They speak very different languages.

   Combined with a coordinator:

   Combined with a subordinator:

Linked with a transition:

WRITING ACTIVITY   COORDINATING AND SUBORDINATING IDEAS

Here is the paragraph from the exercise on page 184 of this chapter. Decide which sentences might sound better if they were combined with a coordinator *or* if they were combined with a subordinator. Write your revision on a separate piece of paper.

(1) Anthropology can be defined as the study of human behavior and culture. (2) Anthropologists can study biological objects. (3) They can study social patterns. (4) Their goal is to understand changes in people's physical and social development over time. (5) Anthropologists achieve this goal by examining the changes that have occurred as people adapted to new environments. (6) They dig up bone fossils. (7) They can compare the fossil forms to living ones. (8) Anthropologists make hypotheses about life in primitive cultures. (9) They cannot prove these hypotheses because the remains of these cultures are rare and in fragments. (10) Anthropologists cannot study early human life. (11) They can do research on ancient documents. (12) They can also study prehistoric artifacts. (13) These artifacts reveal how our human ancestors lived.

A STUDENT RESPONSE

Here is the fourth version of Sonja Rossini's essay on "Women Warriors." The handwritten changes show the author's use of coordination *and* subordination.

FOURTH REVISION: WOMEN WARRIORS

Margaret Mead, the famous anthropologist, was once asked

whether women should be permitted to be combat soldiers. She

answered that they shouldn't~~.~~ₓ *because* ~~She said that~~ they are "too

fierce." I was intrigued by her answer, ^so^ I decided to do
some reading ^because^ I wanted to figure out what Mead meant.

I discovered many historical and modern myths about women
warriors. However, in reality, most primitive and modern
societies do not arm their women. Women can be drafted ~~They~~ ^to^
~~can~~ do non-combat serve in offices. However, they rarely take
part in any real combat or fight in wars. Still, ~~this~~ ^their not fighting^ doesn't
prove that they are "too fierce" to do combat.

Another notable anthropologist, Konrad Lorenz has pointed
out that among most species of animals, it is the males that
fight. He also stated that when female animals do fight, ~~they~~
usually in defense of their babies, ~~and~~ they fight to the
death. This may be a clue into Mead's comment: ^W^omen may
be fiercer, deadlier fighters. In addition, Lorenz noted
that throughout history, in all kinds of cultures and
civilizations, men and boys are the only ones who learn the
rituals and the rules of fighting. Maybe Mead means that
women don't know these rituals and rules. ~~What would happen~~
^If^ ~~women~~ ^they^ were armed? ~~M^aybe they would be ~~too~~ ^so^ fierce~~.~~x ~~Maybe~~ ^that^
they would fight to the death of the world.

Sonja Rossini

Circle every coordinator and every subordinator that Rossini
added.

A Special Case:
Subordination with Relative Pronouns

A **pronoun** is a word that can be used as a substitute for a noun or
a noun phrase (for example, *he, him, your, mine, some,* and so forth). A
relative pronoun is a special type of pronoun that is used simulta-

neously to replace a word or phrase *and* to connect a subordinate idea to another complete idea. The relative pronouns that are used to refer to people are *who, whom,* and *whose.* The relative pronouns that are used to refer to animals, objects, places, or ideas are *that* and *which.* Examples of the way each of these relative pronouns can be used to subordinate ideas follow.

- *who*
  Idea 1: Margaret Mead has written extensively on human relationships.
  Idea 2: Margaret Mead is a noted anthropologist.

  Margaret Mead *who* is a noted anthropologist, has written extensively on human relationships (or Margaret Mead, *who* has written extensively on human relationships, is a noted anthropologist).
- *whom*
  Idea 1: Margaret Mead has written extensively on human relationships.
  Idea 2: I admire Margaret Mead greatly.

  Margaret Mead, *whom* I admire greatly, has written extensively on human relationships.
- *that*
  Idea 1: Margaret Mead's book is *Coming of Age in Samoa.*
  Idea 2: The book established her in the field.

  The book *that* established Margaret Mead in the field is *Coming of Age in Samoa.*
- *which*
  Idea 1: Anthropology was Margaret Mead's passion.
  Idea 2: Anthropology is the study of human culture and evolution.

  Anthropology, *which* is the study of human culture and evolution, was Margaret Mead's passion.
- *whose* (show possession by people or objects)
  Idea 1: Margaret Mead has written extensively on human relationships.
  Idea 2: Margaret Mead's work earned her world-wide recognition.

  Margaret Mead, *whose* work earned her world-wide recognition, has written extensively on human relationships.

Here are two easy guidelines for using *that* and *which*:

- When the idea that you want to subordinate is *necessary for the reader to identify the subject of the main idea,* use *that* (or, if the subject is a person, use *who*), and don't put commas around the subordinated idea.

Mead's belief that nuclear warfare is insane has influenced a whole generation. (The subordinated idea is essential for letting the reader know which of Mead's beliefs is insane.)

• When the idea that you are subordinating *adds information that is not necessary for identifying the subject of the main idea,* use *which* or *who* and put a comma before and a comma after the subordinated idea. The commas indicate that the information between them is not essential for identifying the subject.

Mead's book on Samoa which is still a classic in the field, influenced many anthropologists. (The subordinated idea is not necessary for the reader to identify the book—the main idea makes that clear.)

EXERCISE **SUBORDINATING WITH RELATIVE PRONOUNS**

Examine the following pairs of sentences. In the space below each pair, try to combine them by using a relative pronoun to subordinate the idea that you think should receive less emphasis. The first one has been done as an example.

1. a. Anthropologists have discovered something about human food habits.
   b. Human food habits vary endlessly.

   Anthropologists have discovered that human food habits vary endlessly.

2. a. Various researchers have seen some interesting food habits.
   b. Various researchers have observed almost every living society.

3. a. Eskimos eat meat and fish almost exclusively.
   b. Eskimos live in the Artic.

4. a. Mexican Indians eat mostly grains and vegetables.
    b. Mexican Indians live in the plains.

5. a. Milk is drunk daily by East Africans.
    b. Milk is quite plentiful.

6. a. West Africans consider milk a luxury food.
    b. West Africans have few cows or goats.

   The next six sets have three ideas in each set. Try to combine all three ideas into one sentence using the appropriate relative pronoun. The first one has been done as an example.

7. a. Some Mexicans are repulsed by the food habits of Mexican Indians.
    b. A favorite dish of some Mexican Indians is dog meat.
    c. The dog meat has been aged.

Some Mexicans are repulsed by the food habits of Mexican Indians whose favorite dish is aged dog meat.

8. a. Some tribes in Styria regularly eat arsenic.
    b. Arsenic is a substance.
    c. Arsenic is extremely poisonous.

9. a. The Jappuras of India eat insects.
    b. The diet of the Jappuras of India is lacking in protein.
    c. The insects are crushed and cooked.

10. a. Clay is eaten by several Amazonian tribes.
    b. Clay is a source of minerals.
    c. Several Amazonian tribes soften the clay with water.

EXERCISE   **COMBINING SENTENCES**

Below are some uncorrected sentences about an archaeological finding in Lower Wadi Kubbaniya in Egypt. The people who inhabited Lower Wadi Kubbaniya lived and farmed there over 10,000 years ago. Combine any sentences that might sound better combined. Try to use all of the modification and combination techniques that you learned in this chapter. Write your version of these two paragraphs on a separate piece of paper.

Lower Wadi Kubbaniya must have been an unusually attractive environment. It must have been an attractive place for the people. The people were of the late Paleolithic era. There were fish. The fish were in the river. There were ducks. The ducks were in the marshlands. There were trees and grasses. These trees and grasses were fringing the water. There were antelope and wild cattle. They roamed the vegetated area. There was desert there then. This desert was beyond the narrow band that was watered by the Nile. There is desert there now. We have found the remains of ancient camps. These remains are in several distinct places. These remains are high up on the dunes. The dunes are next to the floodplains. These remains are also lower down on the ridges between the swales in the embayment. The swales are depressions in the ground. And we have found these remains still further down at the mouth of the wadi. The mouth of the wadi is where it empties into the channel. The channel is part of the Nile.

We do not know something. We do not know what the ancient people of Wadi Kubbaniya looked like. We do know something else. We do know how these people went about their lives. We know this in significant detail. In fact, we have pieced together evidence. This evidence was dug up from their campsites. We have reconstructed the annual cycle these ancients lived. They lived this cycle as they moved from place to place. They moved around with the seasons.

When you are finished doing this exercise, turn to page 198 to see the original version of these paragraphs.

EXERCISE **PLAYING WITH A WRITER'S SENTENCES**

Below are nine sentences that have been adapted from a passage in Eldridge Cleaver's *Soul on Ice* in which he writes about the importance of language and of writing. On separate paper, combine them into as many variations as you can think of, using all of the modification and combination techniques.

1. I lost my self-respect.
2. My pride dissolved.
3. My pride was in being a man.
4. My whole moral structure seemed to collapse.
5. My whole moral structure was shattered.
6. It was shattered completely.
7. I started to write because my pride dissolved.
8. I also started to write because my moral structure seemed to collapse.
9. I started to write to save myself.

When you finish this exercise, look at Cleaver's actual sentence which can be found on page 205 of Chapter 9.

WRITING ASSIGNMENT **WRITING AND REVISING AN ESSAY ABOUT THE IMPACT OF TELEVISION**

Here is an excerpt from an essay by G. Comstock, et al., that examines research on the impact of television on children and adults.

Goldbern and Gorn (1977) also exposed four- and five-year olds either to a ten-minute program with no commercials, to the program with two commercials advertising a new version of a familiar toy, or to the program with two commercials on successive days (for a total of four exposures to the commercial). Children were then asked whether they would rather play with friends in the sandbox or with the advertised toy. Almost twice as many children who saw the program without the commercials opted for interaction with friends. Similarly, when faced with an option of playing with a "nice boy" without the toy or with a "not so nice boy" who had it, fewer than 35 percent of those who saw the commercials chose the toyless nice boy compared to 70 percent of those who did not see the commercials. A second set of questions addressed to the children concerned the impact of the commercials on parent-child relations. The children were told their mothers had expressed a preference for a tennis ball over the advertised toy. They were then asked which they liked best. Significantly more children from the control group followed their mother's judgment than did those exposed to the commercials. Moreover, when shown photographs of a father and son and told that the father denied the child's request for the advertised toy over 60 percent of the children who did not see the commercials felt the boy would still want to "play with his daddy," compared to fewer than 40 percent of those who saw the commercials. Finally, children who did not see the commercials were significantly more likely than children who did to state that a child who did not get the toy would remain happy. The authors interpret their results as indicating that television commercials encourage material as opposed to social orientation in children, that exposure to commercials may lead to parent-child conflict, and exposure can lead to disappointment and unhappiness when products are not obtained.

What is your reaction to this excerpt—in particular, to the last sentence of the excerpt? In your experience, do television programs or television commercials have negative effects on children? How should parents deal with their children's desire to watch television? Use the directions below to write a discovery draft about the impact of television on children.

1. Do five minutes of freewriting about the topic. Then, do five minutes of brainstorming and five minutes of clustering to find a focus.
2. Narrow down your purpose for writing and write a brief description of the audience for whom you are writing. Then, write a discovery draft of your essay.
3. Exchange discovery drafts with a classmate. Read your classmate's draft and write down questions about the information that you still need to know in order to understand your classmate's ideas. Also indicate any problems in the believability or the logic of your classmate's supporting details and any problems in organization and coherence. When you are finished, give the draft and your notes back to the writer.
4. Revise the ideas, details, organization, and coherence of your draft using the techniques that you practiced in Chapters 6 and 7.
5. Examine each sentence in your revision. Add adjectives and adverbs in any places where they might make the sentence more interesting or informative. Then decide if any of the adjectives or adverbs should be moved to the front of some sentences. Move them.
6. Examine each sentence again, looking for vague or abstract terms. Circle each one and write in a more specific substitute. Use exact

terms, sensory words, concrete terms, and vivid verbs wherever you can. Then, reexamine each sentence and delete any padding.

7. Use a comma and a coordinator to combine any sentences that would sound better or be clearer if they were coordinated. Use a subordinator or a relative pronoun to subordinate any sentences that would sound better or be clearer if they were subordinated.

8. Rewrite your essay so that it incorporates all of your revisions in sentence structure.

Below are the paragraphs that were adapted for the Exercise on page 195.

Lower Wadi Kubbaniya must have been an unusually attractive environment for people of the late Paleolithic: fish in the river, ducks and geese in the marshlands, various bushes, trees and grasses fringing the water. Antelope and wild cattle roamed the vegetated area. Beyond the narrow band watered by the Nile, there was then, as now, desert. We have found the remains of ancient camps in several distinct places—high up on the dunes next to the floodplains, lower down on the ridges between the swales, or depressions, in the embayment, and still farther down at the mouth of the wadi where it empties into the Nile channel.

Although we do not know what the ancient people of Wadi Kubbaniya looked like, we do know in significant detail how they went about their lives. In fact, by piecing together evidence dug up from their campsites, we have reconstructed the annual cycle these ancients lived as they moved from place to place with the seasons.

ISSUES FOR YOUR JOURNAL

1. Do you watch much television? Why? How does it affect your life or your values?

2. What kinds of writing are you doing for your other courses? How can you use your journal to help you explore material from these courses?

3. How are different groups of people portrayed on television? How do television programs or commercials create or uphold stereotypes?

4. What is "sexist language"? Do you find it offensive? Why or why not?

5. Does your state have a "seat belt" law, a law that requires drivers and passengers to wear their seat belts? If it does have one, how do you feel about it? If not, should it have one? Why or why not?

PART THREE

EDITING

CHAPTER NINE

EDITING
SENTENCE STRUCTURE

*A sentence should read as if its author, had he
held a plough instead of pen, could have
drawn a furrow deep and straight to the end.*
HENRY DAVID THOREAU

INTRODUCTION: THE IMPORTANCE OF EDITING

Editing is the process of identifying and correcting errors and unconventional forms in a piece of writing. When writers edit, they make their writing conform to certain academic, professional, technical, or business conventions. These conventions are simply customs or practices agreed upon by the people acknowledged as experts in the field. All of us follow conventions every day, and these conventions vary in different places or languages. For example, in English, written material is read and written from left to right; in certain other languages it is written from right to left; and in some languages it is written from top to bottom. Writing from left to right is not inherently better or more logical than writing from right to left or from top to bottom; it is simply a convention that has to be followed in many countries if the writer wants to be understood.

Academic writing has its own set of conventions—of sentence structure, grammar, and punctuation—that readers expect to be followed. There are two fundamental reasons why all writers should edit their writing: (1) nonstandard forms interfere with a reader's interpretation of the writer's meaning, and (2) errors are annoying and distracting to most readers. For instance, what is your reaction to this uncorrected paragraph from a student's essay for a sociology course?

The nature/nurture contraversy goes on century after century despite all the research on the effects of genetic inheritance versus the effects of environmental experiences. Studies of identicle twin show that biological heredity is more important for some trates than for others. For example, intelligence and socialability. However, all personality traits are shaped by experience, in fact some researchers claim that individual difference in ability and achievement are almost entirely environmental.

The content, organization, and coherence of this paragraph are fine; but the errors violate our expectations of academic writing, making it difficult to understand what the writer is trying to say. Because readers expect to see Standard Written English in academic essays, this writer's use of unconventional sentence structure, grammar, and spelling is very distracting. Moreover, his errors give the impression that he doesn't care too much about the reader or the topic. If *you* care about your topic and your reader, you should edit your writing.

PAIRED WRITING TASK   EDITING EACH OTHER'S ESSAYS

With a classmate examine a final revision of a piece of writing that you wrote for one of the assignments in this book or for your teacher. Exchange papers with your classmate. After you have read your classmate's paper, write answers to the questions below. Do *not* discuss each other's papers until you are both finished writing your comments.

Your classmate's name:

1. What do you think the writer was trying to say or to show you in this paper?

2. Which sentences have problems, errors, or seem wrong? Which sentences don't seem to make sense? Put a star next to each one and be prepared to discuss it.
3. Which verbs seem incorrect? Which verb or noun endings seem incorrect? Circle each one, and be prepared to discuss it.
4. Which words don't seem to make sense? Underline each one, and be prepared to discuss it.
5. What errors in spelling and punctuation appear in your partner's piece? Be prepared to point each one out to your partner.

EDITING TECHNIQUES AND PROOFREADING

Editing is the final step of the writing process. At some point in the development of a piece of writing, writers stop revising and say, "Enough!" They decide that the piece is as clear, logical, and well-organized as they can make it, given the circumstances in which they are writing it and the deadline for submitting it. Then, they stop revising and start editing. They examine each sentence and each word, slowly and objectively, looking for sources of confusion and ways of improving clarity and correctness. Editing involves identifying and correcting errors in sentence structure, grammar, vocabulary, spelling, and punctuation. Editing is not an easy task. Many writers are so close to their writing that they are often unable to see the errors on the page. All writers need to get some distance from their work in order to proofread objectively. You can get some distance from your writing by following the methods that were discussed on pages 125–126 of Chapter 6. Below are some additional techniques that experienced writers use to identify errors and nonstandard forms in their work.

- Read the piece aloud *slowly*, one word at a time, to another person or into a tape recorder. Reading aloud slowly helps you see errors that you cannot catch when you read silently.
- Place a ruler or a sheet of paper under each line of your writing in order to force your eyes to move more slowly over each line.
- Read your writing from the end to the beginning, one sentence at a time (read the last sentence, then the next to the last, and so forth). Reading each sentence out of its context helps you judge whether it is a complete sentence.
- Every time your teacher returns a paper to you, write down his or her comments related to editing in the Writing Progress Log in this book's Appendix. This will help you track your progress in eliminating errors from your writing.

For example, here is an entry from the Writing Progress Log of one student:

Date   11/5/85   Course   Sociology 101

Title of Paper Reaction to First Set of Readings

Strengths:

Clear analysis of the issues
Effective use of details from the
readings

Problems and Errors:

Word ending errors: *twins, differences*

Sentence structure errors: *1 fragment and 1 run-on*

The appendix of this book also has a Spelling Log to help you keep track of words that you usually misspell. Here is an entry from this student's Spelling Log:

Problem Word	Misspelling	Cause
controversy	contraversy	mixed up "a" and "o"
inheritance	inheratance	mixed up "a" and "i"
environmental	enviromental	forgot the "n"
identical	identicle	spelled "cal" as "cle"
sociability	socialability	added "la" incorrectly

STANDARD WRITTEN ENGLISH (SWE) SENTENCE STRUCTURE

This chapter presents several methods for correcting or eliminating different types of sentence structure errors. However, remember that the rules and conventions of SWE writing are flexible: they depend on the purpose and on the reader. Many professional writers break the rules all the time. For example, most English handbooks advise writers not to begin sentences with "and" or "but" because these coordinators are supposed to be used to combine two complete sentences into one. But I used "and" or "but" to begin many of the sentences in this book, including this!

FRAGMENTS

A sentence begins with a capital letter and ends with a mark of terminal punctuation (a period, question mark, or exclamation point), but not every string of words that begins with a capital and ends with a period is a sentence. For example, here is the excerpt from Eldridge Cleaver's *Soul on Ice* that you worked on in Chapter 8. Which word groups that begin with a capital letter are not complete sentences?

I lost my self-respect. My pride as a man dissolved and my whole moral structure seemed to collapse, completely shattered. That is why I started to write. To save myself.

A **fragment** is an incomplete idea that is punctuated to look like a complete sentence. Many professional writers use fragments for stylistic effects, as Cleaver does in the preceding paragraph in order to emphasize the essence of his point. However, fragments can be very annoying to read, and they often do not let readers see the connections among the writer's ideas. Determining where one sentence should end and the next should begin is a difficult task that gets easier with practice. The more you read and write, the better you will become at seeing sentence boundaries. These boundaries are very important for readers. The following paragraph illustrates an extreme example of what happens when a writer ignores sentence boundaries:

> In any society unpleasant work must be done and some people must be persuaded or forced to do it in most societies some kind of class system works to compel people to do the dirty work these people are excluded from competing for good jobs or professions because of educational limitations, job, discrimination, and cultural background this class of people—usually called the lower class or caste—also includes unemployed unskilled laborers who can survive long periods of unemployment or welfare without guilt.

Because of the absence of sentence boundaries, it's easy to get lost in the preceding paragraph. Although I've never met a writer who omits all terminal punctuation and capital letters, I do know many inexperienced writers who have problems with sentence boundaries, particularly with fragments. Remember that a fragment is *not* simply a short sentence. If a sentence has a complete subject–verb unit, it is a sentence, no matter how short it is. The following three sentences are quite short, but each is a complete sentence:

> "I came. I saw. I conquered."

Here is an even briefer sentence: "Go!" The verb is "go." The subject is not explicitly stated in the sentence, but it is understood to be "you." Fragments may be long or short, and they often seem like complete ideas:

> Studies show that biological heredity is very important for several traits. *Some of which I have already discussed in detail.*

Grammatically, however, fragments are not complete ideas, usually because they are missing a subject or a verb or both. If you read a fragment aloud, it usually sounds correct and almost always makes sense in its context. This is why it is so difficult to find fragments by reading sentences aloud. If you read your sentences aloud and cannot tell whether they are fragments, try examining each to make sure that it has at least one complete subject–verb unit. The **subject** is the person, thing, or idea that is doing the action or experiencing the condition expressed by the sentence:

> In any society, unpleasant *work* must be done.
> Some *people* must be persuaded or forced to do it.

The **verb** is the action that the subject is doing or the condition that it is experiencing:

> In any society, unpleasant work *must be done.*
> Some people *must be persuaded* to do it.

If you are not sure whether a sentence has a complete verb in it, perform this test on it: Find the word that you think is the verb of the sentence. Try putting one of the following pronouns—*I, we, he, you, it,* or *they*—in front of this word. Does the verb make a complete thought with the pronoun? Does it make sense?

> In any society, unpleasant work *done.* ("It done" doesn't make sense.)

> In any society, unpleasant work *is done.* ("It is done" makes sense.)
> *or*
> In any society, unpleasant work *must be done.* ("It must be done" makes sense.)

Another special feature of English verbs is that they can function as other parts of speech as well as verbs. For example, what part of speech is the word "doing" functioning as in the sentences below?

1. Those people were *doing* unpleasant work.
2. *Doing* unpleasant work is dreadful.
3. The people *doing* unpleasant work were miserable.

In sentence 1, *doing* is functioning as half of the two-part verb. Notice that *were* is the first half of this two-part verb and it expresses the time of the action (in the past). *Doing* is the "main" or the "principal" verb, and it expresses the activity that was occurring. In sentence 2, *doing* is functioning as a noun—it is the subject or the thing that is being discussed in this sentence. (The verb in sentence 2 is *is.*) In sentence 3, "doing" introduces a modifying phrase that describes the subject of the sentence. It lets the reader know *which* people were miserable. (The verb in sentence 3 is *were.*)

Thus, only in sentence 1, is *doing* behaving as a verb by letting you know what the action is and when the action occurred. In sentences 2 and 3, *doing* is a **verbal**, a form that looks like a verb but that does not function as a verb. Unlike most verbs, verbals do *not* change their form to indicate the number of subjects in the sentence or the time expressed by the sentence. When you use verbals as verbs, you create fragments instead of complete sentences:

Lower class people excluded from competing for good jobs. (fragment)

Lower class people *are excluded* from competing for good jobs. (complete sentence)

Lower class people, excluded from competing for good jobs, *are forced* to do society's unpleasant work. (complete sentence)

If you have a habit of using verbals instead of verbs, you should look for verbs that end in "ing" or in "ed" and make sure that you include a helper verb *or* add a complete verb.

WRITING ACTIVITY REVISING FRAGMENTS

Here is an advertisement for a sports network. On a separate piece of paper, rewrite the entire ad, turning every fragment into a complete sentence.

Which communicates the ad's message more effectively: the fragments or your complete sentences? Why?

Using a verb instead of a verbal is one way of creating a fragment. Another common way of making a fragment is writing a **subordinator**

fragment. A subordinator fragment is a subject–verb unit that begins with a subordinator but that is not combined with another complete sentence:

> The nature/nurture controversy goes on century after century. *Despite all the research on the effects of genetic inheritance versus the effects of environmental experiences.*

Reread the fragment that begins with "Despite" by itself. If you do this, you will see that it is not a complete idea. It should be connected to the sentence before it:

> The nature/nurture controversy goes on century after century, despite all the research on the effects of genetic inheritance versus the effects of environmental experiences.

Another typical subordinator fragment is one that includes a relative pronoun:

> Studies of identical twins show that biological heredity is more important for particular traits. *Which I have already described.*

This kind of fragment should also be corrected by connecting it to the sentence before it:

> Studies of identical twins show that biological heredity is more important for particular traits, which I have already described.

Methods of Correcting Fragments

There are several ways of correcting or eliminating fragments.

1. If the fragment is a subordinator fragment, a) combine it with the sentence before it or with the sentence after it, *or* b) omit the subordinator:

> Studies of identical twins show that biological heredity is more important for particular traits. *Some of which I have already described.*

a. Studies of identical twins show that biological heredity is more important for particular traits, some of which I have already described.

b. Studies of identical twins show that biological heredity is more important for particular traits. I have already described some of these traits.

2. If the fragment has a verbal instead of a verb, a) add a helper verb, *or* b) change the verbal into a verb, *or* c) add a complete verb:

Studies of identical twins showing that biological heredity is important for particular traits.

a. Studies of identical twins are showing that biological heredity is important for particular traits.
b. Studies of identical twins show that biological heredity is important for particular traits.
c. Studies of identical twins, showing that biological heredity is important for particular traits, have proven that heredity is a critical factor.

3. If the fragment is missing a subject or a verb or both, add the missing part:

The effects of heredity on identical twins.

a. The effects of heredity on identical twins have been examined in recent studies.
b. I have read several studies showing the effects of heredity on identical twins.

EXERCISE   **CORRECTING FRAGMENTS**

Here are three uncorrected paragraphs from a student essay. Identify each fragment and correct it using one of the methods discussed above. You may have to add new words to some of the fragments to make them into complete sentences.

```
    All societies have norms of behavior.  They also have

deviant behavior.  Behavior that violates the society's norms.

All normal people are occasionally deviant.  Doing things, for

instance, that other members of their community might

disapprove of.  But truly deviant behavior is behavior that is

forbidden by the community's laws.  Because it threatens the
```

safety or the social order of the community. Thus, all societies punish deviants who act criminally. Some punishments ranging from ridicule to imprisonment to death.

However deviance can be a positive factor in a society. Because it may slowly change the norms of the society. Especially if the deviant behavior is not extreme. The deviant behavior of a few people may be adopted. By more people and then by larger groups. This behavior may then become the beginnings of a new norm. As more and more people participate in the deviant behavior. People in power slowly begin to accept and even justify the behavior. And eventually it becomes a norm. One striking example of this change from deviance to norm. The earliest Christians were ridiculed, denounced, tortured and killed for their belief in Christ. Their behavior deviated greatly. From the norms of their surrounding Jewish and Roman communities. Slowly as more and more people joined them. Christianity became a respected behavior.

Another example of the way that deviance helps change the norms of society. Twenty years ago, independent women with minds of their own who refused to be bossed around by their husbands. They usually ended up divorced. And married women who worked because they wanted to were considered strange. And married men who stayed home to take care of the children. They were considered really crazy. Their deviant behavior couldn't be understood. Or tolerated by most of our society. Today independent strong women and women who work are everywhere. And more and more men becoming house-husbands.

Yesterday's deviants are today's yuppies!

RUN-ONS

Just as a fragment is not simply a short sentence, a run-on is not merely a long sentence. This passage contains a famous sentence that is 313 words long and grammatically perfect:

Perhaps it is easy for those who have never felt the stinging darts of segregation to say, "Wait." But when you have seen vicious mobs lynch your mothers and fathers at will and drown your sisters and brothers at whim; when you have seen hate-filled policemen curse, kick and even kill your black brothers and sisters; when you see the vast majority of your twenty million Negro brothers smothering in an airtight cage of poverty in the midst of an affluent society; when you suddenly find your tongue twisted and your speech stammering as you seek to explain to your six-year-old daughter why she can't go to the public amusement park that has just been advertised on television, and see tears welling up in her eyes when she is told that Funtown is closed to colored children, and see ominous clouds of inferiority beginning to form in her little mental sky, and see her beginning to distort her personality by developing an unconscious bitterness toward white people; when you have to concoct an answer for a five-year-old son who is asking: "Daddy, why do white people treat colored people so mean?"; when you take a cross-country drive and find it necessary to sleep night after night in the uncomfortable corners of your automobile because no motel will accept you; when you are humiliated day in and day out by nagging signs reading "white" and "colored"; when your first name becomes "nigger," your middle name becomes "boy" (however old you are) and your last name becomes "John," and your wife and mother are never given the respected title "Mrs."; when you are harried by day and haunted by night by the fact that you are a Negro, living constantly at tiptoe stance, never quite knowing what to expect next, and are plagued with inner fears and outer resentments; when you are forever fighting a degenerating sense of "nobodiness"— then you will understand why we find it difficult to wait.

Martin Luther King, Jr.
"Letter from a Birmingham Jail"

If Dr. King had written a period in place of every semicolon in the long sentence above, he would have written a string of subordinator fragments. If he had left out all of the semicolons, he would have written one very long run-on, which would be almost impossible to read. A **run-on** consists of two or more sentences (complete subject–verb units) that are punctuated as one sentence:

> Discrimination is the treatment of people on the basis of their group classification rather than their individual characteristics, it is usually practiced by a group in power in order to preserve its privileges. (run-on)

The run-on above is a special kind of run-on called a **comma splice**: two sentences incorrectly joined with a comma. In Standard Written English, two complete sentences cannot be joined with a comma. As Dr. King's sentence illustrates, the correct way to join two or more complete sentences is to use a semicolon. A semicolon is usually used to join two complete sentences when the second sentence continues the idea expressed in the first sentence:

> Discrimination is the treatment of people on the basis of their group classification rather than their individual characteristics; it is usually practiced by a group in power in order to preserve its privileges.

This sentence could also have been separated into two complete sentences:

> Discrimination is the treatment of people on the basis of their group classification rather than their individual characteristics. It is usually practiced by a group in power in order to preserve its privileges.

Unlike fragments, run-ons are almost never used intentionally for special effects. Long run-ons, in particular, are too difficult to read. For instance, try to make sense of this run-on (which is an adaptation of a sentence that comes from a sociology textbook published in 1963):

> In democratic societies there is at least the tendency for most people to share the values on behalf of which the means of violence are employed this does not mean that these values have to be fine the majority of the white people in some Southern communities may be for instance in favor of using violence as administered by the police agencies in order to uphold segregation but it does

mean that the employment of the means of violence is approved by the bulk of the populace.

This run-on actually consists of four complete sentences:

1. In democratic societies there is at least the tendency for most people to share the values on behalf of which the means of violence are employed.
2. This does not mean that these values have to be fine.
3. The majority of the white people in some Southern communities may be, for instance, in favor of using violence as administered by the police agencies in order to uphold segregation.
4. But it does mean that the employment of the means of violence is approved by the bulk of the populace.

These four sentences could have been written as separate sentences *or* they could have been joined with semicolons *or* they could have been combined with coordinators or subordinators. They could also have been combined into one grammatically correct sentence, as they were in the book from which they were taken:

In democratic societies there is at least the tendency for most people to share the values on behalf of which the means of violence are employed (this does not mean that these values have to be fine—the majority of the white people in some Southern communities may be, for instance, in favor of using violence, as administered by the police agencies, in order to uphold segregation—but it does mean that the employment of the means of violence is approved by the bulk of the populace).

Peter L. Berger
An Invitation to Sociology

Writers often run together two complete sentences when the second complete idea begins with a pronoun or with a transition:

A stereotype is an image of a group of people that is shared by another group of people, *it* is applied indiscriminately to all members of the stereotyped group. A stereotype bears some resemblance to the characteristics of the stereotyped group, *however*, it is always exaggerated and distorted.

In the first run-on above, the pronoun *it* refers to the subject of the first idea (a stereotype), so some writers feel that they should join both ideas in one sentence. These ideas can be joined, but *not* with a comma:

> A stereotype is an image of a group of people that is shared by another group of people; it is applied indiscriminately to all members of the stereotyped group.

Transitions can be used to link ideas, but *not* with a comma:

> A stereotype bears some resemblance to the characteristics of the stereotyped group; however, it is always exaggerated and distorted. (Another way to link these two ideas correctly is to put a period after *group* and begin the second idea with *however*.)

Methods of Correcting Run-Ons

There are several ways of correcting or eliminating run-ons.

1. Find the end of the first complete sentence (subject–verb unit) and put in the appropriate mark of terminal punctuation (a period, a question mark, or an exclamation point). This turns the run-on into two separate sentences.

> *Stereotypes can be positive or negative, usually they are used to emphasize the imperfections of the stereotyped group.* (run-on)

> Stereotypes can be positive or negative. Usually they are used to emphasize the imperfections of the stereotyped group. (two correct sentences)

2. Find the end of the first complete sentence and put in a semi-colon:

> Stereotypes can be positive or negative; usually they are used to emphasize the imperfections of the stereotyped group. (one correct sentence)

3. Combine the two sentences with a comma and an appropriate coordinator:

> Stereotypes can be positive or negative, *but* usually they are used to emphasize the imperfections of the stereotyped group. (one correct sentence)

4. Combine the two sentences with the appropriate subordinator:

While stereotypes can be positive or negative, usually they are used to emphasize the imperfections of the stereotyped group. (one correct sentence)

Stereotypes, *which* can be positive or negative, are usually used to emphasize the imperfections of the stereotyped group. (one correct sentence)

EXERCISE CORRECTING RUN-ONS

Here are three uncorrected paragraphs from an essay. Identify each run-on, and correct it using the method that you think is most appropriate.

People who stereotype are committing injustices, they are depriving other people of their humanity. A stereotype is an image that one group of people share about another group of people, it can be negative, positive, or mixed. When people stereotype, they apply the image to all members of the stereotyped group, they don't see each member's individual characteristics and differences. Although stereotypes are always distorted or exaggerated, they usually bear some resemblance to the characteristics of the stereotyped group. (Otherwise, the stereotype wouldn't be recognized.)

Stereotyping is a very basic means of discrimination. If you stereotype someone as a "cold WASP," a "cheap Jew," or a "lazy Black," you aren't really seeing that person, all you are doing is looking for instances of behavior that prove your stereotype, also you are ignoring behavior that contradicts the stereotype. Treating people on the basis of a stereotype lets you discriminate against them, it makes you feel that it's okay to reject them. In reality, of course, stereotyping is a sign of ignorance, people who stereotype are unwilling or incapable of finding out the facts about other people.

Not only is stereotyping a form of ignorance, it also reveals a lack of emotional maturity. One classic study done by T. W. Adorno showed that insecure and immature people were more likely to accept stereotypes than mature people, another of Adorno's studies showed that people who do not stereotype are more willing to accept others as individuals. They interact with the real person not with the stereotype.

FAULTY PARALLELISM

Parallelism is a way of structuring a sentence so that it places similar ideas in similar grammatical forms. Making similar words or phrases parallel helps readers see the relationships between these words or phrases:

Adorno's research showed that stereotyping is a sign of *insecurity, immaturity, and ignorance.*

Faulty parallelism is distracting because it makes a reader stop to figure out the relationships between ideas that seem similar but that are not in parallel form:

Adorno's research showed that stereotyping is a sign of *insecurity, being immature,* and *people who ignore others.*

In the sentence above, the writer is listing a series of qualities that characterize people who stereotype. When a sentence includes words, phrases, or complete ideas in series, these must be in parallel grammatical form (all nouns, all verbs, all adjectives, and so forth):

- Nouns: Stereotyping is a sign of *insecurity, immaturity, and ignorance.*
- Adjectives: People who stereotype are often *insecure, immature,* and *ignorant.*
- Adverbs: People who stereotype may often act *insecurely, immaturely,* and *ignorantly.*
- Verbs: People who stereotype are often *feeling* insecure, *acting* immaturely, and *ignoring* others.
- Relative Clauses: People who stereotype are usually people *who have little confidence, who have not matured,* and *who have a tendency to ignore others.*

Note that verbs in series must all be in the same form of the verb. If the writer had used different verb forms for this series, the sentence would not be parallel:

People who stereotype are often *feeling* insecure, *act* immaturely, and try *to ignore* others.

EXERCISE **IDENTIFYING AND CORRECTING ERRORS IN PARALLELISM**

The uncorrected paragraphs below have been adapted from a student essay. Underline each sentence that contains grammatical structures which are not parallel and write in a correction above each sentence you underlined.

Most people tend to have sterotyped views of men and women. People usually assume that men are more aggressive, more dominant, and they have more ambition than women. Women, on the other hand, are often stereotyped as being more passive and they show more emotions than men. These beliefs are stereotypes because they are inaccurate in many instances. Not all men are aggressive and ambitious, and not all women are characterized by passivity and show their emotions.

The only sex differences that research has uncovered are differences in upper-body strength, in mathematic skills, and spatially. In particular, males seem to do beter than females in visual-spatial abilities and females are very verbal. In actuality, most sex differences are the results of social training and not coming from biological inheritance.

FAULTY MODIFICATION

Dangling and Misplaced Modifiers

In Chapter 8, you practiced adding modifiers—adjectives and adverbs—to your sentences to make them more informative and more interesting. The placement of these modifiers is very important. If an adjective or an adverb is not next to the word it is describing, then the sentence may sound confusing or unintentionally silly. A **dangling** modifier is a word or a phrase that does not clearly modify any word in the sentence. Here is an example:

Being teenagers, cults can be very attractive.

This sentence is confusing because it implies that cults can be teenagers. Improving this sentence requires rearranging its words:

Cults can be very attractive to *teenagers.*
Teenagers can find cults very attractive.

If a modifying word or phrase is not placed right next to the word it modifies, then it is a **misplaced** modifier. Look at how the misplaced modifier in the following sentence creates unintentional humor:

At an early age, my parents cautioned me about cults.

In this sentence, the initial modifier, "at an early age," sounds silly because it refers to "parents." Moving the modifier next to the word it describes corrects the problem:

My parents cautioned me *at an early age* about cults.

When I was at an early age, my parents cautioned me about cults.

Identifying and Correcting Errors in Modification

The uncorrected paragraphs below are adapted from a student essay. Correct all of the misplaced and dangling modifiers.

What is a "cult" and how is it different from a religion? Defined as deviant groups, sociologists have noted that cults conflict with a society's established religions. Having existed throughout history, people have looked to cults for peace, salvation and mystical experiences. Shrouded in secrecy in today's world, cults are booming. Standing on street corners in every major American city, you can see cult members asking for contributions and trying to get new recruits.

Cults usually recruit members from colleges who are lonely and insecure and seeking easy solutions to the problems of becoming an adult. Using highly sophisticated techniques, the feelings, thoughts and behaviors of new recruits are manipulated. As soon as they enter the cult, cult leaders start their brainwashing. While being deprived of food, sleep and privacy, other cult members put intense peer pressure on the new recruits who are not allowed to discuss their former lives. Within a few weeks, the new recruits undergo a complete personality transformation. By swearing complete allegiance to the cult leader, the leader becomes their new parent. Completely in control, cult members are told what to eat and wear, when to have sex, and even many children they can have.

CONFUSING SUBORDINATION

Sometimes writers try to pack so many ideas in a sentence that they lose track of where the sentence is going. Here is an example of a sentence which has very confusing subordination:

I think that a society is which a religion functions to control the government, like what is going on in Iran now causes serious problems.

Because this sentence seems to be going in several different directions at once, readers get confused about the writer's meaning. Here are three different ideas that I can disentangle from this sentence.

1. I think when a religion functions to control a society's government, it causes serious problems.

or

I think that a society whose government is controlled by religion has serious problems.
2. What is going on in Iran now is an example of a society's government being controlled by religion.
3. What is going on now in Iran now causes serious problems.

I am genuinely unsure of the writer's meaning, but I can think of several ways of rewriting this sentence to make it clearer:

I think that when a religion controls a society's government, as in Iran now, it causes serious problems.

or

I think that a society whose government is controlled by religion, as Iran's is now, has serious problems.

In earlier chapters of this book, you practiced combining ideas by subordinating a part of a sentence to another sentence. Sometimes, when you subordinate several complex ideas, you may accidentally omit a word or phrase that would clarify the relationship among your ideas or you may add words that confuse readers. Most subordinators lead readers to expect specific sentence structures, and if these structures do not follow, readers get confused. For example, read this sentence, and think about how its subordination confuses its meaning:

By deposing the Shah of Iran enabled Muslim leaders to create a religious revolution.

When readers see a sentence that begins with "By" followed by an "ing" verb and a noun, they expect the next word in the sentence to tell who or what is doing the "ing" verb. In the sentence above, readers expect to find out who "is deposing the Shah of Iran" immediately after the word "Iran":

By deposing the Shah of Iran, Muslim leaders were able to create a religious revolution.

If the writer wanted to keep the word "enabled" in the sentence, he would have to change the "By":

Deposing the Shah of Iran enabled Muslim leaders to create a religious revolution.

When you edit your sentences for problems, reread each one aloud to make sure that it states your meaning clearly and that it doesn't mix up the subordinated sentence parts. If a sentence seems very mixed up, reword it or cross it out and rewrite it.

EXERCISE   **IDENTIFYING AND CORRECTING CONFUSING SUBORDINATION**

The paragraph below is adapted from a student essay. Correct each sentence that contains subordination problems.

Although the Middle East is experiencing a major Islamic revival, but Islam has always been a strong independent religion in Iran. By serving the Iranians directly as leaders of the congregations allowed Islamic mullahs to meet the people's needs and to take public positions. During the 1970's, more and more Iranians turned to Islam in which was an outlet for their grievances against the Shah. In January 1979, Ruhollah Khomeini's supporters revolted against the Shah, and he fled to America. Although many Iranians, they supported Khomeini as a symbol of opposition to the Shah, but they didn't really approve of his fundamentalist programs.

They were shocked when Khomeini forced the government and
courts, which these things functioned democratically, to
conform to Islamic laws. Because he was a fundamentalist,
Khomeini wanted that the government to be ruled by religious
authorities who would rule according to God's (Islam's) laws.
Iran is now a total Islamic theocracy.

SENTENCE STRUCTURE CORRECTION SYMBOLS

You might not want to use these symbols to edit your own writing,
but you may need to use them to edit a classmate's writing or to understand your teacher's comments.

Error	Problem
Frag	Fragment (a part of a sentence that is incorrectly punctuated like a complete sentence)
RO	Run-on (two or more complete sentences incorrectly punctuated as one sentence)
CS	Comma Splice (two or more complete sentences incorrectly joined with a comma)
//	Parallelism Error

WRITING ASSIGNMENT WRITING, REVISING AND EDITING AN ESSAY ABOUT STEREOTYPES

Here is an essay by an English teacher about the stereotypes commonly used to describe English teachers. Read the essay and check off
the stereotypes that you think are true.

O WAD SOME POWER THE GIFTIE GIE US . . .

After reading Stevenson's "The Sire de Maltroit's Door," my
class decided that while the characters were romantically con-
ceived, they were not complete stereotypes. Although we expected
Denis to act as a hero should act and "do the right thing by
Blanche," still he was more than just your everyday shining
knight. And while Blanche was a beautiful maiden in distress (has

anyone ever seen an ugly maiden in distress?), she had a nobility that somehow lifted her above the typical heroine tied to the railroad track. Even though the Sire was an evil uncle, or perhaps just an overly suspicious one, he was more interesting and more carefully developed than the fellow in the black cape that wants the rent.

We went on to discuss the idea of stereotypes and managed to get several good ones on the board. Then, in a second's lapse of sanity, I jokingly suggested that it might be fun to make a list of common stereotypes used to describe English teachers. What follows is a list that may amuse and instruct, with some comments I couldn't resist adding.

1. They push books. (I can think of worse things to push.)
2. They always give homework. (But some of them are so dizzy they forget to ask for it.)
3. They lecture a lot. (Time out for soul searching.)
4. They know everything. (About what?)
5. They all wear glasses because when they were little kids they wore our their eyes reading all the time. (Is this any worse than a generation with hearing aids at age 30 from all that rock music?)
6. They tend to be artsy. (Arty?)
7. Their desks are always covered with books and junk. They call this "being creative." (Never trust anyone with a clean desk.)
8. They carry rulers around to whack kids on the knuckles. (I thought math teachers did this.)
9. They are cultured. (See arty, not buttermilk.)
10. They drive junky cars. (We all know the reason for this. Don't we?)
11. They never make mistakes. (The retort to this one is so obvious that I'll leave it to you.)
12. They know how to spell everything. (Don't consult your dictionary; ask your friendly English teacher.)
13. They always have rubber bands around their wrists. (For holding all those homework papers.)
14. Females are usually unmarried and mean. (Some are married and mean.)
15. Males always wear those tweed jackets with reinforced leather patches on the elbows. (They get them from the thrift shop where college professors sold them. This is called "trickledown economics.")
16. They grade papers all the time.
17. They *say* they grade papers all the time.

18. They carry books around all the time.
19. They have big vocabularies and use words like *nadir*. (That's what comes of carrying all those books around.)
20. They are smarter than other teachers. (Well, of course, we wouldn't go so far as to say that, but . . . .)

Carolyn Estes

After you finish reading this essay, do some prewriting for an essay about stereotyping. Think about the stereotypes associated with a particular group (such as elderly people, teenagers, men, women, blacks, homosexuals, Hispanics, Jews, wasps, Orientals, Italians, Poles, "Moonies," Russians, conservatives, liberals, and so forth). Choose one group and think about the ways in which the stereotypes associated with this group hurt or impede individual members of the group.

If you cannot think of much to say about this topic, do some research: watch different television programs *or* examine different magazine advertisements for stereotypes. Pick one of the groups listed above, and take notes about the ways in which group members are portrayed in television or in advertisements. Are they major or minor characters? How are they treated and how do they treat others? How active or passive are they? How do they speak and behave? How educated are they and what are their jobs or professions? How are they dressed and groomed? After you take notes on these details, draw some conclusions about their implications: what stereotypes about the group do the television programs or magazine advertisements uphold or negate? The essay that you develop should be an analysis of the stereotypes of the group or an explanation of the impact of these stereotypes on individual members of the group. When you are finished writing your discovery draft of this essay, revise it using the techniques that you learned in Chapters 6, 7, and 8. Next, proofread this essay by following the proofreading tips described earlier in this chapter. Then, edit the sentence structure of this essay according to the following directions:

1. Reread the essay and circle every fragment that you can find. Correct each one by using one of the methods for correcting fragments discussed in this chapter.
2. Reread the essay and underline every run-on that you can find. Correct each by using one of the methods for correcting run-ons discussed in this chapter.
3. Reread the essay, looking for problems in parallelism and in modification. Correct each error that you find.
4. Reread the essay one more time, looking for confused subordination. Revise or rewrite each sentence that seems confusing.

ISSUES FOR YOUR JOURNAL

1. How important is "correctness"? Do you spend too much or too little time correcting the errors and problems in your writing? Are your attitudes toward correctness in writing related to your attitudes about correctness in other aspects of your life?

2. How do you decide when to stop revising a piece and to start editing it? How do you decide when to stop editing it?

3. Have you ever used a computer and a word processing program to write, revise or edit your writing? If so, what were your reactions to it? If not, would you like to do this? Why or why not?

4. Do you ever see a commercial or read an advertisement and find yourself drawn to the product being advertised? Why? What kinds of images and words do advertisers use to attract and manipulate you?

5. Reread some of your earlier journal entries. How is your writing changing? How are you changing?

CHAPTER TEN

EDITING DICTION

"When I use a word," Humpty Dumpty said, in rather a scornful tone, "it means just what I choose it to mean—neither more nor less."

"The question is," said Alice, "whether you can *make the words mean so many different things."*

"The question is," said Humpty Dumpty, "which is to be the master—that's all."

LEWIS CARROLL

INTRODUCTION:
THE IMPORTANCE OF EDITING DICTION

Like Humpty Dumpty, people often assume that their words mean exactly what they choose them to mean. For example, writers often use words like "great," "terrible," "few," "a lot," and "thing" without stopping to consider whether their readers know exactly what they mean by these terms. How carefully do you choose your words when you are writing? Communication begins with words, and the aim of this chapter is to help you choose and use words more effectively. Your diction (choice of words) reveals your thoughts and attitudes as clearly as your behavior does. For instance, if you label one friend as "cheap" and another as "economical," your label indicates a difference in your attitude toward these friends. In addition, changing one word in a sentence can dramatically change the sentence's emotional impact:

My friend stared at the strangers.
My friend glared at the strangers.

The first statement is neutral; the second implies an opinion about the friend's feelings. When you edit your diction, you must make sure that the words you have selected express the meaning *and* the attitudes that you intended.

A writer's ability to edit diction depends on his or her vocabulary; one cannot choose words one doesn't know. Thus, one of the skills involved in selecting words effectively is building a bigger vocabulary. People have three vocabularies: one for speaking, one for writing, and one for reading. When they write, people often use more precise language than they do when they speak. And when they read, they can understand many words that they might never use when speaking or writing. For example, do you know what the word "incarcerated" means? If you do, did you ever use it when you were speaking to someone? Did you ever use it in your writing? If you aren't familiar with this word, can you figure out what it means when you read it in the context of a sentence such as the following?

After the prisoner had been incarcerated for twenty years, the parole board finally decided to examine his appeal for freedom.

Since each type of vocabulary affects the other types, the more you read, the larger your writing and speaking vocabularies will grow. The more attention you pay to learning unfamiliar words in the material you read, the more words you will have at your command to convey ideas effectively to your readers.

PAIRED WRITING TASK **IDENTIFYING PROBLEMS IN DICTION**

Work with a classmate on this task. Examine a revision that you wrote for one of the assignments in this book or for your teacher. Exchange papers with your classmate. After you read your partner's paper, write answers to the questions below. Do *not* discuss each other's papers until you are both finished writing your comments.

Your partner's name:

1. What do you think the writer was trying to say or to show you in this paper?

2. Which words don't seem to make much sense? List them in the space below.

3. Which words seem vague, unclear, or too general? List them below.

4. Which words don't seem appropriate for the topic or for the purpose of the essay? Which words are too formal or too informal (or sound like slang)? List them below.

When you are finished answering the questions above, return the essay to your partner and discuss it. Suggest alternate words for any of the words that you listed above.

INACCURACY AND INAPPROPRIATENESS

When they edit their writing, experienced writers make sure that the words they have used are **accurate** and are **appropriate** for their purpose and readers. Accuracy is extremely important: if writers use words incorrectly or if they use vague words, their writing will be confusing or unintentionally humorous. Here is an example of a sentence with words that are vague and misused:

> The Lakers' loss was not such a big deal and I hope that they don't succor to the Celtics next week.

I have no idea what this writer means by the phrase "such a big deal." And I'm sure that he didn't want me to giggle at his misuse of "succor." If this writer had edited his diction, he would have looked up the word "succor" in a dictionary and discovered that it didn't communicate the point he was trying to make (that the Lakers shouldn't yield to the Celtics). Or he might have used a *thesaurus* (a dictionary of synonyms) to look up the word "succor." If he had, he would have found the following entry:

> Succor, v.   1. Aid, assist, help relieve
> 2. Cherish, foster, encourage, comfort
> n.   Relief, aid, assistance, help

The writer would have seen that he had misused "succor" and he might have realized that the word that he meant was "succumb" (which means "yield" or "give in"). Looking up a word to make sure that you are using it correctly or to find a better synonym is one of the best ways of increasing your vocabulary. Unfortunately, many writing textbooks warn students not to use "big words" or synonyms that they haven't used before because they might use them incorrectly. I think these warnings are counterproductive. How can you learn the precise meaning of a word unless you try it out in a sentence and see how your reader reacts to it? Furthermore, if you always play it safe as a writer—using simple words whose meanings you are sure of—your writing will be technically correct but very monotonous. Thus, my advice is to learn and to use as many new words and synonyms as you can. Just make sure that you edit them for accuracy and appropriatenesss *before* you hand in a piece of writing to a teacher or an employer.

INAPPROPRIATE CONNOTATIONS

Why do so many textbook writers warn inexperienced writers against using synonyms that they have looked up in a dictionary or in a thesaurus? Because words have different **denotative** and **connotative** meanings. A dictionary lists the denotations of a word: the objective, literal meanings of the word at the particular point in time that the dictionary was written. Many words also have connotations: emotional associations and personal meanings that individuals attach to the word. For example, here are one dictionary's denotations of the word "thin":

thin, adj. 1. having relatively little depth
            2. having little fat or flesh; lean; gaunt

The denotation of the word "thin" is neutral, but each person's connotation of this word differs, depending on the person's sex, experiences, and opinions. For some people the connotation will be neutral: "Everyone is my family tends to be thin." For others, the word "thin" may have a positive connotation: "My sister is so thin that she looks stunning in this year's fashions. She could be a model." And for others, the word carries a negative connotation: "My sister is so thin that she looks sick. She should get some meat on her bones." Although connotations are often private and individual, many words carry universal connotations that writers can use to create different impressions. For instance, here are three descriptions of a person:

1. James is an overweight, shy man who is firm about his beliefs.
2. James is a fat, withdrawn man who is rigid about his beliefs.
3. James is a well-nourished, reserved man who is resolute about his beliefs.

The adjectives in the first description ("overweight," "shy," "firm") are neutral. The adjectives in the second and the third descriptions have the same denotations as the adjectives in the first, but their connotations are quite different! Editing diction involves examining the connotations of the words you have written and figuring out if they carry the emotional shades of meaning that you intended them to convey. Two words may be synonymous, but no two words have exactly the same connotations. Select your words carefully: synonyms may share the same basic denotation, but their connotations may be so different that they cannot be substituted for one another. It's important to be sensitive to the connotations of words when you are writing and when you are reading. The more you understand the emotional power of connotations, the less you will be manipulated by words. For instance, advertisers sell their products by exploiting the connotative power of words: everything is either *new, improved,* or *revolutionized*—words that connote desirable qualities for most Americans. Here are some more examples of this manipulative use of the connotations of words:

1. (about a motorcycle) "It's a mean marauder, tough, maneuverable. It makes you feel good and look bad."

2. (about a cigarette) "Alive with pleasure. Light, cool, refreshingly smooth."

Using connotations in this manner is a form of dishonest, manipulative writing. Be aware of it, and edit it out of your writing.

EXERCISE **EXAMINING CONNOTATIONS**

Below are two versions of an evaluation of the movie *Shoah*. The first is a letter to a friend; the second is a movie review for an English class. These evaluations have been adapted so that you can choose the most appropriate word or phrase in each sentence. Examine each set of choices and circle the word whose connotations are most appropriate for the purpose and the audience. If you are not sure of the meaning of any of the words, look it up in your dictionary.

January 2, 1986

Dear Alex:

When you (arrive, get, come) here next week, you must see Shoah. This (film, picture, movie) is about the (killing, annihilation, extermination) of the Jews in Germany in the Holocaust. I thought it was (astonishing, great, wonderful) and movie critics have (hailed it, called it as, termed it) a masterpiece. It's a ten hour documentary and it's being (exhibited, displayed, shown) in two parts.

When I first (ascertained, found out, discovered) how (lengthy, long, prolonged) the movie was, I didn't think I could (handle, bear, take) ten hours of watching people being (killed, slain, murdered) and (corpses, dead bodies, carcasses) being shoveled into graves. But Shoah doesn't have even one of these types of (shots, scenes, sights). The

whole movie is about the people who (took part in,
participated in, had a role in) the Holocaust. It's got
stories from the (martyrs, victims, sufferers) and from
(murderers, torturers, killers).

I think I'm going to see it again with you because I was
really (stunned, surprised, shocked) and moved by it. Anyway,
I've got (many, lots, numerous) of other things planned for us
to do. See you soon.

> Love,
>
> Amy

A REVIEW OF SHOAH

The word "Shoah" is the Hebrew word for "annihilation,"
and this (film, picture, movie) is about the (killing,
annihilation, extermination) of the Jews in Germany in
the Holocaust. It was written and directed by Claude
Lanzmann and movie critics have (called it, hailed it as,
termed it) a masterpiece. The movie is a documentary that is
ten hours long; it is being (exhibited, shown, displayed) in
two parts.

When I first (ascertained, found out, discovered) how
(lengthy, long, prolonged) the movie was, I wondered how I
would be able to sit through ten hours of watching people
being (killed, slain, murdered) and (corpses, dead bodies,
carcasses) being shoveled into graves. But Shoah doesn't have
even one of these types of (shots, scenes, sights). Instead
the whole movie is about the people who (took part in,

participated in, had a role in) the Holocaust. We hear
stories from the (martyrs, victims, sufferers) and from
(murderers, torturers, killers) and we see the concentration
camps as they are today--(beautiful, peaceful villages).

I am not Jewish but I was (stunned, surprised, shocked)
and moved by this (impassioned, eloquent, amazing) movie. It
taught me important lessons about people's inhumanity.

Amy White

VAGUE TERMS

In addition to examining the denotations and connotations of words, another way to ensure that you are using accurate diction is to edit your writing for vague, general words. Some writers use a kind of shorthand language in their discovery drafts and even in their revisions. They know what they mean by their vague terms and they expect their readers to know too. However, most readers have no interest in trying to guess at a writer's meaning. Here are some of these vague "all-purpose" terms that can ruin the precision of your writing:

- great, good, fine, nice, okay, all right
- terrible, awful, bad
- big, huge, gigantic
- funny, strange, interesting
- a lot, lots, many, plenty
- things, aspects, factors, stuff
- kind of, sort of

These words could have so many different meanings that they don't communicate anything clearly. For instance, if someone told you that she had read *a lot* of books for her sociology course, how many books would you assume she read? Five? Ten? Twenty? If the same person then told you that she learned important *things* from these books, what would you assume that she learned? Facts? Stories? Observations? Lessons? When you edit your diction, check for these all-purpose words and substitute more specific terms.

EXERCISE   EDITING ALL-PURPOSE WORDS

Here is an uncorrected paragraph that has been adapted from a student essay. Circle every vague word and write in a more precise substitute.

Why do the superpowers spend a lot of money on weapons and so little on their people? I think that the arms race is a terrible thing. The superpowers have a lot of weapons. They could blow up the earth many times. It's so strange that they continue to build more. And the bad thing is that while Russia and the U.S. spend lots of money on weapons, children are starving or dying from awful diseases. Supporters of nuclear weapons say that there are many factors affecting the buildup of weapons. They worry that if Russia has more or better weapons than us, it will attack us or our friends. This means that the U.S. and Russia have to build up arms at the same rate. This idea was okay for many years, but now other countries have nuclear weapons. This is terrible because a maniac like Libya's Khaddafi might bomb us without caring about the consequences. I think the arms race is really bad.

CLICHÉS

Another form of shorthand language that all writers should eliminate from the final revisions of their writing is the **cliché** (pronounced "klee-shay"). A cliché is a phrase that has been used so often that it no longer means much, and readers don't pay much attention to it. Expressions such as "pretty as a picture," "apple of my eye," and "worked like a dog" give readers the impression that the writer is too lazy or too dull to think of an interesting way of saying something. Because clichés come to mind so easily, people frequently include them in their discovery drafts. However, experienced writers always look for them and edit them out when they are checking their work for accuracy and appropriateness.

EXERCISE REWRITING CLICHÉS

Rewrite each of the underlined clichés in the following paragraph. On a separate piece of paper, rewrite the entire paragraph, *substituting* a new expression or phrase in place of every cliché.

My mom is <u>second to none</u>. She's as <u>pretty as a picture</u> and as <u>sweet as honey</u>. I know <u>beyond a shadow of a doubt</u> that I am my mom's <u>pride and joy</u>, and her love has always kept me <u>safe and sound</u>. My mom works hard for <u>the finer things in life</u>, and she's usually as <u>busy as a bee</u>. But she always has time for me and lends me <u>a helping hand</u>, especially when I'm <u>down and out</u>. In <u>this day and age</u>, teenagers often put their parents down, but not me. My mom is <u>one in a million</u>. I want to <u>follow in her footsteps</u>.

Many clichés are based on comparisons between two dissimilar things: "pretty as a picture," "happy as a lark," "smart as a whip," "proud as a peacock." Because clichéd comparisons are used so often, they lose their originality and their meaning. Instead of falling back on clichés, writers should try to develop their own fresh, interesting comparisons that can capture their readers' attention and imagination. Comparisons that include the words *like* or *as* are called **similes**, and similes can help readers see things in new ways:

An hour after the bomb was dropped, Hiroshima looked like an oozing wound.

The image "an oozing wound" stirs readers' imaginations and enables them to understand how the writer feels about this topic. Metaphors—implied comparisons that do not use *like* or *as*—also have this emotional power:

Hiroshima was no longer a city but a decaying barren riverbed.

The writer of this metaphor invites readers to see a once bustling city as a riverbed that is rotting away from the effects of the atomic bomb. When you edit your diction, try to include similes and metaphors that are rich in sensory details. Try to think of fresh, original details that will capture your ideas exactly.

EXERCISE **WRITING SIMILES**

Use your imagination to finish each of the following comparisons with a fresh, vivid image:

1. This classroom looks like

2. Going to school is like

3. Brainstorming is like

4. Editing an essay is like

INAPPROPRIATE LEVEL OF USAGE

Usages are customary ways of speaking and writing. In Chapter 1, you read about some of the conventions of Standard Written English (SWE) usage. SWE is a dialect, and like all spoken and written dialects, it has at least two different usage levels: **formal** and **informal**. Usage levels are always linked to social situations and are affected by the age, sex, race, and social background of the speaker/writer and of the audience. The ability to change one's usage level to fit the situation and the audience is a survival skill needed in school and at work. You know intuitively that the language you use with your best friend is often inappropriate for your teacher or your employer. For instance, think about the consequences of using slang or obscene words with some of your teachers or employers.

The ability to choose appropriate words for different writing contexts develops with practice. Students who have not received much feedback on their writing often try to make their writing sound more "academic" by selecting words that are too formal for their purposes and readers. Instead of impressing readers, they often confuse readers or unintentionally amuse them. Here is an example of overly formal diction:

> I have perused the essay and found the author's protestations to be preposterous.

The language is pretentious and offensive. If the diction in this sentence were less formal, it would be easier to read:

> I have read the essay and found the author's assertions to be unreasonable.

The most difficult part of editing one's diction for academic writing is finding a balance between extreme informality and extreme formality. This is not easy to do, particularly for writers who have not done much academic reading and writing or who have not worked at building their vocabulary. If you learn a new word and try it out in a sentence, you run the risk of it being inappropriate in the particular sentence or essay. However, I always advise students to take this risk.

EXERCISE CHOOSING APPROPRIATE DICTION FOR DIFFERENT CONTEXTS

Here are two versions of a statement made by Harold M. Agnew, a nuclear physicist who worked on the atomic bomb that the United States dropped on Hiroshima in 1945. I have made adaptations of his statement for different purposes and readers. In each version, examine each set of choices and choose the most appropriate word or phrase.

Assume that Agnew wrote the following paragraph in a letter to his wife. In this letter he was trying to justify his current work on nuclear arms.

(<u>I've</u>, <u>I have</u>) always felt that science and the military (<u>are obligated to</u>, <u>should</u>, <u>ought to</u>) work together. And they have, from (<u>the beginning</u>, <u>day one</u>, <u>the outset</u>), whether it was Leonardo da Vinci or Michaelangelo or whoever. They were always (<u>planning</u>, <u>concocting</u>, <u>designing</u>) things for the people in charge. . . . War is too (<u>serious</u>, <u>important</u>, <u>momentous</u>)

to be left to (the rising generation, the young, kids). The
young people who go around yelling "(Get rid of, dismantle,
kill) the Bomb!" ought to be careful, (because, 'cause, for
the reason that) the politicians might put a bow and arrow in
their hands and make the (young people, kids, youths) (go,
sally forth, rush out) again, knowing that nothing is going to
happen to them [the politicans]. With the (progressive
growth, development, proliferation) of nuclear weapons, the
(man, guy, chap) who says "Go fight a war" is talking to
himself.

Now assume that Agnew wrote the following paragraph in a press
release for reporters who wanted to interview him about his views on
nuclear weapons.

(I've, I have) always felt that science and the military
(are obligated to, should, ought to) work together. And they
have, from (the beginning, day one, the outset), whether it was
Leonardo da Vinci or Michaelangelo or whoever. They were
always (planning, concocting, designing) things for the people
in charge. . . . War is too (serious, important, momentous)
to be left to (the rising generation, the young, kids). The
young people who go around yelling "(Get rid of, dismantle,
kill) the Bomb!" ought to be careful, (because, 'cause, for
the reason that) the politicans might put a bow and arrow in
their hands and make the (young people, kids, youths) (go,
sally forth, rush out) again, knowing that nothing is going to
happen to them [the politicians]. With the (progressive

<u>growth</u>, <u>development</u>, <u>proliferation</u>) of nuclear weapons, the

(<u>man</u>, <u>guy</u>, <u>chap</u>) who says "Go fight a war" is talking to

himself.

When you have completely finished this exercise, turn to page 247 of this chapter to see Agnew's actual statement.

THE AUTHORIAL "I"

Student writers are often puzzled by the recommendation made by many teachers and textbooks that they should "avoid the frequent use of the first-person pronouns *I* and *we* and the second-person pronoun *you*." There are two reasons behind this advice: (1) these pronouns make a piece of writing sound conversational and informal, as if the writer knows the reader well, and (2) if many sentences include *I* and *we*, the piece of writing seems focused on the writer rather than on the topic. For instance, read the two paragraphs that follow. How do they differ in tone?

I think the arms race is terribly destructive: we have enough weapons to blow each other up six times. You may say that building our nuclear defenses is a protective device, but we cannot protect ourselves against maniacs like Colonel Khaddafi who might decide to bomb us without caring about the results.

The arms race is terribly destructive: the United States and Russia have enough weapons to blow each other up six times. Supporters of nuclear weapons believe that building America's nuclear defenses is a protective device, but the United States cannot protect itself against maniacs like Colonel Khaddafi who might decide to bomb an American city without caring about the results.

In the second paragraph, the writer has substituted clear specific nouns for the vague *we, you,* and *us:* and she has deleted the unnecessary introducer "I think." This makes the second paragraph sound more objective and more focused on the arms race (rather than on the writer). For many types of academic writing, the conversational tone of the first paragraph is inappropriate since it gives the impression that the writer is relying solely on her personal experience for support rather than on objective evidence. However, first- and second-person pronouns may be absolutely appropriate for some types of academic writing, particularly if the assignment asks writers to share their experiences or their reactions to something. In addition, writers should use *I* if avoiding it would make their writing sound awkward. For example, here are two sentences in which the writer's avoidance of *I* sounds silly:

> When considering the personal consequences of nuclear war, this writer gets quite worried. It is believed by this writer that atomic war will devastate life on this planet.

Contrast these sentences with the following one:

> I am quite worried about the consequences of nuclear war since I believe that atomic war will devastate life on this planet.

You have to make a decision about how you want to sound.

WRITING ACTIVITY   CHANGING USAGE LEVELS FOR DIFFERENT AUDIENCES

The focus of this activity is a movie that you recently saw or a book that you recently read. Think about your responses to this movie or book and consider why you would or would not recommend it to others. Then write *two* reviews of the movie or book: one review should take the form of a letter to your best friend; the other should be an essay for your school's newspaper.

Remember, a movie or book review is not merely a description of the plot and characters. A review should express the writer's overall judgment about the worth of the work and it should support that judgment with direct references to specific features of the work (such as the ideas, the characters, the action, the setting, the acting, the language, and the style).

Write the letter to your friend first. Then, adapt the details, vocabulary, and the sentence structure of your letter to change it into a formal review essay that would be appropriate for a newspaper. When you are finished writing both versions, examine and revise and edit each one so that it is appropriate for your purpose and your reader.

WORDINESS

Wordiness—the use of several words instead of a single word—often results when writers strain to make their diction sound academic or overly formal. For instance, a writer who thinks that a wordy phrase is more forceful than a single word will write that his essay "concerns the subject of . . ." or "pertains to the topic of . . ." instead of writing that it is "about" the issue. Inexperienced writers may think that wordy phrases make their writing more impressive; experienced writers know that excess words slow sentences down, obscure meaning, and bore readers. Here are a few comments about wordiness by some famous writers:

If it is possible to cut a word out, always cut it out. *George Orwell*

Clutter is the disease of American writing. We are a society strangling in unnecessary words, circular constructions, pompous frills, and meaningless jargon. *William Zinsser*

To write simply is as difficult as to be good. *Somerset Maugham*

Striking a balance between sketchiness and wordiness, like finding the appropriate word for a context, is a difficult skill that develops with practice. One trick for editing wordiness is to identify and eliminate the following common wordy phrases and to substitute their single-word alternatives.

"Wordy" Phrases and Their Alternatives	
the fact that phrases	
due to the fact that	because
regardless of the fact that	although
in view of the fact that	since
in light of the fact that	because
aware of the fact that	know
in spite of the fact that	despite
that phrases	
for reasons that	for
it is important that	should
in the event that	if
on the condition that	if
of phrases	
on the subject of	about
pertaining to the subject of	about
in lieu of	instead
make an attempt to	try

EXERCISE **EDITING WORDINESS**

Examine an essay that you wrote for an assignment in this book or for your teacher. Underline every wordy phrase that you find and substitute a single-word alternative for it. Be ruthless: cross out every word that isn't absolutely necessary for expressing your meaning.

SEXIST LANGUAGE

Sexist language is often in the eye of the beholder. Many people see nothing wrong with the following sentence:

When a student has finished planning his ideas, he should try to organize them in a logical sequence.

The use of masculine pronouns and nouns to refer to both genders is a historic tradition in our society and our language. However, this tradition is changing. More and more people are finding the sentence above sexist and therefore offensive. Moreover, sexist language is often inaccurate. For instance, can you find possible inaccuracies in the sentences below?

The typical student at my college is trying hard to improve his communication skills. Also, everyone in my English class is concerned about his writing.

Both uses of the pronoun ''his'' are probably inaccurate: few American colleges admit males only, so the typical student in most colleges is a woman or a man. Similarly, English classes are composed of male and female students. These sexist inaccuracies are just as incorrect as are other types of errors. For example, the pronoun agreement error in the following sentence is no different or worse than the errors in the sentences above:

The typical student at my college is trying hard to improve their life.

Here are some guidelines for you to follow for sentences in which you have used a pronoun to refer back to a noun that is singular and not necessarily male (such as ''the typical student'').

Guidelines for Non-Sexist Diction

1. Use plural nouns instead of singular ones:

   Most students at Hunter College are trying hard to improve their lives.

2. Use *he or she*, *his or her*, and *him or her* to refer to indefinite pronouns:

   Everyone in Prof. Greenberg's class is concerned about his or her writing.

   Note: Use this alternative sparingly because it gets tiresome to read. If you think you are using it too often, convert the indefinite pronoun into a plural noun:

   All of the students in Prof. Greenberg's class are concerned about their writing.

3. Use the indefinite pronoun *one:*

   One should try hard to improve one's writing.

4. Omit unnecessary pronouns wherever you can:

   Each student should hand in the essay next week (instead of *his essay* or *his or her essay*).

5. Use *Ms.* instead of *Mrs.* or *Miss* (unless you are writing a letter to a woman who has a professional title—like *Dr.*—or who has requested that you use *Mrs.* or *Miss*):

   Ms. Williams is planning on becoming a lawyer.

Unfortunately, sexism, like racism and ageism, won't disappear from our language as long as it exists in our lives. Nevertheless, as an educated, intelligent member of our society, you have an obligation to use language impartially and accurately.

EXERCISE EDITING SEXIST LANGUAGE

Take out an essay that you wrote for an assignment in this book or for your teacher. Circle every instance of sexist language and rewrite the essay, using non-sexist diction.

DICTION AND DICTIONARIES

A dictionary is a valuable learning tool: in addition to giving the spelling, the meaning, and the pronunciation of words, a good college dictionary also presents information about the history of each word, about its modern usage, and about its synonyms and their connotations. While I am not recommending that you take up dictionary-reading as a new pastime, I do advocate the regular use of a standard college dictionary as an excellent way to learn new words, to check the accuracy of one's diction, and to improve one's spelling. Do not waste your money on a pocket dictionary: it doesn't include as many words or as much information about each word as does a college dictionary. Here are four standard college dictionaries:

- *The American Heritage Dictionary of the English Language* (Boston: Houghton Mifflin)
- *Funk & Wagnalls Standard College Dictionary* (New York: Harcourt Brace Jovanovich)
- *The Random House College Dictionary* (New York: Random House)
- *Webster's New World Dictionary of the American Language, College Edition* (Cleveland: Collins-World)

Here is an entry for the word "remunerate" from the 1966 edition of *Webster's Third New International Dictionary:*

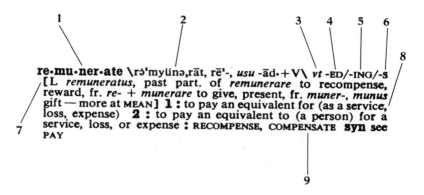

1. correct spelling of the word with dots indicating the separate syllables
2. pronunciation key
3. part of speech (v.t. = **transitive** verb or a verb that needs an object)
4. correct spelling of the past tense ending (which is the same as the past participle ending for this verb)
5. correct spelling of the "ing" ending for this verb
6. correct spelling of the third person present tense ending
7. derivation of the word (L = Latin)
8. definitions of the word
9. synonyms

Be aware that different dictionaries offer different information. Each dictionary represents the judgments of the group of people who wrote it, and these judgments mirror the constantly changing nature of language itself. Finally, no matter which dictionary you buy, it won't help you make decisions about diction if it sits on your shelf. Read the introductory material (so you know how to use the dictionary properly) and then USE IT.

EXERCISE USING THE DICTIONARY

Get a copy of a standard college dictionary and follow the directions below:

1. Look up the word *mature*.
   a. How do you spell each of the syllables that make up this word?

   b. What are the different ways of pronouncing this word?

   c. What language did this word come from, and what did it mean in that language?

   d. What part of speech is this word defined as *first*?

   e. How many definitions are given for this word and what are they?

   f. How many synonyms are given for this word, and what are they?

   g. What other part of speech can this word be?

    h. Write two sentences: In one, use this word as one part of speech; in the other, use the word as the other part of speech.

  2. Look up the verb *lie.*
    a. What language did this word come from, and what did it mean in this language?

    b. What are the definitions of the verb *lie*?

    c. What words does your dictionary give as synonyms for *lie* (as a verb)?

    d. Look up each synonym and explain how the connotation of each one differs slightly from the connotation of *lie.*

    e. Write a sentence using the verb *lie.* Then, write a sentence for each of the synonyms for this verb.

A PROFESSIONAL RESPONSE

Here is Harold Agnew's statement that was adapted earlier in this chapter. Compare the words and phrases that he used to the choices that you selected in the exercise.

I have always felt that science and the military *should* work together. And they *have*, from Day One, whether it was Leonardo da Vinci or Michaelangelo who whoever. They were always designing things for the people in charge. . . . War is too important to be left to the young. The young people who go around yelling "Get rid of the Bomb!" ought to be careful, 'cause the politicians might put a bow and arrow in their hands and make the kids sally forth again, knowing that nothing is going to happen to *them* [the politicians]. With the development of nuclear weapons, the guy who says "Go fight a war" is talking to *himself.*

The actual context of this statement was an interview between Agnew and a reporter for *Time* magazine on the fortieth anniversary of the bombing of Hiroshima. Is Agnew's vocabulary appropriate for this context? Why or why not?

DICTION CORRECTION SYMBOLS

Use these symbols to edit your own writing, edit a classmate's writing, or to understand your teacher's comments.

Error	Problem
WW	Wrong word (word doesn't make sense in the context of the sentence)
Con	Inappropriate connotation
Vague	Term is too vague or unclear
Cl	Cliché
Usage	Inappropriate usage level

WRITING ASSIGNMENT WRITING, REVISING, AND EDITING
AN ESSAY ABOUT NUCLEAR WEAPONS

Here is an essay on nuclear war by Theo Summer, the editor of *Die Zeit*, a weekly magazine published in Hamburg, Germany. It was written on the fortieth anniversary of America's bombing of Hiroshima.

A NEW ERA
from Hiroshima to a Balance of Terror

The nuclear age began in the early hours of Aug. 6, 1945, when the bomb bay of the *Enola Gay* opened and the first atomic bomb used in anger was dropped. It weighed about four tons and had a destructive power equivalent to that of 20,000 tons of conventional explosive. It exploded forty-three seconds later above Hiroshima.

Virtually nothing was left of the city. Tens of thousands died instantly, as they would three days later in Nagasaki—killed by radiation, burned to a cinder, or torn apart by the shock wave. There were probably 200,000 dead in two cities.

"My God, what have we done?" the copilot asked when the *Enola Gay* turned to steer clear of the mushroom cloud. This question has preoccupied humanity ever since, and the answers have differed.

As the streets of Hiroshima and Nagasaki still lay in ruins a thirty-six-year-old Yale professor, Bernard Brodie, wrote a book, *The Absolute Weapon—Atomic Power and the World Order*. His basic tenet was that "hitherto the aim of the military has been to win wars. From now on its main aim must be to prevent them." Deterrent strategy was born.

The diametrically opposite conclusion was reached, at the same time and also at Yale, by a twenty-five-year-old law student, William Borden who had served in World War II as a bomber pilot. His book, *There Will Be No Time—The Revolution in Strategy*, was based on the assumption that America's enemies would soon have atomic weapons. An armed peace could not last forever. He advised the U.S. to prepare for a nuclear war so that it could win if necessary.

These two viewpoints have held sway in the debate on war and peace in the nuclear age. In practice they often have merged.

If deterrence is to work, the argument runs, the opponent must be told repeatedly that should it fail, the other side would be well able to wage and even win a nuclear war. The contradiction thus arose between a proclaimed strategy of nuclear deterrence and an actual strategy of nuclear war.

Several U.S. presidents have been tempted to resort to a nuclear strike to gain an advantage—in Korea and Indochina, and during the Berlin and Cuban crises. Nikita Khrushchev played nuclear poker in the Caribbean, and Leonid Brezhnev did so in the Yom Kippur War. Yet in the end world leaders realized that to use nuclear weapons was a risk they could not afford.

But can we rely on the common sense of world leaders in years to come? Does the fact that the balance of terror has kept the peace for decades insure that it will continue to do so?

The nuclear powers have increased in number. There are five: the U.S., the Soviet Union, Britain, France, and China. Several others have the technological capability to manufacture nuclear weapons, including Israel, India, Pakistan, and South Africa. The larger the number of nuclear powers, the greater the risk.

The nuclear powers' stockpiles now amount to a staggering 50,000 warheads, whereas two years after Hiroshima the Americans had a mere thirteen devices, and the Soviets had none. Moreover, the explosive power of nuclear warheads has been increased to an incredible degree. There has yet to be an answer to former U.S. Defense Secretary Robert S. McNamara's question, "How much is enough?"

A final alarming fact is that the superpowers have not conducted serious disarmament and arms control negotiations for six years. Meanwhile, nuclear stockpiles grow. Bids to control the arms race are weaker than the inclination to boost it in exotic ways.

The idea of a nuclear holocaust by no means appalls only people inclined to hysteria. It also causes gooseflesh among many who are aware of the deterrent system's advantages.

At a gathering of scientists who built the first atomic bomb forty years ago, Nobel Laureate Isidor Isaac Rabi made a frightening comment. The nations of the world, he said, were like people lining up in front of the gas chambers at Auschwitz while scientists were busy perfecting the gas chambers.

Statesmen must take heart if there is to be any change. That is the only possible lesson on the 40th anniversary of Hiroshima.

Theo Sommer

After you finish reading the essay, do some prewriting for an essay about nuclear weapons or about nuclear war. Think about the two different viewpoints that were described in the essay (the viewpoints of Bernard Brodie and of William Borden). Which viewpoint do you share? How do you feel about the possibility of a nuclear war? Should our country prepare for a nuclear war? Is a nuclear war "winnable" or "survivable"? Can anything be done to prevent a nuclear war?

If you cannot think of anything to say about this topic, do some research: read magazines, journals, and books that discuss this topic and take notes. Do some freewriting, brainstorming, and clustering about the topic. Then write a discovery draft of an essay that describes your view about the nuclear arms race or that describes your reaction to living with the threat of nuclear war. When you are finished writing your discovery draft of this essay, revise it using the techniques that you practiced in Chapters 6, 7, and 8. Next, edit your sentence structure using the methods that you learned in this chapter.

Exchange essays with a classmate. After you read your classmate's essay, edit its sentence structure *and* diction. Circle every problem that you find. Return the essays and discuss them. Then correct every problem or error that your classmate found in your essay.

ISSUES FOR YOUR JOURNAL

1. Were you ever in a situation in which you were aware that people spoke "differently" from you (much more formally or informally)? How did it make you feel?
2. Write a description of a situation in which you deliberately adapted your spoken diction to fit an audience whom you wanted to impress. What did you do? Why? What were the results? What might have happened if you had not changed your diction?
3. How has your education changed your diction? Do you use different words (or do you use words differently) than do relatives or friends who have not has as much schooling as you? How do these differences make you feel?
4. Look back over your journal entries. Has your diction changed at all? If so, in what ways? If not, select a journal entry and rewrite it using more specific or more formal language. Then compare it to the original entry.
5. What are some of the advantages and disadvantages of computers? How can computers help people? How will the increasing use of computers hurt some people?

EDITING GRAMMAR AND USAGE

Every person has a grammar which is just a little bit different from anybody else's—grammars are like snowflakes—and we all sort of get together and decide on what things we have enough in common to call a language.

SUZETTE HADEN ELGIN

INTRODUCTION: THE IMPORTANCE OF EDITING GRAMMAR AND USAGE

As the linguist Suzette Elgin says, "Every person has a grammar." All people with normal hearing will have mastered the rules of their languages' grammar by the time they are five-years old. This unconscious grammar—that enables us to speak, and eventually, to write our language—is different from the lists of rules in the "Grammar and Usage" sections of handbooks and textbooks. So why am I devoting a chapter to grammar and usage? Because the grammar that some students use in writing may not follow the conventions that readers expect to see in academic or business writing, and if readers get distracted by nonstandard forms, they will not attend to meaning. For example, consider your reactions to the following sentences, only one of which has been edited for correct Standard Written English (SWE) grammar and usage:

1. The reader ain't got no idea what the writer mean in that essay.
2. The reader don't have any idea what the writer mean in that essay.
3. The reader doesn't have any idea what the writer means in that essay.

The meaning of these three sentences is basically identical. How do they differ? How do you think a teacher or an employer might respond to each of them? Most readers expect to see SWE grammar and usage in writing, and many readers get annoyed when their expectations are disappointed. Writers who use unconventional forms of grammar in their academic writing make it more difficult for readers to understand their ideas. Thus, part of the process of communicating ideas effectively in writing involves expressing these ideas in grammatical forms that do not violate readers' expectations.

PAIRED EDITING TASK **ANALYZING PROBLEMS IN GRAMMAR AND USAGE**

Work with another classmate on this task. Below is an uncorrected placement test essay written by a college freshman. Read it carefully and then circle every nonstandard grammatical form that you find. Above each circle, write in the correct SWE form.

CHILDREN AND VIOLENCE

I believe that children learn violent behavior from their

parents. Children, especially a young child, is influence by parental behavior. Children look up to their parents and tend to imitate him.

Children also are influence by television (TV) and movies but to a less degree. If a child from a non-violent home see violence on TV, he don't automatically assume that the TV characters are acting appropriate. However, the child who been condition to seeing adults act violent may think there is nothing wrong with the violent behavior he see on TV, and he may try to imitate them.

Children learn way of coping with frustration and anger from their parents, not from their TV heros. Therefore, parent should be less worry about television and more about they own behavior.

VERB FORMS

Every English verb has three forms that are called its "principal parts." These forms are the **present**, the **past**, and the **past participle**. All of the verb tenses in English are made from these three principal parts.

The Present and the Future Tenses

The **present** tense in English indicates that the action or the condition expressed by a sentence is happening right now or is a general truth. For most verbs, the present is the form of the verb that can follow the word *to*. It is the form of the verb that is listed in the dictionary:

(to cause)   Certain tests *cause* problems for some foreign-born students.

(to require)   These tests *require* fluency in English.

In order to form the **future** tense of verbs, simply put "will" or "shall" in front of the present tense form:

These tests *will cause* problems for them in college because college tests also *will be written* in English.

EXERCISE   **USING THE PRESENT AND FUTURE TENSES**

Write a paragraph describing your usual method of getting to school each day. If you live in a school dormitory, describe the way you get from your room to your first class. (Describe the hallways, corridors, staircases, and streets.) If you walk or drive to school, describe the route that you take. Do you use public transportation? If so, which buses and trains do you usually take? Where do you get on and off them? Use specific details and exact names. For this description, all of your main verbs should be in the present tense because the present is the form that is appropriate for actions that are repeated habitually (for example, "Every Monday at 8:15 a.m., I *walk* to the bus stop at the corner of First Street and Maple Avenue, and I *wait* for the number six bus").

When you are finished revising and editing your paragraph, circle every main verb. Above each one, write its future form. Then cross out all of the references to time in the paragraph, and above each one that you crossed out write "next week." By doing this, you will be changing your paragraph from a description of your general method of getting to school to a description of how you will get to school next week. Here is an example:

    Next Monday   will walk
~~Every Monday~~ at 8:15 a.m., I ~~walk~~ to the bus stop at the corner of First Street and Maple Avenue, and ~~I wait~~ for the number six bus.
                              will wait

The Past

The **past** tense indicates that the action or the condition expressed by a sentence happened in the past and is over. It is expressed by means of the past form, which usually ends in "ed." In fact, you can produce the past form of most verbs by merely adding *ed* to their present forms:

Multiple-choice tests *caused* problems for those students because the tests *required* fluency in English.

However, a number of verbs do *not* follow this rule. Instead, their past form is produced by changing the spelling of their present forms. These verbs are called **irregular** verbs, and they cause many problems for students who have not yet memorized how to spell them:

> Those students *found* multiple-choice tests difficult because they *were* not familiar with the procedures for answering these tests.

The Past Participle

In contrast to the past tense, which expresses actions or conditions that were completed in the past, tenses using the **past participle** express actions or conditions that began in the past and that are still occurring. Often, the past participle is the form of the verb that follows a helping verb such as *have, has, had, am, is, are, was*, and *were*. Like the past form, the past participle of most verbs is produced by adding *ed* to their present forms. In other words, the past and the past participle of most verbs look exactly the same:

> These tests *caused* problems recently because they *required* fluency in English.

> These tests *have caused* problems for the past fifty years, and some of these tests *have required* fluency in English.

However, many irregular verbs have different past and past participle forms:

> Many students *chose* incorrect answers on the test.

> Many students *have chosen* these incorrect answers before.

An important part of editing grammar and usage is learning to identify and correct unconventional verb forms. If you are ever unsure about the past or the past participle of an irregular verb, look up the present form of the verb in the dictionary. Almost every dictionary lists the present, the past, and the past participle forms of every irregular verb (in that order).

The English language enables you to use or to combine different verb forms to refer to different times. For example, if you want to refer to an action that is occurring as you are writing, you can use the present tense form ("I ask myself that question now") or you can use the *-ing* form ("I am asking myself that question now"). If you want to refer to an action that has been occurring over a period of time and is still occurring, you can combine the past participle form and the *-ing* form ("I have been asking myself that question for quite a long time now").

EXERCISE **EDITING PAST AND PAST PARTICIPLE VERB FORMS**

Below is a student's report of an interview with a computer "hacker." Only the first paragraph has been edited for correct SWE verb forms. As you read the report, circle every nonstandard verb form, and write in the correct SWE form.

I interviewed Martin X four times. He is twenty years old and he lives in New York City. During the past two years, he has been a student at City College, majoring in computer programming.

Martin X is a "hacker"--a person who illegally taps into other people's computer systems and reads or steals their data. This delinquent career begun with Martin's desire to solve computer puzzles. He seen his older brother and sisters tap into computer bulletin boards across the country and he has wanted to prove that he could do it too. He always been mathematically talented, and he learn how to program a microcomputer by the time he was ten. Although his family forbid him to do anything illegal, he had did his first "hacking" at the age of twelve--he tap into employee data bank of the company where his mother worked and he discover confidential information about every employee in the firm. Slowly, he become addicted to the challenge of unlocking the security systems of the major computer networks in his neighborhood. He spended more and more of his time at his computer terminal, despite the adverse effects that hacking had on his schoolwork and his social life. He brang his friends over to see his accomplishments, but they all thought he was weird. His family worry about him too, although he had swore to them that he wasn't doing anything illegal.

Martin was unable to admit that hacking had became an obsession. It was only after he had broke the security code of his bank that his hacking was discovered. The bank didn't press charges against Martin, but they did threatened to do so if he resumed his illegal trespassing. His parents become so upset that they taken him to a psychiatrist. During therapy, Martin stop hacking, but then he begun doing it again after he stopped seeing the doctor. He claims that he has never stoled any valuable information from anyone and that he has not made any profits from his activities. He believes that hacking is a "harmless educational pursuit."

WRITING ACTIVITY   USING THE PAST PARTICIPLE

Have you ever thought about what you might be doing now if you had not gone to college? Would you have stayed home? Would you have worked? What job would you have chosen? Why? Would you have been happy or unhappy? On a separate piece of paper, do some prewriting about these questions. Then, write an essay about what you would have done if you had not gone to college. Use as many past participles as you can. When you are finished writing, revise your essay to make it clearer, more specific, and more interesting. After you revise your essay, edit it for Standard Written English verb forms. Use a dictionary to check the spelling of every past participle.

SUBJECT-VERB AGREEMENT

Another important editing skill is checking to see that all of one's verbs "agree" with their subjects. **Agreement** means that the form of the verb matches the **person** and the **number** of the subject of the sentence. **Person** is a grammatical term that refers to the speaker's or the writer's relationship to the subject of his or her sentence. If the writer is talking about herself, she must use a *first person* subject—*I* (if she is talking about herself alone) or *we* (if she is talking about herself as part of a group):

I rushed out to join the crowd, and *we* began marching.

If the writer is talking to someone or to something, he or she must use the *second person* subject—*you*. *You* can be used to address a single person or a group.

You are the person who must lead the march. The rest of *you* are all courageous and unyielding.

If the writer is talking about someone or about something, he must use a *third person* subject—*he, she,* or *it* (for a single person, thing, or idea) or *they* (for a group). If the subject of a sentence can be replaced by the words, *he, she, it,* or *they,* then it is a third person subject. Each italicized subject in the following paragraph is a third person subject:

Nancy West leads this march on the White House. *This rest of the group* follows her. *The rally* is scheduled for 1:15 p.m. *Some marchers* may arrive early. *They* should wait for the rest of the group before raising their placards.

Remember that the term "person" has nothing to do with humans ("a house" can be a third person subject). The subject of a sentence also has "number." A subject can be **singular**—one person or thing—(*I, you, he, she, it,* or *one thing*) or **plural**—more than one—(*we, you, they, several things*). Problems in subject–verb agreement usually arise in the present tense with *third person singular* subjects since these subjects require a verb with an "s" ending. Look at each of the italicized third person singular subjects in the paragraph that follows: each one needs a verb ending in "s":

Nancy West lead**s** this march on the White House. *The group* fol-low**s** her. *The rally* **is** scheduled for 1:15 p.m. If some marchers ar-rive early, they are to wait for the rest of the group before raising their placards.

Here is a chart of present-tense verb forms:

Present Tense Verb Chart		
	Singluar	*Plural*
First person	I walk	we walk
Second person	you walk	you walk
Third person	she/he walks	they walk
	it walks	

In the present tense of Standard Written English, a third person singu-lar subject needs an "s" ending on a regular verb.

EXERCISE **USING PRESENT TENSE VERBS**

Here is a paragraph that was written in the present tense. Fill in each blank space with the present tense form of any verb that makes sense.

Computers _____ in a variety of sizes and prices. Some

people _____ intimidated by computers. They _____ that a

computer _____ a powerful machine with many mysterious

buttons. Other people _____ it to be an overgrown

calculator. In reality, a computer _____ a machine that

_____ many types of arithmetic and logical operations. The

computer _____ complex and powerful operations and it _____

them quickly, efficiently, and reliably. The heart of the

computer _____ the Central Processing Unit or CPU. It _____

all of the "memory" needed to interpret instructions and to

perform operations. Memory _____ the amount of information

that the computer can store. Computers _____ two types of

memory: "random access memory" or RAM and "read only memory"

or ROM.

SPECIAL PROBLEMS IN SUBJECT-VERB AGREEMENT

There are several sentence structures that make it difficult to determine whether the subject is singular or plural.

When Words Separate a Subject from Its Verb

Words that come between a subject and its verb do *not* affect the number of the subject. You must determine which word is the sentence's subject and then use it to decide whether the verb needs an "s" ending.

The *color* of that computer *seems* drab.

The *colors* of that computer *seem* drab.

Be particularly careful editing subject-verb agreement when the words that separate a singular subject from its verb sound like they are making the subject plural. These words include expressions such as "in addition to," "as well as," "including," and "together with." These expressions do *not* make the subject plural even though they sound like they do.

A *microcomputer*, as well as a main-frame, *uses* silicon chips.

A *microcomputer and a main-frame use* silicon chips.

EXERCISE   IDENTIFYING AND CORRECTING AGREEMENT ERRORS

In the uncorrected paragraph that follows, underline the subject of each sentence and put two lines under the main verb of the sentence. Then, circle every verb that does not agree with its subject and write the correct form of the verb above each error that you have circled. The first sentence has been corrected as an example.

Recently, the number of computer programs for

has

preschoolers (have) increased dramatically. Most types of this

so-called "toddler software" uses music, color, and animation
to attract young children. The typical program prepared by
many publishers teach shapes, colors, and reading readiness.
The program, including the disk and the directions, are easy
to use. Furthermore, one of the features that make this
software so attractive to parents are that they make learning
entertaining. A child between the ages of three and five need
to be instructed only once in how to use the program. Then
the child, together with his or her parents, simply work
through the "game" hitting number and letter keys. Programs
that require a child to make a decision or to solve a problem
seems to be the most popular. This type of program, as well
as programs that ask children to create imaginary things, also
foster reading readiness.

When a Subject Comes After Its Verb

In some sentences, you may reverse the order of your subject and
its verb in order to achieve an interesting effect. When you do this, remember that the subject determines the form of the verb regardless of
whether it precedes or follows the verb:

At the end of the list *is* the *toddler program.*

At the end of the list *are* the *toddler programs.*

In other sentences, you may want to begin with the words "There" or
"Here." These sentence openers move the true subject to a position after its verb:

There *is* one significant *reason* why these programs are fun.

There *are* many *reasons* why these programs are fun.

When you edit your verbs, make sure that you check these sentences to find the subject and to determine the correct form of its verb.

When Two or More Subjects Are Joined by "or" or "nor"

When two or more subjects in a sentence are joined by *or* or *nor*, the verb form is usually determined by the subject that is closest to the verb.

Neither the child nor her *parents like* the program.

Neither the parents nor their *child likes* the program.

EXERCISE   **IDENTIFYING AND CORRECTING AGREEMENT ERRORS**

In the paragraph that follows, fill in each blank space with the correct SWE form of any verb that makes sense in the sentence.

While there _____ no up-to-date figures on the number of

English teachers using computers, it _____ that many teachers

are incorporating them in their lessons. Either a creative

writing program or drill and practice programs _____ a

teacher to provide individualized instruction for each

student. In addition, there _____ some software programs

that _____ a teacher to tailor the lesson to each student's

needs. A drill program or a set of tutorial lessons _____

questions for students to answer and _____ also each of their

responses. A good tutorial that provides many appropriate

options _____ students plenty of opportunities to practice

their skills at their own pace.

When the Subject Is a Singular Pronoun

When used as subjects, the following pronouns are always considered singular and need verbs with "s" endings on them in the present tense:

each	anyone
either	anything
neither	somebody
every	someone
everybody	something
everyone	nobody
everthing	none
anybody	nothing

Everything contributes to the program's success.

Someone doing remedial work *is* likely to enjoy the computer's endless patience and flexibility.

Either, neither, each, and *every* are always singular subjects unless they are used with *or* or *nor*.

Neither tutorial *is* difficult.

Either this program or those *drills are* appropriate.

When Words Separate a Singular Pronoun Subject from Its Verb

When a singular pronoun such as *either, neither, each*, and *every*, is separated from its verb by other words, it is easy to get confused about the form of the verb. Remember that words that come between a subject and its verb do *not* affect the number of the subject or the form of the verb.

Neither program *is* difficult.

Each of these programs *has* a different focus.

The pronouns *some, none, any*, and *most* may be either singular or plural depending upon the meaning of the sentence.

Some of the programs *are* boring to use.

Some of this problem *is* caused by dull graphics.

EXERCISE IDENTIFYING AND CORRECTING AGREEMENT ERRORS

In the paragraph that follows, fill in each blank space with the correct SWE form of any verb that makes sense in the sentence.

Some of the most interesting educational software _____

"creativity" programs. Each of these programs _____ users

to stretch their imagination as they solve complex problems.

None of these programs _____ exactly the same. One

particularly challenging one _____ "The Robot Factory."

This program _____ you to design a robot. Each of your

robots _____ to move through a maze that _____ on the

screen. You _____ the robot move by selecting thrusters,

grabbers, eyes, wheels, and many other components for it.

Every robot that you create _____ different, and each _____

different technological concepts.

When the Subject Is a Collective Noun or a Quantity

A collective noun is the name of a group that usually functions as a single unit. Some examples include *family, class, audience, committee,* and *group.* If you are referring to the group as a single unit, then the noun is a singular subject (and needs an "s" ending on its verb). If you are referring to the individual members of the group, then the noun is a plural subject.

This *group* of programs *is* known as "Creativity Software."

That *group* of programs *have* been separated onto different disks.

Like collective nouns, words that state a quantity or an amount usually function like singular subjects, but they can function like plural subjects when they refer to individual items. Words of quantity include amounts of time, money, height, length, width, space, and weight.

Two hours is the usual time it takes to complete a whole program.

Two-thirds of the programs *are* made by the same manufacturers.

When the Subject Looks Plural
but Is Singular in Meaning

There are many subjects that look plural (in other words, that end in "s") but that are singular in meaning. These include names of some school subjects, names of some diseases, titles, and miscellaneous words like *politics* and *news*.

Mathematics is the focus of the *news* which *is* on television now.

Computing Professionals is an excellent journal.

EXERCISE   **IDENTIFYING AND CORRECTING AGREEMENT ERRORS**

In the paragraph that follows, fill in each blank space with the correct SWE form of the verb provided after the space. The first one has been done for you.

Computers *have* [to have] become indispensable in

solving crime. The number of crime labs in urban cities

_____ [to be] increasing each month. A recent report

entitled "Computers and Law Enforcement Agencies" _____ [to

offer] some reasons for the growing use of computers. First,

the most recent group of crime-fighting computer programs

_____ [to be] able to analyze a variety of unidentified

substances. Moreover, a number of these programs _____ [to

contain] millions of records about people who have been

officially accused of crimes. Finally, $500 _____ [to be]

not too much money to pay for programs that _____ [to access]

information from thousands of state and local law enforcement

agencies. These programs, which _____ [to be] growing in

number, _____ [to save] time, money, and energy.

VERB TENSE CONSISTENCY

After you edit your writing for verb forms and for subject-verb agreement, check to see that your verbs are consistent in tense. The verb tense that you select—past, present, or future—lets your reader know the time frame of the events that you are discussing. If you switch verb tenses without any logical reason, you will confuse your reader. For example, read the following excerpt from the uncorrected first draft of a student paragraph about writing:

> Many teenagers today do not write very well. Most of the blame for this problem can be attributed to a society that permits children to be promoted year after year without learning basic literacy skills. Teachers were not accountable for their students' failures. And technology made it easy to communicate without writing. However, writing skills will always be necessary learning tools.

Doesn't this paragraph make you want to ask the writer, "Why did you switch from the present tense to the past and then to the future?" This is the exact question that a classmate posed to the writer, and he revised his draft. Below is his revision. How does it differ from his first draft above? Why is the last sentence in both versions written in the future tense?

> Many teenagers today do not write very well. Most of the blame for this problem can be attributed to a society that has permitted children to be promoted year after year without learning the basic literacy skills. For years, teachers have not been accountable for their students' failures. And technology has made it easy to communicate without writing.

However, basic writing skills will always be necessary and
valuable learning tools.

WRITING ACTIVITY MAKING VERBS CONSISTENT

On a separate piece of paper, do some prewriting activities to help
you plan a brief essay that compares the high school that you attended
to the college (or other learning institution) that you are currently attending. The readers for this essay are seniors in your old high school
who want to know more about your current school. Choose *one* specific
feature to compare in this essay: the teachers (in both schools), the caf-
eteria, the course registration process, the students, the library, the
classes, or some other feature of the two schools. When you discuss
your high school, use the past tense, and when you discuss your current school, use the present tense. Write your first draft of the essay on
a separate piece of paper. When you are finished writing, revise your
essay and edit it for SWE verb forms and verb consistency.

PRONOUN FORM, REFERENCE, AND AGREEMENT

A **noun** is a word that names a person, a place, a thing, a quality,
an action, or an idea. A **pronoun** is a word that can replace a specific
noun or that can be used instead of a noun. Usually a pronoun is used
to replace a previously stated noun (called its *antecedent*). Pronouns
help writers avoid repetition and they provide connections among sentences. For example, read the following student paragraph to see how
pronouns help knit sentences together.

The computer center in my high school was very small and
uninviting. It didn't have many programs and the ones it did
have were very old. It was directed by an ogre of a director
who wanted to protect the disks from us. He didn't like the
way we handled them and he was forever criticizing us.

When editing your writing, you may want to refer to the pronoun chart below. It shows the correct forms of three different types of SWE pronouns: *subject, object,* and *possessive*:

Chart of Pronoun Forms			
	Subject	*Object*	*Possessive*
First person			
Singular	I	me	mine, my
Plural	we	us	ours, our
Second Person			
Singular and Plural	you	you	yours, your
Third person			
Singular	he	him	his
	she	her	hers, her
	it	it	its
Plural	they	them	theirs, their

Every pronoun that you write should refer clearly to an antecedent noun stated earlier in the same sentence or in a preceding sentence. Unclear pronoun references confuse readers. If a pronoun doesn't have an obvious antecedent, or if the reader might be unsure about the pronoun's antecedent, replace the pronoun with the specific noun (even if this means that you have to repeat the noun a few times):

In my high school, *they* loaded the programs for *you* in advance. (Who loaded the programs for whom?)

In my high school, the *computer teachers* did the *students'* program loading in advance.

Just as verbs have to agree with their subjects, pronouns must agree with the nouns that they refer to or with the nouns that they replace. When you edit your pronouns, make sure that they agree with three characteristics of their antecedent nouns: **gender** (female, male, or neuter—*it*), **person** (first, second, or third), and **number** (singular or plural):

I liked my high school computer teacher the most out of all of my teachers. *She* knew every student by name, and *her* grading policies were fair. I owe *her* a great deal.

SPECIAL PROBLEMS IN PRONOUN-ANTECEDENT AGREEMENT

When the Antecedent Is an Indefinite Pronoun

Instead of referring to a noun, a pronoun may refer to another pronoun called an **indefinite pronoun**. Indefinite pronouns are usually used when speakers or writers do not know the name of the specific person or thing that they are discussing or when they want to discuss people in general. This group of pronouns includes the following:

anyone	nothing
anybody	everyone
anything	everybody
someone	everything
somebody	each
something	either
no one	neither
nobody	

These indefinite pronouns require a singular pronoun when referred to.

Everyone in my school likes *her* courses.

When *one* registers for computer courses, *he* has to consider who is teaching them.

When the Antecedent Is a Collective Noun

A collective noun—*family, group, audience, committee, team, class*—requires a singular pronoun when the noun refers to the group as a single unit. If a collective noun refers to the individual members of the group, it requires a plural pronoun.

The *Computer Committee* usually makes *its* choices quickly, but the *members of the Software Committee* reach *their* separate decisions rather slowly.

When Two or More Antecedents Are Joined by "or" or "nor"

When two or more nouns are joined by *or* or *nor*, the pronoun should agree with the noun that is closest to it.

Neither my professors nor my *tutor* allows students to be late to *his* programming sessions.

Neither my tutor nor my *professors* allow students to be late for *their* programming sessions.

EXERCISE   **DETERMINING PRONOUN FORM, REFERENCE, AND AGREEMENT**

Fill in each blank below with the correct pronoun.

Many teachers believe that most educational software is garbage. Much of this software has fancy colors and graphics but _____ doesn't have sound enough educational content to justify _____ high price. The developers of most software have tried to disguise _____ programs' educational content with slick gimmicks _____ attract attention but _____ don't really teach anything. For example, each of the English programs that I have reviewed presents _____ lessons in a video game format, but _____ lacks a logical sequence of concepts and meaningful content. Many of these programs reflect the "game mentality" of the programmer who developed _____: learning seems secondary to having fun. Teachers are the people _____ ought to be directly involved in the development of educational software. A teacher is the only person who knows _____ school's curriculum; thus, _____ is the best person to determine the appropriateness of the content of educational software for students.

PLURALS AND POSSESSIVES

It's easy to get confused about "s" endings. When you edit your writing, look for the three types of words that need "s" endings: (1)

present-tense verbs that agree with singular subjects, (2) plural nouns, and (3) possessives.

Plural Nouns

To form the plural of most nouns, simply add "s" to the end of the noun.

teacher	teachers
day	days
Reagan	Reagans

To form the plural of a noun that ends in "s," "x," "z," "ch," or sh," add "es."

boss	bosses
wish	wishes
Jones	Joneses

To form the plural of a noun that ends in "y" preceded by a consonant, change the "y" to "i" and add "es" (except for a proper name, which keeps its "s" in the plural).

galaxy	galaxies
dictionary	dictionaries
Holly	Holly*s*

To form the plural of a number, a letter, or a symbol, add an apostrophe and an "s." If you write out the number, letter, or symbol, add only the "s."

V	V's
8	8's
vee	vees
eight	eights

Possessives

To form the possessive of most nouns, simply add an apostrophe and an "s" to the end of the noun.

teacher	teacher's
Reagan	Reagan's

To form the possessive of singular nouns that end in "s," also add an apostrophe and an "s" to the end of the noun.

Adams   Adams's

To form the possessive of plural nouns, add only the apostrophe.

teachers   teachers'
Reagans   Reagans'

Never add an apostrophe or an apostrophe and an "s" to possessive pronouns. The possessive pronoun that most writers make this error with is *its*. *It's* is the contraction of *it is*, not the possessive form of *it*.

EXERCISE   **USING PLURALS AND POSSESSIVES**

Below is an excerpt of a student's essay about computers and education. On a separate piece of paper, rewrite this excerpt, changing the word "computers" from plural to singular (that is, every time you see "computers," change it to "a computer" or to "the computer"). This change in the number of the subject of each sentence will require a change in the form of the corresponding verb. You will also have to make corresponding changes in the pronouns that refer to the subjects, and you may have to change the wording of some of the sentences.

```
    Personal computers are an inevitable part of the future
of education because of their many capabilities.  Computers'
abilities to organize information, to retrieve research, and
to solve problems will probably make them indispensable to
teachers and students alike.
    What do computers have to offer for learners?  First,
they are fun to use, particularly for a generation whose best
friends are television sets and video games.  Second, thanks
to their ability to present the same material over and over
again endlessly, computers are infinitely patient tutors.
```

Moreover, computers are "interactive"--they provide feedback appropriate to the users' responses. Thus, they can provide students with more individualized attention in one day than they can get from a month of classroom experience.

Furthermore, computers are able to store incredible amounts of data and information. For example, recent computers' hard disks are able to store entire encyclopedias, including diagrams, pictures, and photographs. And computers--actually computers' programs--have the ability to cross-reference all of this information and provide indexes of them.

In the not-too-distant future, students and teachers will tap computers' vast potential, and everyone will benefit.

EXERCISE **IDENTIFYING AND CORRECTING ERRORS IN THE THREE DIFFERENT "S" ENDINGS**

In the essay below, circle all of the words that have incorrect SWE "s" endings (verbs, plural nouns, and possessives). Then write your correction above each error that you have circled.

Computers' cannot think. Or can they? Recently, Soft Path Systems' new creative software program, "Brainstormer" was introduced on the American market, and it enable computer to do much of the busy-work usually involved in creative thinking. Brainstormer don't actually comes up with original ideas, but it do create new combination of the basic ideas that a person type in. It's goal is to shuffle and display all of the possible variation of ones' original ideas.

In order to use the program, you types in a few basic themes and some variation on these themes. The program then mixs up the themes and variations, producing hundred of thousands of possible storys. These story's value is in helping you generate a multitude of options for developing your ideas. The program enable you to explore possibilitys and it helps you break out of ruts.

Brainstormer is also useful for teachers. It's ability to spew out endless variations can help a teacher to creates many different student's learning activitys. Furthermore, Brainstormer create individualized activitys to fit each students' needs so that different students' can work simultaneously on problem requiring different level of skills.

However, Brainstormer do has some drawback. It cannot develops original ideas, and it do not chooses the best or most logical combinations of ideas. In other word, it really do not think! But for those writer who frequently experiences difficulty in generating ideas, Brainstormer may be just the answer. Its a tool that can helps them produce ideas and it may improve their' creativity.

GRAMMAR AND USAGE CORRECTION SYMBOLS

Use these symbols to edit your own writing, edit a classmate's writing, or to understand your teacher's comments.

Error	Problem
VERBS	
Vb	Incorrect verb form or verb ending
PP	Incorrect use of the past participle
Agr	Subject-verb agreement error
T	Incorrect verb tense
Vb Cons	Incorrect switch in verb tenses
PRONOUNS	
Pro	Incorrect pronoun form
Pro Agr	Pronoun-antecedent error
Pro Ref	Unclear pronoun reference or missing antecedent
PLURALS	
Pl	Incorrect plural ending on a noun
POSSESSIVES	
Poss	Incorrect possessive form or ending

WRITING ASSIGNMENT WRITING, REVISING, AND EDITING AN ESSAY ABOUT COMPUTERS

Below is an essay about computers by Lewis Thomas. After you read it, follow the directions below it and write an essay about computers.

TO ERR IS HUMAN

Everyone must have had at least one personal experience with a computer error by this time. Bank balances are suddenly reported to have jumped from 379 dollars into the millions, appeals for charitable contributions are mailed over and over to people with crazy-sounding names at your address, utility companies write that they're turning everything off—that sort of thing. If you manage to get in touch with someone and complain, you then get instantaneously typed, guilty letters from the same computer, saying, "Our computer was in error, and an adjustment is being made in your account."

These are supposed to be the sheerest, blindest accidents. Mistakes are not believed to be part of the normal behavior of a good machine. If things go wrong, it must be a personal, human error, the result of fingering, tampering, a button getting stuck. The computer, at its normal best, is infallible.

I wonder whether this can be true. After all, the whole point of computers is that they represent an extension of the human brain, vastly improved upon but nonetheless human, superhuman

The focus of this essay is the current or potential value of computers in your life. Your readers are your classmates and your teacher. When you are finished writing your discovery draft, get feedback on it, and then revise and edit it using the techniques that you have practiced in this book.

ISSUES FOR YOUR JOURNAL

1. Has grammar been a problem for you? If so, why and how?
2. Are there any errors in your writing that you feel are impossible to correct, no matter how hard you try? What kinds of errors are these? Why do you think that they are so difficult for you to identify or to correct?
3. Did you enjoy reading and writing about computers? Why or why not?
4. What age is the drinking age in your state? What age do you think it should be? Why?
5. How do you feel about guns and about gun control? Who should be allowed to own guns? Who shouldn't be? Why?

CHAPTER TWELVE

EDITING SPELLING AND PUNCTUATION

A word is a design, once committed to memory, we can recognize when we meet it again. We do not learn to spell in obedience to any "laws" of correctness. We learn to spell merely because it is more convenient to re-identify the picture we call the word if its form, its outline, is standard and invariable ... two sum up the prakticle cas fer korekt spelin and fer crekt punctueshn too deepens on the advantejiz of won aksepted cod over meny indavidule coads kurect speling savs the tim of both reeder and riter.

CLIFTON FADIMAN AND JAMES HOWARD

INTRODUCTION: THE IMPORTANCE OF EDITING SPELLING AND PUNCTUATION

The English language is difficult to spell because its spelling system is based primarily on meaning rather than on sound. Often, it is pointless to try to "sound out" the spelling of a word because a particular sound in it may be represented by several different combinations of letters. For instance, the "long a" sound can be spelled five different ways in English: "a" (paste), "ai" (bait), "ay" (may), "ei" (weigh), and "et" (bouquet). The playwright George Bernard Shaw once wrote that the word "fish" ought to be spelled "ghoti": "gh" can make an "f" sound (as in "rough"), "o" can make a "short i" sound (as in "women"), and "ti" can make an "sh" sound (as in "motion"). Complicating matters is the fact that there are very few useful spelling rules, and all of them have several exceptions.

Nevertheless, writers have to edit their spelling and punctuation because spelling and punctuation errors distract readers and can distort the meaning of a piece of writing so that it cannot even be understood. Furthermore, many readers have prejudices about people whose writing is filled with spelling and punctuation errors: the common stereotype associated with people who cannot spell or punctuate well is that they are less intelligent and less educated than people who can spell and punctuate well. Unfortunately, some teachers also believe this stereotype, and they fail essays that are intelligently written and coherently developed but are filled with spelling and punctuation errors. Don't let this happen to you. Proofread for your typical errors and correct them. In addition, don't let fear of misspelling certain words keep you from using them. As you write and revise, choose words to convey your ideas and feelings and don't worry whether you have spelled them correctly. Just remember that you will have to look them up in a dictionary when you are finished revising.

PAIRED WRITING TASK   **IDENTIFYING PROBLEMS IN SPELLING AND IN PUNCTUATION**

Work with another classmate on this task. Below is Sonja Rossini's essay that was discussed in Chapter 8. This is how the essay looked *before* she edited it for errors in spelling and punctuation. Read the essay. Then, reread it and circle every error in spelling and in punctuation that you can find. Work with your partner on correcting each error. When you are finished, compare your corrections to Rossini's edited version on page 190 of Chapter 8.

WOMEN WARRIORS

Margaret Mead, the famous anthrapologist, was once asked, weather women should be permitted to be combat soldiers. She answered, that they shouldn't because they are "Too Feirce". I was intrigued by her answer; so I decided to do some reading because I wanted to figure out what Mead meant.

I discovered many historical and modern myths about Women Warriors. However in reality most primitive and modern societies, do not arm their women. Women can be drafted to do non-combat service in offices. However they rarely take part in any real combat or fight in wars. Still their not fighting doesn't prove that they are "Too Feirce" to fight.

Another notable anthrapologist Konrad Lorenz has pointed out that, among most species of animals it is the males that fight. He also stated that when female animals do fight usually in defense of their babies they fight--to the death. This may be a clue into Meads' comment; women may be feircer deadlier fighters. In addition Lorenz noted, that throughout history; in all kinds of cultures and civilazations men and boys are the only ones who learn the rituels and the rules of fighting. Maybe Mead means, that women don't know these rituels and rules. If they were armed maybe they would be so Feirce, that they would fight to the death of the world.

Sonja Rossini

COMMON CAUSES OF SPELLING ERRORS

As Rossini's essay illustrates, writers usually have patterns of spelling errors that they repeat over and over again in their writing. If a writer has *not* been diagnosed as learning-disabled, then most of his or her typical spelling errors will result from one or more of the following causes:

1. *addition*: a letter is added to a word, usually because the writer pronounces the additional letter
   inter*r*gration—integration
   ath*e*lete—athlete
2. *deletion:* a letter is dropped from a word, usually because the writer doesn't pronounce it
   la*b*ratory—laboratory
   gove*r*ment—government
3. *transposition:* a letter is interchanged with the letter next to it, usually because the writer hasn't memorized a rule governing a tricky combination of letters
   rec*ie*ve—receive
   effic*ei*nt—efficient
4. *substitution:* a letter is substituted for a letter that sounds similar, usually because the writer is unsure of the exact spelling of the sound
   add*i*tude—attitude
   civil*a*zation—civilization
5. *confusion about a spelling "demon":* a word that is difficult to spell has been spelled incorrectly, usually because the writer didn't look up the correct spelling in a dictionary
   di*s*sappear—disappear
   exist*a*nce—existence
6. *confusion with a homonym:* a word spelled like its homonym, usually because the writer doesn't know the spelling of the two homonyms (words that sound alike but that are spelled differently and have different meanings)
   principle—principal
   sight—cite—site

Here are some of Sonja Rossini's spelling errors. Can you figure out the most typical cause of her spelling problems?

anthr*a*pologist	—anthropologist
prim*a*tive	—primitive

civil*a*zations —civilizations
ritu*e*ls —rituals

These are "intelligent" spelling errors—each one represents the way that the writer pronounces the word. Rossini clearly has a pattern of problems with substitutions: all of these errors indicate confusion over the spelling of sounds that can be spelled several different ways. Since this type of error is so difficult to catch (because the writer isn't even aware that she has misspelled words), the only way to edit it is to ask someone else to help find it. Most writing textbooks present lengthy lists of homonyms and spelling demons, but this seems pointless because each writer has his or her own set of troublesome words to look for and correct. Experienced writers don't refer to lists or homonyms or demons, and most of them don't memorize or use many of the rules of spelling. Instead, they proofread for their typical errors, they examine tricky words to see if these "look right," and they use a dictionary to check the spelling of troublesome words.

TECHNIQUES FOR IMPROVING SPELLING

Here are some suggestions for dealing with spelling problems and for improving spelling ability.

1. Don't worry about spelling while you are writing or revising a piece of writing; wait until you are finished revising before you check your spelling. If you are writing an essay examination and you don't have time to edit, reread your paper carefully and look for any words whose spelling you are unsure of. If a dictionary is permitted on the test, look up each troublesome word. If not, try writing alternative spellings for each troublesome word and pick up the one that looks right.
2. Write down every word that you misspell in the Spelling Log on page 339 at the end of your notebook. This is the best way to figure out your own spelling problems. By listing every misspelled word (and its correct spelling), you will accomplish two important things: (a) you will see the correct spelling of a word that usually confuses you and (b) you will see your typical patterns of errors (additions, deletions, substitutions, transpositions, homonym confusions, or "demon" confusions). If you have trouble determining your pattern of spelling errors, ask your teacher to help diagnose your problem. Once you have figured out the particular words or patterns that are causing problems for you, you will know exactly what to look for when you edit your spelling.

3. Use a standard college dictionary to look up the spelling and the punctuation of words when you are editing. If you don't know the first few letters of a word (which you must know in order to look it up), ask a classmate, a teacher, or a friend to help.

4. Create your own set of hints for remembering words that give you problems. For example, one student told me that she always uses the following sentence when she edits to help her remember how to spell the "there" homonyms: *They're* home in *their* house over *there*. And I still use the hints that my elementary school teacher taught me: The *principal* is my *pal* (not *ple*), and There's a *dance* in *attendance*.

5. Read material of increasing difficulty. Research on student's vocabulary development and on spelling skill indicates that both of these abilities are related to quantity and quality of reading. The more you read, the more words you will learn and the more you will be able to identify the correct spellings of words.

6. Do crossword puzzles and other word games that require you to match meaning and spelling. Do *not* do "word search" or "word hunt" puzzles since these don't include any information about the words' meanings and they only stress letter shapes.

EXERCISE **IDENTIFYING PATTERNS OF SPELLING ERRORS**

Use the proofreading techniques discussed in Chapter 9 to find and circle every spelling error in the uncorrected paragraph that follows. Then look up the correct spelling of each misspelled word and write it in above the error. The first one has been done as an example.

> If someone crashes into my car, destroying it and killing
>
> me because I am not wearing my seat belt, so be it. I made a
>
> *consequences*
> decision and I must take the (consquences.) I and millions of
>
> other Americans are willing to do this, but our government
>
> won't let us. Many states have past "seat belt laws" that
>
> perscribe stiff fines for people who don't buckle up. I think
>
> these laws are disasterous because they take away people's
>
> indavidual rights. Each person has the right to decide how
>
> much protection he or she needs. Its not fare for legaslators

to decide that every person in the state must wear a seat belt

at all times. I am an intellagent women and an excellent

driver, and I am capable of determining when I need to wear a

seat belt. Seat belt laws are more than an annoying

hinderance; they are an assault on our personal freedom.

SPELLING RULES

I have little faith in spelling rules. There are only three that I have found helpful in editing my own spelling:

First Rule: Doubling a Final Consonant

If you want to add a suffix to a word that ends in a single consonant, double this final consonant *if* three conditions are met:

a. The suffix begins with a vowel.
b. The original word consists of only one syllable or is accented on the final syllable.
c. In the original word a single vowel precedes a final single consonant.

Doubled	*Not Doubled*
control—controlled	peel—peeled
got—gotten	beat—beaten

The exception to this rule is any word that ends in an "x": tax—taxed

Second Rule: Silent "e"

If you want to add a suffix to a word that ends in a silent (unpronounced) "e," drop the "e" *if* the suffix begins with a vowel, *but* keep the "e" if the suffix begins with a consonant.

hate—hating	hate—hateful
rare—rarity	rare—rarely

Some exceptions to this rule include the following words:

true—truly   mile—mileage
argue—argument   agree—agreeable

Other exceptions include any word that ends in an "e" that is preceded by a "g," "c," "o," or "y":

notice—noticeable
hoe—hoeing

An exception is the word "judge"—judgment

Third Rule: Changing "y" to "i"

If you want to add a suffix to a word that ends in a "y," change this "y" to an "i" *if* the suffix begins with any letter except "i." (Keep the final "y" if the suffix begins with "i.")

marry—marriage   marry—marrying
satisfy—satisfied   satisfy—satisfying

The exceptions to this rule include four words:

day + ly = daily
pay + ed = paid
say + ed = said

Many teachers recommend that writers learn the "i/e" jingle ("i" before "e" except after "c" or when sounded like "a" as in "neighbor and weigh"). This jingle may be helpful, but it doesn't acknowledge all of the exceptions (including words like "either," "seize," "financier," and "height"). If "e/i" or "i/e" transpositions are a problem for you, resign yourself to looking up every word that contains these combinations.

EXERCISE   **USING SPELLING RULES TO EDIT SPELLING**

Read the two uncorrected paragraphs below, and circle each misspelled word. Then try to use the spelling rules discussed on the preceding pages to correct each spelling error. When you are finished, use a dictionary to look up each word that you corrected in order to confirm that your spelling is correct.

Recently, more and more public institutions have stopped permiting people to smoke. Smokers are now restrictted to one small area in public rooms or they are forbiden to smoke at all. As a longtime smoker, I am more annoied at these restrictions; I am outraged that my individual rights are being completly ignored. It has goten to the point where I am afraid to smoke in public for fear that some wierdo will attack me, demanding that I put out my cigarette immediatly. Since I hate getting into arguements with people I usually comply. But I am getting angryer and angryer at this denyal of my rights.

Although I smoke only occasionaly, I feel that smoking is my privilege. I know that smoking is bad for my health (and for my surviveal), but I have the right to do what I want to my body. I find it truely outragous that our government is granting non-smokers more legal rights than smokers have. This is irrational and inexcuseable. There has been a noticable decrease in the number of places where smokers are allowwed to smoke peacefully, and I think this is an illegal infringment of our rights.

EXERCISE   EDITING SPELLING

Practice your proofreading and editing skills by finding and correcting every spelling error in the following uncorrected essay. Work with another classmate on this essay and take turns looking up every word whose spelling you are unsure of.

Recently, there have been many laws passed aim at ensureing public safety: laws prohibitting drinking and driving, laws forbiding people to smoke in some areas, and laws requireing people to wear safety equipement in cars or motorcycles. Many Americans oppose these laws because they percieve them as infringments on their right to do whatever they want with their lives and their bodys. They feel that the goverment should not pass laws regulatting people's indavidual rights.

However, I beleive that the people who complian about the abridgement of their personal rights are basicly selfish and aren't considerring the consaquences of their actions. For instance, how many smokers consider how irratateing their habit is to non-smokers. Moreover, recent resaerch has shown that breatheing the smoke from someone else's cigerette can increase a nonsmoker's chances of getting cancer? Since when do smokers have the "right" to give other people cancer? And when the smokers themselfs get cancer or emphasyma, who has to pay their medical and hospital bills? All of us do, in the form of our medical insurence premiums and our taxes.

Moreover, I particuly rezent people who choose to drive without seat belts. In an accident, they will not be able to retane control of their cars and thus they are more likely to injure pedestrains and other drivers around them. Their contemt for seat belts jepordizes other people's safety. Therefore, when it is apparant than an indavidual's behavior has (or can potentialy have) adverce affects on those around

```
him or her, then that behavior has to be controled.  This is

the principle reason why I support our societies' laws

protecting public safety.
```

CAPITALIZATION RULES

There are several rules governing the conventions of capitalization in Standard Written English. Since readers expect these conventions to be followed (and get distracted or annoyed if they aren't), writers have to memorize these rules or look them up when they are editing their writing.

1. Capitalize the first word of every sentence and of every sentence within a sentence.
   He said, "This is the book that I need."
2. Capitalize the names of specific people, places, groups, businesses, and events.
   Jack Logan was wounded in the Vietnam War while fighting in the Fifth Division in Cambodia.
3. Capitalize people's titles and their abbreviations.
   Karen L. Greenberg, Ph.D. or Dr. Karen L. Greenberg
4. Capitalize the names of specific courses, religions, languages, and organizations.
   This semester, I studied Republican politics in my Political Science 101 course, and I learned some Greek in my World Religions course.
   (Note: If the writer of the sentence above had left out "101," then "political science" would *not* be capitalized.)
5. Capitalize titles of works (except words of three letters or fewer).
   "Women Warriors"
   Death of a Salesman

EXERCISE **EDITING CAPITALIZATION**

Edit the following uncorrected paragraph by finding and correcting every error in capitalization.

```
    although i am not the least bit suicidal, i believe that

all humans deserve the right to die when and how they wish to.
```

self-inflicted death is not murder. I strongly oppose new york state's law making suicide illegal and punishing people who help others commit suicide. Also, even though i am a devout protestant, i do not regard suicide as a violation of god's laws. For example, ten years ago, when dr. henry p. van dusen and his wife committed suicide, i felt that god would not damn them since they were simply exercising their free will. dr. van dusen was the president of the union theological seminary (the most famous protestant seminary in the world). the van dusens were famous here in america and in many european and african countries where they lectured extensively. however, no one knew how ill they had become and how much they depended on nurses for even basic functions like eating and bathing. their suicides, which were discussed in detail in the "people" sections of <u>time</u> and <u>newsweek</u> magazines, shocked and angered many people. however, many others, including myself, understood that the van dusens wanted to live and die with dignity and they did. everyone deserves these rights.

THE APOSTROPHE: USES AND RULES

The most frequent spelling error in student essays seems to be the incorrect use of the apostrophe. Incorrect apostrophes can distort your meaning, so proofread for them every time you edit a piece of writing. Here are some guidelines for using apostrophes:

1. Add an apostrophe and an "s" to form the possessive of nouns that do not end in "s."

    Dr. **Van Dusen's** suicide shocked the world, but his **family's** response was sympathetic.

2. Add an apostrophe to a singular noun that ends in "s."

   Revered James **Lewis's** response was that "they died with dignity."

3. Add the apostrophe alone to form the possessive of plural nouns that already end in "s."

   The **Van Dusens'** suicide shocked the world, but their **friends'** reactions were sympathetic.

4. Do *not* add an apostrophe to a possessive pronoun.

   Although suicide is a way of dying with dignity, **its** effects are felt by family and friends.

5. Use an apostrophe to replace omitted letters in contractions.

   We **shouldn't** say that suicide is wrong because we **don't** have the right to judge other people's decisions.

Note: Remember that many teachers and employers think that contractions are inappropriate for formal writing. If you want to make your writing sound more academic or more formal, rewrite all of your contractions and any other abbreviations. For instance, read the sentence in the preceding example and then read the following sentence:

   We should not say that suicide is wrong because we do not have the right to judge other people's decisions.

The sentence with contractions sounds less formal than the one without contractions.

EXERCISE **EDITING APOSTROPHES**

Practice your skills at proofreading and editing unconventional uses of apostrophes by finding and correcting all of the problems in the following uncorrected paragraphs.

I just turned eighteen; now I am legally an adult. I can be drafted to fight for my country and die defending it's freedom. But I cannot buy a drink because most state's drinking age is now 21. The public and many congressmen and women believe a higher drinking age will save lives. They believe that most of the alcohol-related car crashes in this country are caused by drunken teenagers' aged 18-21. However they never cite evidence supporting their' beliefs. And after

extensive research on this topic, I have not seen one study
that provides reliable scientific evidence for raising our
countrys' drinking age from 18 to 21. Higher drinking ages do
not reduce the number of accidents or deaths' due to alcohol
abuse.

In fact, the people responsible for most drunken driven
accidents and fatalities are 21-24 year-old drivers'. Maybe
our congresspeople would like to raise the drinking age to 25!
Moreover, I think that Americas' history shows that
prohibition is not an effective deterrent to alcohol abuse.
If you make it illegal for people under 21 to drink in the
open, they will drink anyway, and probably drink more and get
into more trouble than if they could drink in places where
their behavior could be supervised by adult's. I think
congress should trust us and should lower the drinking age
to 18.

PUNCTUATION PROBLEMS

Many writers have one of the two basic problems with punctuation—underpunctuating or overpunctuating—and either problem can drive readers to distraction. Read each of the following "sentences" aloud to see an example of each problem:

1. Another notable anthropologist Konrad Lorenz has pointed out that among most species of animals it is the males who fight when females do fight usually in defense of their babies they fight to the death.
2. Another notable anthropologist, Konrad Lorenz, has pointed out, that among most species of animals, it is the males, who fight; when females do fight, usually in defense (of their babies), they fight—to the death.

Why did you have trouble understanding each of these "sentences"? One reason is that punctuation signals "chunks" of meaning. Here are the chunks of meanings in the preceding "sentence":

Another notable anthropologist / Konrad Lorenz / has pointed out that among most species of animals / it is the males who fight / when females do fight / usually in defense of their babies / they fight to the death

When we speak, we signal these chunks by pausing briefly after meaningful word groups and by stressing specific words. When we write, we use punctuation marks to represent these pauses and stresses. For this reason, it is difficult to grasp the meaning of the underpunctuated "sentence" above. For the same reason, an overpunctuated piece is even more difficult to read. In "sentence" 2, the unnecessary punctuation keeps forcing the reader to stop in the middle of a chunk of meaning, and this is extremely annoying. Some writers can read their writing aloud and hear where the various punctuation marks belong. For example, read aloud the correctly punctuated paragraph below, and consider whether you pause very briefly at the commas.

Another notable anthropologist, Konrad Lorenz, has pointed out that among most species of animals, it is the males who fight. When females do fight, usually in defense of their babies, they fight to the death.

Many writer has difficulty "hearing" punctuation, and they have to learn to punctuate by trying out all of the different punctuation marks and examining readers' responses to them. Punctuation serves five basic functions of punctuation:

1. Punctuation ends sentences.
2. Punctuation connects sentences.
3. Punctuation separates items in a series within a sentence.
4. Punctuation separates words or phrases that modify a sentence.
5. Punctuation separates quoted words or phrases from the rest of a sentence.

These five basic functions will be used to categorize the rules of punctuation that follow.

Ending Sentences

Once writers have decided whether their ideas should be expressed as statements, exclamations, or questions, they have to follow the conventions of Standard Written English punctuation. They must use a period to end each statement, an exclamation point to end a strongly worded statement, and a question mark to end a question. Here is an example of each "terminal" punctuation mark:

I think playing with punctuation is fun.

I think playing with punctuation is terrific!

Is playing with punctuation really so terrific?

Connecting Sentences

The conventions of Standard Written English allow writers to use a semicolon, a colon, or a comma (with a coordinator) to connect sentences.

- A semicolon can be used to join two sentences when the idea in the second sentence is a continuation of the one in the first. It indicates a pause that is greater than a comma's but not as great as a period's.
    I just turned eighteen; now I am legally an adult.

- A colon can be used to connect two sentences when the second sentence contains an illustration of the first.
    I am now legally an adult: I can drive and I can be drafted to fight for my country.

- A comma and a coordinator can be used to link two sentences.
    I am legally an adult, but I am prohibited from drinking.

Separating Three or More Words or Phrases Used in a Series

A comma should be used to separate words or phrases or sentences in a series within a sentence.

New York, Connecticut, and Rhode Island have raised the drinking age from 18 to 21.

Separating Modifiers from the Rest of the Sentence

In Chapter 8, you practiced adding and moving descriptive words and phrases to sentences to make them more interesting and informative. Descriptive modifiers can be placed at the beginning, the middle, or the end of a sentence:

> In New York, and many other states, teenagers cannot drink until they are twenty-one years old.

Different handbooks give different rules about using commas to punctuate modifiers that are used to introduce or to end a sentence. In general, here are the conventional rules for punctuating material that introduces or interrupts a sentence:

- A comma should be used to separate an introductory word or phrase from the main sentence, but it is *not* necessary to separate a descriptive word or phrase at the end of a sentence.

> In New York, teenagers cannot drink until they are twenty-one years old.

> Teenagers cannot drink until they are twenty-one years old in New York.

- A comma can be used before *and* after descriptive words or phrases that interrupt the flow of a sentence, if these descriptive words or phrases are not necessary for identifying the subject of the sentence.

> Teenagers in New York, who may want to drink only rarely, cannot drink until they are twenty-one.

In this sentence, "who may want to drink only rarely," is not essential to the meaning. Do *not* use commas to surround interrupting modifiers that *are* essential to the meaning of the sentence.

> Teenagers in New York who want to drink illegally will always find a way to do so.

In this sentence, the phrase "who want to drink illegally" is necessary for letting the reader know exactly which teenagers the writer is discussing.

EXERCISE EDITING COMMAS

Proofread the following uncorrected paragraphs for comma errors. Insert commas where they have been omitted and cross out commas that are not necessary. Some of the commas are used correctly.

I have known how to use guns, since I was ten years old. My dad taught me how to shoot a gun, just as, his dad had taught him when he was ten. When I was younger, my family would go hunting, in the woods, every fall and spring. We would set traps, to catch rabbits raccoons and muskrats, and we would use rifles to shoot deer and birds. Shooting and trapping, was our way of life. These activities bound us all together, and provided us, with tons of food.

Recently, however, I have begun to question the "innocent" pleasure that I felt, in those days. I keep reading, about how hunting and trapping is making some animals extinct, and is destroying the breeding habitats of others. I think about animals that chewed their legs off, so as to free themselves from traps. I wonder about how animals who did not escape our traps felt, when we clubbed them to death. I wonder how innocent, or how guilty I was. Lately when I read all of the posters of the National Rifle Association, that talk about the glories of hunting the rewards of trapping and the joy of using guns I get a little nauseous. I think the "gun tradition," has ended in my family. I will not teach my son to shoot.

Separating Quoted Material from the Rest of the Sentence

A pair of quotation marks should be used to set off the exact words that someone has spoken or written. Quotations of three or more words are usually preceded by a comma:

President Reagan said, "I believe in raising the national drinking age to twenty-one."

When the quotation opens the sentence, the comma goes inside the closing quotation marks.

"I believe in raising the national drinking age to twenty-one," said President Reagan.

The above quotations are "direct"; the exact words that someone has spoken are recorded. The following sentences contain "indirect" quotations; a summary of what was spoken or written are presented. Quotation marks should *not* be used to set off an indirect quotation.

A pair of quotation marks is also used to set off titles of stories, poems, magazine articles, and chapters of books:

I read an article called "Teenage Alcohol Abuse Today" in *Newsweek* magazine.

Periods and commas are always placed inside the closing quotation marks:

The president said, "I will sign a drinking-age bill if Congress passes it."

Colons and semicolons are always placed outside the closing quotation marks:

The president said, "I will sign a drinking-age bill if the Congress passes it"; however, later he added that the bill "has to be bipartisan."

Question marks, exclamation points, and dashes are placed inside the closing quotation marks when they are part of the quoted material:

The president asked, "Will the bill be bipartisan?"

(The question mark is part of the direct question being quoted.)

They are placed outside the closing quotation marks when they are part of a larger sentence.

What does the president mean by "bipartisan"?

(The question mark ends the question in which the word ''bipartisan'' is enclosed.)

EXERCISE **CHOOSING AND USING PUNCTUATION**

Here are two uncorrected paragraphs without any punctuation. Insert punctuation marks (periods, question marks, semicolons, colons, commas, apostrophes, dashes, or quotation marks) wherever they are needed. Make sure that you capitalize the first letter of every new sentence that you create.

Why is the speeding limit in our nation cities 55 miles per hour has any study ever shown that a 55 mile per hour speed limit saves gasoline and if so how much gas does this speed limit actually save I have yet to see some solid evidence supporting a speed limit last week I heard our governor say that he wants to raise the highway speed limit to 60 miles per hour he said I believe that raising the speeding limit will lessen the number of fatalities on our states roads I disagree with him I doubt that a legal speed limit whether it is 55 or any other number of miles per hour really saves as many lives as our politicians tell us it does most accidents particularly fatal ones are caused by drunken or otherwise incapacitated drivers not by drivers who are speeding

As anyone who has ever driven in our major cities knows no one can speed the traffic is usually too heavy there are too many pedestrians and there are frequent traffic lights and stop signs thus the real issue is the speed limit on highways why shouldnt drivers go as fast as they want on Americas highways most highways in America are long open stretches of

road you can drive for miles and miles on most highways and
never even see a car except for the traffic cop who is hiding
behind a billboard waiting to catch speeders all in all I
think the 55 mile per hour speed limit is absurd.

SPELLING AND PUNCTUATION CORRECTION SYMBOLS

Use these symbols to edit your own writing, edit a classmate's
writing, or to understand your teacher's comments.

Error	Problem
sp	spelling error
'	insert an apostrophe
:	insert a colon
,	insert a comma
—	insert a dash
=	insert a hyphen
.	insert a period
?	insert a question mark
"	insert a quotation mark
;	insert a semicolon

WRITING ASSIGNMENT WRITING, REVISING, AND EDITING
AN ESSAY ABOUT INDIVIDUAL RIGHTS

Most of the readings and exercises in this unit concerned controversial "individual rights": smoking, drinking and driving, refusing to
wear seat belts, committing suicide, and using guns. Choose one of
these issues for an essay that will convince your classmates of the
soundness of your opinions on the topic. Write a discovery draft and
get feedback from your classmates. Then revise your draft using the
techniques that you practiced in Chapters 6, 7, and 8. Next, edit your
revisions using the methods that you learned in Chapters 9, 19, 11, and
in this chapter. When you are finished editing, exchange essays with a
classmate. After you read your classmate's essay, circle every unconventional form and every problem and error that you find. Return the
essays and discuss them. Then correct every problem or error that
your classmate found in your essay.

ISSUES FOR YOUR JOURNAL

1. How do you feel about always having to look up troublesome words in a dictionary? Is doing this worth the effort? Why or why not?
2. What courses are required at your school? How do you feel about these courses? Should more liberal arts courses be required? Why or why not?
3. What are your strengths and weaknesses as a student? How can you become a better student?
4. How effective are you at controlling time? How well do you plan and organize your time? Do you keep a daily list of things "to do"? Why or why not?
5. Are you continuing to write on a regular basis in your journal? Why or why not?

PART FOUR

APPLYING YOUR WRITING SKILLS

CHAPTER THIRTEEN

APPLYING YOUR WRITING SKILLS

Every time a student sits down to write for us, he has to invent the university for the occasion—invent the university, that is, or a branch of it, like history or anthropology or economics or English. The student has to learn to speak our language, to speak as we do, to try on the peculiar ways of knowing, selecting, evaluating, reporting, concluding, and arguing that define the discourse of our community.

DAVID BARTHOLOMAE

INTRODUCTION: WRITING AND REVISING FOR SPECIAL PURPOSES

What does David Bartholomae mean? Do you feel as if you are "inventing a branch of your university" every time you sit down to write a term paper in a different course? Do styles and strategies of writing in the various academic disciplines differ? Most of us who study writing and writers would probably answer "yes"—scholars in different fields think and write differently. Think again about what Bartholomae is saying: in school, students are constantly asked to do different types of writing—to write as a literary critic for literature courses, as an experimental psychologist for psychology courses, as a programmer for computer courses. For each course, students need to figure out how experts in that discipline write: What kinds of examples are appropriate? Which types of arguments are convincing? How should the material be organized? What is the appropriate jargon or the correct technical vocabulary? Since most students are not yet experts in the various disciplines they are studying, they have to read widely and consult sources in order to "invent" the style and logic of any particular discipline.

Thus, not only are student writers faced with the difficult task of learning to write more effectively, but they are also being asked to use their writing to learn about new subjects *and* to demonstrate what they have learned. No wonder some students feel overwhelmed by the writing demands placed on them! However, these three tasks or goals—learning to write better, using writing to learn something new, and writing to show learning—are all interrelated. When one writes about the material in a course, one can simultaneously learn the material, figure out how to write effectively about it, *and* improve one's writing skills. Although different disciplines do require different strategies for organizing and presenting material, the techniques of effective writing are the same in every discipline. These techniques are the ones that you have been practicing in this book: prewriting; limiting a topic; writing a working thesis statement; considering focus, purpose, and audience; developing appropriate supporting details; and revising several times. There are, however, specialized conventions and formats for each discipline, and this chapter will help you examine and apply these conventions and formats.

GROUP WRITING TASK **ANALYZING WRITING ASSIGNMENTS IN DIFFERENT DISCIPLINES**

Often, an assignment from an academic course will contain clues about how the teacher expects students to develop a response to the assignment. A writer's success depends on his or her ability to analyze these clues and to respond to them appropriately. In order to practice analyzing these clues, get into a group and examine the assignments below. In the space below each, write down what you think the assignment is asking writers to do. Be specific and don't merely repeat the words in the assignment. The first one has been done as an example.

1. (Sociology) Select any society that we have studied and discuss its social stratification.

   Choose one society that the course included and describe its social classes. Explain how each social class is determined, and give examples of each class.

2. (Economics) Which of the various taxation policies that we have discussed is the fairest to all Americans? Justify your selection.

3. (Art History) In a concise, organized fashion, outline the contemporary art trends that we have discussed in the past five sessions. Then, choose two of these trends and compare them.

4. (Political Science) Select one of the congressional bills that we have discussed and explain its development from a draft bill into the current law.

CUES AND CLUES IN SPECIALIZED WRITING ASSIGNMENTS

When David Bartholomae says that students have to learn to "speak the language" of each discipline, he is implying that different disciplines organize and present material in different ways. How are students supposed to know these various approaches to presenting material? One way is to examine the cues and clues in the writing assignments of different courses. A **cue** is a word that suggests the strategy to be used in responding to the assignment. Cue words signal different methods of selecting, developing, and presenting details. Here are some cue words and the strategies that they suggest:

Analyze: Describe each part of an object, an idea, or a problem separately and show how they relate to one another and to the whole.

Argue: State your point of view and provide support or proof.

Classify: Separate the parts of an object, an idea, or a problem into groups according to characteristics that group members share.

Compare: Describe each object, person, or idea and show how they are similar.

Contrast: Describe each object, person, or idea and show only how they are different.

Define: Explain what the object, person or idea is and is not and give some examples of it.

Describe: Give details about a person, object, or idea using sensory language so readers can experience it the way that you do.

Discuss: This catch-all term usually means "analyze and illustrate."

Evaluate: Explain the worth or value of something or someone by examining its good and bad points.

Explain: Like "discuss," this usually means "analyze and illustrate."

Illustrate: Present several examples.

Narrate: Relate a sequence of events.

Outline: List the main ideas and the most important details within each idea.

Summarize: Select the main points and briefly describe them in a paragraph or two.

Trace: Begin with the first occurrence of the event and describe its progress up to the present.

DOUBLE-ENTRY NOTEBOOKS

The best way to prepare for writing assignments and essay exams in various disciplines is to take notes on the lectures, discussions, labs, and readings. Here is a technique that will enable you to record your notes *and* to think about the material and shape a response to it. Instead of writing on every page of your notebook, write your notes on the right pages only. On the left pages, write your responses to your notes: the questions, comments, and reactions you have as you write your notes and as you review them later on in the day or the week. Here is a sample:

[left]	[right]
Reactions	*Notes*
	Humans have altered the population dynamics of many species.
The guy brought the starling over cause he liked it and now they cause problems at airports and buildings.	Now 900 million starlings in U.S. (brought over by an Englishman in 1890).
What should we do about these birds?	
Why don't people care about killing these animals? And how come they don't attack people back?	Thousands of deer and bears are killed by motorists each year.
Can't we figure out a way to get rid of the mice and rats without killing them?	Millions of mice and rats exterminated each year—several species are rapidly becoming extinct.
Can't they be moved to different habitats? Why do we have the right to "exterminate" a species?	Most human-animal encounters are hostile and end with the animal dying.
What do others do?	

If you keep a double-entry notebook, not only will you have notes on a subject, but you will also have your reactions to it—your insights, concerns, and questions. These reactions will provide many ideas for you to explore in essays and research papers, and it will also help you study for tests.

SUMMARIES

Summary writing is the most frequently assigned type of writing in college courses *and* in most jobs. A summary is a brief description of the main idea and key supporting points of something you have read, heard, or experienced. Teachers often ask students to summarize lectures or reading material because summarizing is an excellent way of learning: writing a summary requires a writer to identify the most important parts of an explanation or an argument and to present these parts in his or her own words. In order to write a summary of a discussion or a reading, you need to take notes on the main ideas and the most important details. Turn these notes into a summary by asking yourself what the main point of the reading or lecture was: "What was I supposed to learn from this?" State this main idea as the opening sentence of your summary. Then, in your own words, briefly state the key ideas and the important details. Present these ideas and details in the order in which they occurred in the material that you are summarizing; do *not* rearrange the organization of the details. For example, here is a classmate's uncorrected summary of Shaun Morrissey's brief essay on page 136 of Chapter 6:

```
Shaun Morrissey has always wanted to be a civil liberties

lawyer.  He wants to protect the constitutional rights of

minorities and poor people and businesses.  He has had some

volunteer experience in legal aid and he thinks that the

responsibilities, the salary and the working conditions will

be fine for him.
```

Reread Shaun Morrissey's essay. How is the summary above different from Morrissey's essay?

WRITING ACTIVITY WRITING A SUMMARY

Here is the editorial essay about liberal arts courses written by Richard J. Del Guidice, a dean at the State University of New York at Potsdam. Read this essay, and write a one-paragraph summary of it. Do *not* let your opinion of the author's viewpoint affect your summary.

LIBERAL ARTS COURSES
SHOULD BE REQUIRED FOR COLLEGE STUDENTS

Confronted with unfavorable demographic trends, a student population that is more interested in professional training than education and shrinking financial support, higher education institutions have been forced to rethink their missions in order to survive. Some have chosen to invest heavily in those programs that students demand, those that provide narrow job skills which assure that a position will await the student after graduation.

But are we not surrendering to the passions of the moment, sacrificing the real mission of the university in our stampede to teach a business curriculum, to offer data processing? In permitting our students to tell us what to teach them, we are not serving them well at all. What we are doing is giving them marketable skills that will be obsolete five years from the day they graduate. They will be left with nothing, their investment in higher education having paid only short-run transitory dividends.

There is an even more important implication in the rush to the marketplace. And that is that there is no central body of knowledge with which all of us should be familiar. It is as if the accumulated wisdom of humankind is defined anew by each generation of college students.

We cannot lose touch with the bedrock of human experience, those components of knowledge generally referred to as the liberal arts. And it is in reference to the liberal arts that an institution's general education curriculum is most important.

General education curricula are built on each institution's characteristics. In designing such a curriculum, one begins by assessing the institution's particular strengths. And here I must speak of our situation at Potsdam to demonstrate the general rule: We have one of the finest schools of music in the United States, the Crane School. For this college to institute a general education program that does not include music would be truly bizarre.

Once an institution understands how it is unique, once there is general agreement on how that uniqueness will be translated into a general education curriculum, one must then decide how to bring it to the student body. If we expect today's career-oriented student to select courses that are not useful in the market sense, then we are truly removed from reality. Given their choice, a substantial portion of our students would follow as narrow a course of study as possible, rejecting all that could not be connected to future salary. Therefore, we must require our general education curriculum of all our students and I would hope that our new design would include a music component.

If, in fact, we are experts in education, we should know what our students must learn. We too often stress the service nature of education, that which we do *for* our students. We must also keep in mind that to make education a meaningful experience for them, we must also do *to* them. Part of what we do to them should be to expose them to that part of human heritage called music and the arts. But we cannot simply put music requirements into place and insist that all students take them. All we would accomplish would be to add another piece to the mountain of fragments we are already giving them.

Unless we make music and the arts a required part of our general education system, we have failed to accomplish what I believe must be the goal of a liberal arts education—to make our students, as Plato wrote, "lovers not of a part of wisdom only, but of the whole. . . . "

Richard J. Del Guidice

Write your summary of this essay in the space below.

ANALYSES

Another type of writing frequently assigned in college and business is the analysis. When you analyze something, you break it down to learn about its parts and to show how they are related to one another and to the whole. Although you may not be aware of it, you are analyzing all the time that you are awake: noticing things and people and considering how they have or haven't changed, examining problems and figuring them out, seeing something enjoyable and thinking about why you liked it. Analysis is a basic human thought process.

In college, a typical analytic assignment is the "critical review" (of a book, a poem, a play, a film, a television show, a piece of music, a dance, or a piece of art). The first step in writing a critical analysis is to determine the overall effect of the work on you: What message did you

get, and how did it make you feel? Once you have clarified your response, you have to explain how the creator of the work communicated
this message and achieved this effect. Breaking the work down to its
individual components helps you understand its effect. How would you
go about analyzing a fictional book, story, play, film, or television
show? In secondary school, students are usually asked merely to "report" on a book or a show—to summarize its main elements and their
reactions. In college or in a professional setting, you are expected to go
beyond the report and offer an evaluation based on a fuller analysis.
You can begin by thinking about how the work made you feel and about
the impression it made on you. What point was the writer trying to
make, and how did he or she communicate this point? Which parts of
the work affected you most? In what ways does the work relate to your
life or to your experiences? Next, you could develop a working thesis
statement about the relationship of the various elements of the work to
its overall effect. As you develop your ideas and details, this working
thesis statement may change to reflect your increased knowledge
about your topic.

A STUDENT RESPONSE

Here is a student's uncorrected summary and analysis of a nonfic-
tion book on writing about art.

A SHORT GUIDE TO WRITING ABOUT ART BY SYLVAN BARNET

(Boston: Little, Brown and Co., 1981)

This new writing textbook is for art students in high

schools, colleges and vocational schools. The author's goal

is to help students write more intelligently about art and

also become more critical about art criticism. Barnet

stresses the need for students to pay careful attention to the

different aspects of a work of art and he teaches students how

to use these aspects as evidence for their evaluations. This

book also has specific strategies for writing about art and

also general guidelines for doing research.

As an art major, I think this is a very valuable "how-to" book. The author's guidelines about how to analyze different types of work of art make a lot of sense. He teaches readers how to look at a work of art and write about it. I particularly like his questions that readers are supposed to ask themselves when they look at an art work. I tried out these questions and found that they helped me see a painting in a whole new way. The part of the book that I didn't find so useful was the last third on research. There are dozens of research handbooks in the library and art students can use them if they need to know how to do research. The author should have stuck to teaching writing about art instead of trying to include a research handbook too. Still I think most art students would benefit from reading this book. Also, I think Mr. Barnet is a wonderful writer himself, and that made this book a pleasure to read.

Marie Miller

Which aspect of the book contributed most to Miller's impression of the book?

WRITING ACTIVITY WRITING AND REVISING ANALYSES
FOR DIFFERENT PURPOSES AND AUDIENCES

For this activity, you will have to write two different analyses of a problem. The problem that you will be analyzing is "the writing problem" at your school. Assume that administrators, teachers, and students at your school are concerned because many of the students are experiencing difficulties in writing their assignments satisfactorily.

Analysis 1

Analyze your school's writing problem from the students' point of view. Interview friends and classmates about the elements of their writing problems and about the factors that are causing these problems or making them worse. Based on your interviews, define the writing problem at your school and analyze the causes of the problem *from the students' point of view*. Then use the notes that you took during your interviews to prewrite, write, and revise a brief analysis.

Analysis 2

Analyze your school's writing problem from the teachers' perspective. Interview teachers about the characteristics of students' writing problems and about the factors that are causing these problems or making them worse. Based on your interviews, define the writing problem at your school and analyze the causes of the problem *from the teachers' perspective*. Use the notes that you took during your interviews to prewrite, write, and revise a brief analysis.

EVALUATIONS

Teachers of every academic subject frequently ask students to write evaluations because the process of evaluating requires students to explore topics in depth: one cannot judge something—an idea, a viewpoint, a theory—until one truly understands it. Typically, an evaluation assignment asks writers to defend or attack a point of view or to compare it to competing viewpoints. Also, when an assignment asks writers to "respond to" or "react to" a viewpoint, it is asking them to evaluate it—to judge it according to criteria that are appropriate for the subject. When you do freewriting and brainstorming for an evaluation assignment, think about whether you agree or disagree totally with the view or if you agree or disagree only partially. If you agree with the view, you can defend it by using one or more of the following strategies:

- Explain your reasons for agreeing with it.
- Do research and offer supporting evidence for the view from experts in the field.
- Describe any criticisms of the view (that have been discussed in class or that you have read about) and show why each is not valid or conclusive.

If you disagree with the view, you can attack it by using one or more of the following strategies:

- Describe all of the problems in the view and explain why the view is not accurate or not logical.
- Do research and explain the criticisms of the view offered by experts in the field.
- Explain why the view has not been supported logically or with enough evidence.

If you have mixed responses to the view, you will have to provide reasons why you agree in part and disagree in part. You can use the same prewriting techniques—freewriting, brainstorming, and clustering—that you would use for any essay to develop your initial responses to the issue or viewpoint. Then, write a working thesis statement that presents your subject and your evaluation or judgment of it. Next, write out the criteria or the standards by which you will evaluate your subject. In any evaluation, it is important for the writer to let the reader know, at the beginning of the essay, what criteria he or she is using. This lets the reader know what to expect. For example, what is your reaction to the following brief evaluation of a word processing program?

"Volkswriter Deluxe is terrific. It's the best program that I've used and I recommend it highly."

This writer has given her judgment but hasn't provided any criteria—she hasn't told us *why*, or according to what standards, Volkswriter Deluxe is so good. Now look at her revision:

Volkswriter Deluxe is the best program on the market. It is easy to learn and use and it performs a wide range of tasks. And best of all, it's less expensive that its competitors.

This revision presents the three criteria that are most important to this writer: ease of learning and use, comprehensiveness, and price. Each discipline has its own set of criteria. For example, when you analyze a fictional work of literature, you might evaluate it according to criteria such as "believability of characters" or "effectiveness of language." If you were asked to evaluate an economic theory, you might use criteria such as "comprehensiveness" and "validity."

In order to write an effective evaluation, you need to choose criteria that are appropriate for your readers and that are most likely to convince them. Although your audience is usually your teacher, don't assume that he or she knows everything about the topic and that it is acceptable to leave out information. In fact, the first information that you should present is a precise, accurate statement of the view that you are evaluating. Then, give your opinion about it (in your introduction), so that your reader will know what to expect from your essay. Make a list of your criteria, and under each criterion list all of the reasons for your judgment. Then write a discovery draft of your essay. Your goals in this discovery draft are to judge your subject and to justify your evaluation according to appropriate criteria. If your reasons and evidence conflict with your working thesis statement, develop a new one. If you need to consult public sources, consult them, take notes, and incorporate these notes into your discovery draft.

A PROFESSIONAL RESPONSE

Here is a draft of an evaluation of a word processing program. I wrote the evaluation for a magazine for writers. The program is the one that I used for this book.

```
            AN EVALUATION OF VOLKSWRITER DELUXE

    If you write for a living or for pleasure, you probably

do your writing on a computer with a word-processing program.

If not, you should get one immediately, and the one you should

get is Volkswriter Deluxe, version 2.1, from Lifetree

Software.  The acid test for any word-processing program is

its power--how well and how quickly it performs a wide variety

of tasks.  Volkswriter Deluxe is one powerful little program,

and--like its automotive namesake--it's also easy to learn,

fun to use, relatively cheap.

    Volkswriter Deluxe is not a luxury program--it doesn't

create footnotes or endnotes, it doesn't have a spelling

checker in it, and it doesn't compute mathematics.  However,

it does just about anything else you might want to do to a
```

piece of text--creating, modifying, formatting, and printing
quickly and easily. The program is packed with features for
creating, moving, adding, and deleting text. It uses the IBM
PC's function keys to invoke all editing commands, so you
don't have to worry about key combinations. If you forget any
function key's command, you can call up an on-screen outline
that tells you (in four short lines) what every key (and every
combination of keys) does.

I am not particularly adept with computers, and I almost
gave up word-processing totally when I first tried to learn
Wordstar and Microsoft Word. Then I found Volkswriter Deluxe,
and life got easier. Its set-up is almost completely
automated, and its on-disk tutorials are excellent. It is
truly easy to use, and best of all, it offers power and fun
for a relatively cheap price (about $250). I recommend it
highly.

Karen L. Greenberg

1. What are the criteria I am using to judge this product?

2. What evidence do I provide to support my judgment? How convincing is this evidence?

WRITING ACTIVITY WRITING AN EVALUATION

Use the techniques for writing an evaluation described on the preceding pages of this chapter to write a discovery draft of an essay that evaluates your school. Imagine that some high school seniors in your neighborhood have asked you (and several other students at different colleges) to write this essay for their school newspaper. Keep this audience—high school seniors in your neighborhood—in mind, and draft an evaluative essay that will help them decide whether to apply to your school.

Your evaluation must support your judgment as fully and as clearly as possible. Remember that you must provide evidence (facts, statistics, observations, and experiences) to support each of the reasons for your judgment. And most importantly, make sure that your supporting evidence is appropriate for your audience.

ESSAY EXAMINATIONS

Essay examinations are gaining in popularity among American teachers because they enable them to determine the extent to which students can think critically and write analytically about a subject. There is no way that anyone can write an effective response to an essay exam unless he or she has kept up with the material being tested. Cramming the night before a test cannot substitute for doing the readings, taking notes on them, and discussing the readings and the class lectures or labs in study groups. When you receive an essay examination, the first thing you should do is read it through carefully in its entirety. This will give you a sense of the number of questions you will have to answer, the amount of writing you will have to do, and the amount of time you should devote to each answer. Next, examine each question for its cues and clues. If you misinterpret the question or ignore its directions, you cannot answer it correctly. Here are some sample essay questions with comments about the strategies that each seems to require:

1. "Discuss the concept of 'negative feedback' and its role in maintaining homeostasis (the steady state)."

   This question, from a biology final exam, asks for information from a reading or lecture. It begins with the vague cue *discuss* but it does indicate that students should define "negative feedback" and give examples of it. Then, they should define "homeostasis" and give examples of the ways in which negative feedback helps maintain it.

2. "Most poets use music—stress and tonal patterns—to achieve meaning and mood. Analyze the contribution of music to the meaning and the mood of one poem by three of the following poets: Emily Dickinson, Walt Whitman, Robert Lowell, John Crowe Ransom, or Wallace Stevens."

   This question, from an English literature midterm, also requires students to respond with information that they have learned in the course. In addition, it requires students to present their personal interpretations. The question seems complicated, but the clues are clear: choose *three poets* and choose *one poem* written by each poet. Then for *each* of these three poems, describe how its metrical pattern, rhythm, and rhyme schemes set up the mood and help communicate the meaning of the poem.

3. "Attack or defend this thesis: all fascist movements are really anti-movements—they define themselves by the things against which they stand."

   This question, from a political science final, asks for an evaluation. It has no right or wrong answer; answers either make sense and are supported by appropriate evidence or they are unreasonable or unsupported. Students would have to explain what the thesis means and then give their opinion about its accuracy or validity, providing specific evidence for their judgment and their reasons.

Every essay examination question contains at least one cue about the strategy that students should use to respond to it, as well as clues about the information that should be included in the answer. Never write a response until you are sure that you know what the question is asking you! Analyze an essay exam question carefully before you begin answering it, try to relax, and remember that you have a large repertoire of strategies to use to develop your response: narrating, defining, describing, comparing, contrasting, analyzing, evaluating, and arguing. Your goals in writing an essay exam are always the same: (1) to state your answer as clearly and as directly as possible and (2) to signal the relationships among your ideas so that your answer is easy to read. The time limits of essay exams force writers to compress the processes of writing: prewriting may consist of merely jotting down notes or making a scratch outline. Often, there is not enough time to revise and rewrite, so writers have to draft and revise simultaneously. In addition, on an essay test, you can state your thesis statement immediately without worrying about getting and holding the reader's attention. Also, your conclusion can be briefer, simply summing up your main points. Make sure that you leave time to reread your answers and to write your corrections neatly.

STUDENT RESPONSES

Here are some actual student essays written in response to essay examination questions. Be prepared to discuss why you think each one did or did not answer the questions effectively.

1. Discuss the various ways in which color is measured. Then describe the relationship between color and light variation.

Student's notes:

munsell's hue system   hue chrome
→   → values
—more light →   Decribe each
(moonlight / daylight)   more color
Light makes different effects

Student's answer:

The most widely used system for measuring colors is the Munsell system named for its inventor Albert Munsell. The system consists of a tree that shows the hue, chroma and value of different colors. Hue is the basic quality of a color (red, yellow, green, blue and purple). Value is each color's degree of whiteness or blackness. Chroma is the color's strength or degree of contrast. Color can also be measured in math terms: the product of value times chroma is a color's power.

Colors vary according to how much light hits them. The more light that hits the color the more the color is visible to our eyes. If you look at a color picture in the moonlight you can't see the color in the picture. If you look at the same picture in the day, the colors are sharp. Light produces different effects on color its measurement.

2. Discuss this recent statement made by Yitzhak Shamir, Foreign Minister of Israel: "Soviet actions demonstrate clearly that the Soviet Union is opposed to peace in the Middle East."

Student's notes:

Russia → increasing support for PLO & ARF ✓
↳ speeches, money, arms ✓
↳ treaties with Syria, Iraq, & Yemen ✓

If it wanted peace, it wouldn't attack ✓
& boycott Israel & it would have
supported Geneva Conf. & Camp David

Student's response:

I agree totally with Minister Shamir's statement that the Soviet Union is opposed to peace in the Middle East. Russia has been increasing its support for the PLO and the Arab Rejectionist Front in terms of speeches at the U.N. and money and arms. It has formed treaties with Syria, Iraq and Yemen and it sends all kinds of technology to Libya whose leader is committed to the destruction of Israel.

If Russia or the Arab countries in the Middle East
seriously want peace, they would not spend so much time
attacking and boycotting Israel and they would not spend so
much money on stockpiling arms to wipe Israel off the face of
the earth. And also, the more arms that Moscow gives to the
Arabs, the more arms we have to give to Israel just to
maintain the balance of power. This certainly doesn't
contribute to peace in the Middle East. America was willing
to support the Geneva Conference and the Camp David accords,
but Russia did not. This shows how clearly they are opposed
to peace.

3. List the different types of galaxies and their characteristics.
Then explain why the different shapes of galaxies do *NOT* represent
stages in the life cycle of a galaxy.

Student's notes:

> I. Elliptical (egg-shaped, old)
> II. Spiral (circular, all ages)
> III. Irregular (no shape, old & young)
> Young and old stars in all 3 types.

Student's answer:

1. Elliptical galaxies are egg-shaped and they range from a
   full sphere to a flat narrow one. They contain mostly old
   stars.

2. Spiral galaxies have a circular center with spiral arms
   radiating out from them. They have young, middle aged, and
   old stars in them.

3. Irregular galaxies have no regular shape. They contain
   some young and old stars.

   Some scientists believe that galaxies start out as
elliptical, then change to spiral and then end as irregular.
But this doesn't seem true because there are young and old
stars in all three types of galaxies. If irregular galaxies
were the last stage of a galaxy's life cycle, then it would
have only old stars in it.

RESEARCH ESSAYS

Many college teachers assign research essays in order to help students learn to use sources intelligently. In Chapter 6, you learned how to consult public sources—people, books, periodicals, and reference works—to gather additional details for an essay and to revise a working thesis statement. Writing a research essay requires a writer to consult a wide variety of sources of information and to sort out, analyze, and organize this information logically and coherently. The process of producing an effective research essay is basically a process of becoming an independent learner: one learns where and how to get the best information about a question or a problem, and one learns how to evaluate and present this information. This process has eight steps:

1. selecting a topic and narrowing it down to a manageable question or problem
2. compiling a "working bibliography"
3. exploring these sources and taking notes
4. developing a working thesis statement and an outline
5. writing a discovery draft of the essay
6. revising it
7. editing it
8. using the appropriate format and the appropriate method of documentation

Selecting and Narrowing Down a Topic

Choose a topic that really interests you: you will have to read about it for several weeks, so you might as well start with a topic that is important to you. If you are assigned a subject to write about, use the techniques that you practiced in Chapters 2 and 3 to narrow down the topic:

- Do some freewriting about it and find a focus or two.
- Do some brainstorming to develop the focus and to clarify your purpose and audience.
- Do some clustering to elaborate details about your focus, purpose, and audience.
- Jot down notes about the topic's parts, characteristics, processes, or stages.
- Jot down notes about the topic's causes, effects or implications for various groups of people.
- Do a brief discovery draft of your ideas about the focus.

A STUDENT RESPONSE

Here is an example of a student's effort to narrow down a topic that was assigned to him for a research paper in his Communication course: "The Impact of the Media on Our Society." This topic is too broad for an 8–10 page essay.

Impact of Media

Effects on adults and children

Television

Audience – Communications teacher who knows most of these impacts

Research Sources – Books and articles on how television programming (affects Americans)

(entertainment and news)

(teachers them certain values as kids – reinforces these values as they grow-up)

Focus—Effects of television programming on Americans

(These effects are probably negative.)

Compiling a Working Bibliography

When you have an idea of the problem or question that you want to examine, go to the library and prepare a list of the possible sources of information about this focus. Begin with the **catalogue**, the alphabetical index of all of the materials in the library. In some libraries, the catalogue consists of cards in drawers; in others, these cards have been converted into pieces of data on computer terminals. The catalogue lists all of the library's books by their title, author, and subject. Here is an example of each card for the book *You and Media*:

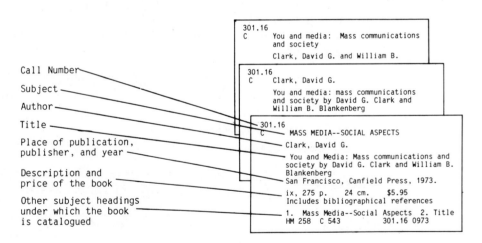

Call Number

Subject

Author

Title

Place of publication, publisher, and year

Description and price of the book

Other subject headings under which the book is catalogued

> 301.16
> C   You and media: Mass communications and society
>   Clark, David G. and William B.

> 301.16
> C   Clark, David G.
>   You and media: mass communications and society by David G. Clark and William B. Blankenberg

> 301.16
> C   MASS MEDIA--SOCIAL ASPECTS
>   Clark, David G.
>   You and Media: Mass communications and society by David G. Clark and William B. Blankenberg
>   San Francisco, Canfield Press, 1973.
>   ix, 275 p.   24 cm. $5.95
>   Includes bibliographical references
>   1. Mass Media--Social Aspects 2. Title
>   HM 258 C 543   301.16 0973

Begin your working bibliography by looking up all of the books on the subject of your topic. The subject card for each book indicates whether it has a bibliography. On a separate 3" by 5" index card, write down the author (last name first), title (underlined), date of publication, place of publication, publisher, and call number of each book that seems relevant to your topic. The catalogue will indicate the books on your topic that have bibliographies. Write down the call numbers of books with bibliographies, and find and examine each of them. Make out a separate index card for each of the books that you select from these bibliographies.

Next, check the appropriate indexes of periodicals—the journals, magazines, and newspapers—stored in the library. Since periodicals are current, they are valuable sources of information. In order to find periodicals that include information about your topic, consult several periodical indexes. The two most useful are the *Reader's Guide to Periodicals*, which is a monthly index of the articles in about 200 magazines and which lists articles under both subject and author, and the *New York Times Index*, which is a monthly index of major news events and feature articles and which lists articles by their subjects. Essays in academic, business, and professional journals can be found by consulting periodical subject indexes in specific fields, such as the *Humanities Index*, the *General Science Index*, the *Business Periodicals Index*, and the *Social Science Index*.

When you consult these indexes, use a separate 3" by 5" index card for each article or essay that seems relevant to your topic and include the author (last name first), title of the article (in quotation marks), title of the periodical (underlined), volume number, complete date, and page numbers. The Reference Section of most libraries has additional resources that may be very valuable for compiling a preliminary working bibliography. These include guides to government publications, yearbooks, indexes of pamphlets, brochures, clippings, indexes of book reviews, and indexes of biographies. Many libraries also have indexes ofaudiovisual materials (such as film, videotapes, slides, records, and audiotapes).

Exploring Sources and Taking Notes

As you read the various sources of information in your working bibliography, keep your specific topic and your purpose for writing about this topic in mind. Select information that is relevant to this topic and record your notes on your index cards. Most often, your notes should be a summary, *in your own words*, of the information contained in the source. If you record an author's specific points—even in your own words—you are paraphrasing, not summarizing. Make sure you note the page number of material that you paraphrase because you will need to indicate it in your paper. If you think that the author's exact words are very important for clarifying a point, copy them exactly, put a quotation mark at the beginning and end of the quote, and note the page number from which it came. Here are two bibliographical note cards: the first shows the material from the source in a quotation, and the second shows a paraphrase of the quoted material.

Barnouw, Erik. *The Sponsor* NY: Oxford
University Press, 1978. (301.161B)

p. 105 - "the action in episodic drama
can be quickly understood, and
invites emotional identification"...
"Such programming undoubtedly forms
patterns of ideas and attitudes about
the world"... "On television it is
drama, not news programming, that
takes the lead in setting patterns."

Barnouw, Erik. *The Sponsor*. NY Oxford
University Press, 1978. (301.161B)

P. 105 - Barnow says that people
understand and identify with
episodic drama ("action/adventure"
shows) and this affects their
ideas and attitudes about life
more than the information
presented in news programs.

WRITING ACTIVITY USING THE LIBRARY CATALOGUE

Use your library's catalogue to find out the following information about the book *News From Nowhere:*

Book's complete title_____

Author's complete name_____

Date of publication_____

Place of publication_____

Publisher_____

Subject headings_____

Call number_____

Developing a Working Thesis Statement and an Outline

As you read the various sources of information in your working bibliography, you may change your focus based on the material that you are reading and the ideas that occur to you when you think about the significance of what you have read. For example, here is a student's initial focus for her essay:

Most people watch several hours of TV every day and tend to accept the values portrayed in the shows.

And here is the working thesis statement that she developed after consulting several sources about her focus and after thinking about what she had read in these sources:

Television sponsors have become the ones who define society's values and who transmit these values through their commercials and their control of TV programming.

A working thesis statement helps you keep track of what your research essay will explain, describe, or prove. Just remember that you can revise this thesis statement as often as you want while you are doing your research *and* while you are drafting and revising your essay. After you have done extensive reading about your focus, examine your note cards to get a sense of the kinds of information you have collected and to get an idea of what issues still need further research. As you read through your note cards, think about some ways in which you might apply the information that you have collected.

- Do you want to review prior research on the topic, pointing out areas of agreement or conflict among researchers?
- Do you want to compare the work of competing researchers and explain whose view(s) seems more logical and why?
- Do you want to use a theory (or a set of interrelated theories) to explain a specific phenomenon?
- Do you want to confirm or refute the assertions, methods, or findings of other research on the topic?
- Do you want to show how research on one field of study relates to research in another field?

As you clarify your purpose in doing research, you may have to modify your thesis statement. You may also want to write an informal outline of the information that you have collected. One way to do this is to separate your note cards into groups pertaining to the same subtopics. Here is an example of part of an outline based on a group of note cards:

Section II. Sources of power of TV sponsors
(How does the sponsor transmit its idea of what is good, important, or valuable to viewers?)
  A. Commercials
    1. Spokespersons
      a. Entertainment or sports stars
      b. Authority figures
    2. Idealized world
      a. People always wealthy, clean, and happy
      b. People have plenty of time to relax, clean, and use the sponsors' products
  B. Programs
    1. Entertainment programs
      a. Idealized people, families, and lives
      b. Neat, clear solutions to every problem
    2. News programs
      a. Only "entertaining" news is shown
      b. Editorials and interpretations of news events depend on sponsors' values

The writer can use this outline to arrange her note cards so that she can start writing a draft of this section of the essay.

Writing a Discovery Draft of the Essay

A research essay calls for many of the strategies that you have been practicing: describing, defining, summarizing, explaining, comparing, contrasting, analyzing, and evaluating. As you reexamine each group of notes and try to make the information meaningful to a reader, you will have to choose the strategy that is most appropriate for your purpose and for the information. Think about ways of presenting the information that you have collected and consider the background details that should be presented before a specific piece of information is discussed in your draft. Consider why the information that you have collected is important. Also, think carefully about your point of view and about how the information makes sense in terms of your point of view?

Use your own words as much as possible. When you refer your sources to support your points, paraphrase them or quote them and cite the source by author and the page number(s). A **paraphrase** is a point-by-point summary of another writer's idea—in your own words—and you should paraphrase more often than quote. In fact, you should only quote the exact words of another writer if these words are particularly striking or memorable. Otherwise, when you want to present the ideas or evidence from the sources you have consulted, paraphrase these ideas accurately, simply, and clearly. *And cite the source's author* and page number(s). If you do not cite the source of paraphrases and quotes, you are **plagiarizing**—borrowing someone else's ideas and words and trying to pass them off as your own. The best way to make sure that you do not accidentally plagiarize is to put quotation marks around all of the material taken from sources that you record in your notes. When you write your draft of the essay, put quotation marks around all of the source material that you quote directly (and cite the source) or paraphrase the material and cite the source. Here is an example of a piece of writing; a student's discussion of it, using accurate paraphrases and quotes; and another student's plagiarized paraphrase of the original piece:

EXCERPT FROM A SOURCE

The dependence on camera events, pseudo-events, gives enormous power to those in a position to create such events. No network dares ignore a White House rose garden "scenario" or a military "photo opportunity." Thus, in regard to current happenings, the arrangers tend to set the agenda for national discussions, directing our attention *to* some events, some problems—and, far more significantly, *away from* others.

STUDENT REFERENCE TO THIS SOURCE

Another subtle way in which the government controls the news is through the events that it plans. As Erik Barnouw has pointed out, "No network dares ignore a White House rose garden 'scenario' or a military 'photo opportunity' (127). National and local government agencies have the power to focus our society's attention on some events and to make us ignore other events (Barnouw, 128).

STUDENT PLAGIARISM OF THIS SOURCE

The government has enormous power over network news. For example, no network can ignore an event at the White House or at the State Department or at a military base. Thus, government agencies can almost set the agenda for national discussions by focusing our attention on some events and, more importantly, away from others.

WRITING ACTIVITY PARAPHRASING

Here is a passage from a chapter by Paul Weaver on "Newspaper News and Television News" in the book *Television as a Social Force*. On a separate piece of paper, write a brief paraphrase of Weaver's points and include the appropriate citation.

Faced with a choice between two potential newsworthy events, the American TV news organizations will prefer, other things being equal, the one for which there is better film. What film they have for an event tentatively identified as newsworthy ordinarily guides, and in some cases may completely determine, the way the event is defined and the theme chosen for a story—a practice which could easily cause the story to misrepresent the situation as it really was. And in rare instances, television news organizations have been known to "create" film, to stage spectacles for purposes of being filmed, in order to have something newsworthy to report. (page 92)

Revising the Essay

A research paper should show the writer's mind at work: it reveals the significance of the information to the writer. An ineffective research paper merely strings together a series of paraphrases and quotations from experts on the topic. An effective one synthesizes the theories and views of experts in a field and uses this information to present a new understanding of the topic. As you revise your essay, make sure that you have incorporated paraphrases and quotations smoothly into your writing. Each one should be introduced by a brief comment and should serve a specific function (such as illustrating your point, backing up your assertion, or giving an example of the author's language).

Also, check to make sure that you have given credit to the author whenever you have used his or her ideas to support yours. Remember, if you have merely changed a few words of another writer's sentence or paragraph, you are plagiarizing, not paraphrasing. All of your paraphrases must state the original writer's meaning *in your own words*. Also, make sure that you give credit to the writer, either by citing the author's last name and the page number in parentheses at the end of the paraphrase or by writing an introductory comment at the beginning of the paraphrase (such as "according to Erik Barnouw" or "as Erik Barnouw has noted"). Then, revise your essay using all of the strategies that you have learned and practiced in this book.

Editing the Essay

A research essay has to be edited for errors and for unconventional forms, just as does any other essay you write for a teacher or an employer. Use the techniques that you have learned in this book to edit your sentence structure, diction, grammar and usage, spelling, and punctuation.

Using the Appropriate Format and the Appropriate Method of Documentation

Different academic disciplines have different formats for research essays. Generally, a research essay should be typed, double-spaced, on one side of each piece of paper. All pages should be numbered consecutively in the top right hand corner and should have one-inch margins on all four sides. Different academic disciplines also have different styles for citing sources within the text, in footnotes or in endnotes, and within bibliographies. Your teacher will tell you which style manual to use to document your sources. Below are some guidelines from the documentation recommendations of the Modern Language Association (MLA), the style that is used most often for essays in the humanities and that resembles the style of the American

Psychological Association (APA), the style used in the social and the natural sciences:

- When you paraphrase or quote a source in your text for the first time, you must cite the author's name and the relevant page number(s). Put parentheses around the page number, but don't write the word "page" or "p."
- If you do not mention the author's name in your brief introduction to the paraphrase or quote, then state the author's last name and the page number(s) within parentheses at the end of your paraphrase or quote.
- At the end of your essay, provide a bibliography—called "Works Cited"—which includes all of the sources mentioned in the essay, arranged alphabetically according to the author's last names. When you include more than one source by the same author, list these alphabetically by title; instead of repeating the author's name, use three hyphens followed by a period. Here is an example of part of a list of Works Cited:

Works Cited

Barnouw, Erik. The Sponsor. New York: Oxford University

Press, 1978.

Clark, David, and William Blankenburg. You and Media: Mass

Communication and Society. New York: Harper and Row,

1973.

Griffith, Thomas. "From Monitor to Public Echo." Time 124

(13 Nov. 1984): 89.

Weaver, Paul. "Newspaper News and Television News."

Television as a Social Force. Ed. Richard Adler. New

York: Prager Publishers, 1975. 81-96.

WRITING ASSIGNMENT **WRITING, REVISING, EDITING,**
AND DOCUMENTING A RESEARCH ESSAY

Reread the editorial essay about liberal arts courses by Dean Richard Del Guidice earlier in this chapter. Next, reread your summary of this essay. Then, consult *at least* three books and four periodicals for additional information about the issue of increasing the number of required liberal arts courses in American colleges and universities. You will be using this information to develop a research essay that defends or criticizes Del Guidice's thesis and supporting reasons. Your audience for this essay consists of administrators and teachers at your school who want to increase the number of liberal arts courses that every student must take and decrease the number of electives. Use the following guidelines to help you plan and write your evaluation of Del Guidice's points.

Guidelines
1. Reread Del Guidice's essay, and do some freewriting, brainstorming, and clustering about your reactions to it.
2. Specify your focus:
   What exactly is Del Guidice's thesis?
   How much do you already know about this issue?
   What else do you need to find out about it, and what kinds of sources should you consult?
3. Determine your audience:
   Who is your audience for this essay?
   What does your audience already know about this topic, and how do they feel about it?
   What kind of evidence will you need to present in order to convince this audience of your view?
4. Refine your purpose for writing this essay:
   What do you want your readers to understand?
   What do you want your readers to think, to feel, or to do when they are finished reading your essay?
5. Write a sentence that can serve as your working thesis statement. (Feel free to change this thesis statement as you do research and write a discovery draft.)
6. Carefully reread your freewriting, your brainstorming, and your clustering. Consider the ways in which your details relate to your focus, audience, purpose, and working thesis statement.
7. Go to the library to find relevant sources, take notes on them, and keep a working bibliography.
8. Write a discovery draft of your essay.
9. Get as many responses to your discovery draft as you can (from classmates, teachers, tutors, friends, and family).
10. Revise your discovery draft by answering the questions for revising an evaluation on page 315 of this chapter. Then revise it again by using the techniques that you practiced in Chapters 6, 7, and 8.

11. Edit your essay using the techniques that you practiced in Chapters 9, 10, 11, and 12.
12. Consult your library's copy of the *MLA Handbook for Writers of Research Papers*, second edition, edited by Joseph Ginaldi and Walter Achtert, (New York: Modern Language Association, 1984). Follow its directions for the format of your essay and for documenting sources within the essay and at the end of the essay.

ISSUES FOR YOUR JOURNAL

1. What kinds of writing do professionals in your major (or in your current job) have to do? How do you feel about your ability to do these writing tasks?
2. Collect interesting quotations from lectures or from readings in your courses. Write them down in your journal, and write your responses to each one.
3. What books, journals, or magazines have you read in the past month? What do these reveal about your reading habits and your life?
4. How do you see yourself changing—as a student, as an employee, a son or daughter, a parent, or a friend?
5. What do you want to change most about your life? How will you go about making this change?

INDIVIDUALIZED PROGRESS LOGS

1. Writing Progress Log

2. Spelling Log

3. Conference Log

     The three charts that follow will help you keep track of your writing progress and problems *if you use them.*

1. WRITING PROGRESS LOG

Every time your teacher returns a piece of your writing—in your writing course *and* in every other course—make notes about the piece in this log. By doing this, you will be able to see your progress and also focus on the areas that need further improvement. If you need more writing log pages, make copies of this page.

Date _____   Course _____

Title of Paper _____

Strengths:

Problems and Errors:

2. SPELLING LOG

List in this log every word that you misspell or that you are not sure how to spell. In your spare time, make up a sentence for each of the words in the log (on a separate piece of paper). If you need more Spelling Log pages, make copies of this page.

PROBLEM WORD (spelled correctly)	**MY MISSPELLING**	**TYPE or CAUSE** (of this spelling error)

3. CONFERENCE LOG

Every time you have a conference with your writing teacher, summarize that conference in the space below. Use the notes that you write in this log to help you remember your teacher's comments and suggestions and to help you keep track of your progress. If you need more Conference Log pages, make copies of this page.

Date of Conference _____

Material Discussed _____

Teacher's Comments, Suggestions, and Assignments:

Dear Student,

   Writing this book was a labor of love and anxiety for me. Now I need your help to revise it. When you are finished using this book, please write me a letter about its strengths and its weaknesses. What did you like about it? What did you dislike? How can I improve it? Please mail your letter to me at the address below. If you include your name and address, I will write back to you. Thank You.

Gratefully,

Karen Greenberg
c/o College Division
St. Martin's Press
175 Fifth Avenue
New York, NY 10010

Chapter 5
"Knowing Little About How Things Work." I. Peterson. Reprinted with permission from *Science News,* the weekly news magazine of science, copyright 1986 by Science Service, Inc.
Life Manipulation (excerpt) by David Lygre and published by Walker and Co. Reprinted by permission of the publisher. Copyright © 1979.
Science and Survival by Barry Commoner (excerpt). Copyright © 1963, 1964, 1966 by Barry Commoner. Reprinted by permission of Viking Penguin Inc.
Chapter 6
"Dwight Gooden," © 1985, LeRoy Neiman, Inc.
Chapter 7
Donald M. Murray, *A Writer Teaches Writing.* Copyright © 1968, by Donald M. Murray. Used by permission of the publishers.
"Careers That Promise Big Payoffs," by William C. Banks. Reprinted from the November 1985 issue of *Money Magazine* by special permission; © 1985, Time Inc.
Chapter 8
Handycam ad, reprinted by special permission of Sony and McCann-Erickson.
Television and Human Behavior, Comstock, Chaffee, Katzman, McCombs, Roberts. Reprinted by permission of New York—Columbia University Press, 1978 by the Rand Corporation.
Chapter 9
"Letter from a Birmingham Jail, April 16, 1963" (pages 83–84) from *Why We Can't Wait* by Martin Luther King, Jr. Copyright © 1963, 1964 by Martin Luther King, Jr. Reprinted by permission of Harper & Row, Publishers, Inc.
Chapter 10
Reprinted by permission from *The Random House College Dictionary, Revised Edition.* Copyright © 1984 by Random House, Inc.
Theo Sommer, "A New Era" excerpted from *Die Zeit,* Hamburg, Germany. Reprinted by permission of *World Press Review,* copyright © 1985.
Chapter 11
The Medusa and the Snail by Lewis Thomas (excerpt). Copyright © 1976 by Lewis Thomas. Originally published in the New England Journal of Medicine. Reprinted by permission of Viking Press Penguin Inc.
Chapter 13
Richard J. Del Guidice, "Liberal Arts Courses Should Be Required for College Students." Reprinted by permission of Richard J. Del Guidice, © 1985.

INDEX